Prospect
and
Retrospect

Selected Essays of James Britton

Prospect
and
Retrospect

Selected Essays of James Britton

edited by Gordon M. Pradl
New York University

BOYNTON/COOK PUBLISHERS, INC.
MONTCLAIR, NEW JERSEY

HEINEMANN EDUCATIONAL BOOKS
LONDON

Library of Congress Cataloging in Publication Data

Britton, James
    Prospect and retrospect.

    1. English philology—Study and teaching—Addresses,
essays, lectures. 2. Education—Great Britain—Addresses,
essays, lectures. 3. Language arts—Addresses, essays,
lectures. 4. Literature—Study and teaching—Addresses,
essays, lectures. I. Pradl, Gordon M. II. Title.
PE65.B74   1982   420'.7   82-14608
ISBN 0-86709-043-X

For information address Boynton/Cook Publishers, Inc.
206 Claremont Avenue, Montclair, NJ 07042

ISBN   0-86709-043-X

Printed in the United States of America

82 83 84 85 10 9 8 7 6 5 4 3 2 1

Published in Great Britain by Heinemann Educational
Books Ltd. 22 Bedford Square, London WC1B 3HH.
ISBN 0 435 10115 3

Contents

Introduction

Restriction of the peculiar human powers made possible by language should be cause for unease, if not alarm. Denied the integrity of our own words, we lose possibility. In this sense our freedom depends directly upon our ability to represent the events of our lives. Through the web of syntax we infuse the world with play and in the process become masters of our own destinies. In telling the stories of our reality, both private and public, spiritual and material, we assert a future. The future, though always apparently beyond our control, is in actuality a continuing alternative, one we actively construct out of our understanding of past events. Gain control of a person's language and you determine his fortune, because you have usurped his natural capacity to interpret his own perceptions, indeed you narrow the very range of those perceptions.

Language powers the future, and thus the recent energies of researchers and educators in exploring the connections between language and behavior are not surprising. The complex contradictions of literacy provoke endless inquiry as we seek to expand the ways of fulfilling our unique symbol-making needs. Heirs to that majestic evolutionary development, the human brain, the only living organ which produces in excess of what it takes in through its sensorium, we are insatiably propelled forward by meaning. It is our wisdom to intend toward interpretations, however mistaken they may be in both individual and collective instances, because all our prospects grow inexorably out of what we can command retrospectively. What this suggests is that the teaching of English implies nothing if it does not somehow impinge upon our students' nascent powers to shape tomorrow.

Such paradoxes and loyalties mark the ongoing quest manifested in the writings of James Britton. Taking seriously the power that is literature residing in each of our lives, he has spent a lifetime closely observing children and adults as they make sense of their worlds by assimilating, manipulating, and inventing the endless structures of language. His observations and resulting insights serve to heighten our awareness of how the English curriculum might foster the creative exploration of the tension between self and society through the dialectical interplay of word and intention. Drawing in rich synthetic ways on the ideas of philosophers, psychologists, and linguists—from Langer and Polanyi, Vygotsky and Kelly, Jakobson and Chomsky— Britton has developed a model of language use that seeks to account for the varying ways individuals mediate their personal meanings amid the existing constraints and conventions of cultural institutions. Such mediation constitutes *learning*, with both its subjective and objective dimensions, and it is the positive thrust of this growth metaphor which has dominated Britton's intellectual concerns, even as it is reflected in the title of his major work, *Language and Learning*, published in 1970.

Sensitive to what both youngsters and adults can and want to accomplish when they are speaking and listening, writing and reading, Britton has tried to avoid a linguistic category system that depends exclusively upon the quality of the attained performance. Rather, he concentrates on distinctions that grow naturally out of the functional roles individuals find themselves in when they are using language. The first crucial division is between *participant* and *spectator* functions of language. As participants in the events of the world we use language instrumentally to get things done. We send messages, write up reports, give directions, and do a thousand other things in order to keep activities moving. On the other hand, in a contempletive mood, we reflect on the meaning and significance of these activities, thus assuming the role of spectator. We use language in this way to generate and refine our value systems, and characteristically what we create are the stories of the events of our lives spun from the thematic interpretive frameworks which serve to define our identities.

In classifying the linguistic products that result from these two language functions, Britton distinguishes between *transactional* and *poetic*. In the first case what predominates is the message. In receiving transactional language, we all but see through the transparency of its form, seeking to understand the text by matching up its meanings and referents with our pre-existing knowledge in a *piecemeal* fashion. Poetic texts, on the other hand, call attention to the opacity of their forms. Our interpretation, or perhaps our celebration, of them is never directly utilitarian; rather, as with music, our immediate concern is with overarching patterns and repetitions. In this way the world created in the poetic text is finally understood as a whole, or to use Britton's term it is *globally contextualized*. The spectator role in which we create poetic texts, however high or however low, points to our ongoing need to extract meaning, to make sense of our varied existence, as we seek confirmation from our audience, which initially is ourself. In the retelling we discover our themes and project possibility forward.

In the midst of generating these categories Britton makes an important allowance for an obvious truth: by no means are all speech situations and written texts highly stylized and formal. Indeed the majority of our linguistic utterances are colloquially self-reflexive. In other words, they call as much attention to ourselves as speakers as they do to the message or form. When another person receives such utterances, we share a special bond with them, for it means that they are concerned with us as an individual. Through such relationships, marked by the tentative exploratory quality of our words, our intermixing of fact and observation with emotive evaluatory commentary, we *learn* about the world and grow increasingly confident about our capacities to affect the future.

Such language performance, Britton appropriately labels *expressive*, for during such utterances we both exclaim what is without while expressing our emerging inner relationships with it. Developmentally, of course, expressive language characterizes the speech and writing of children as they learn how to differentiate among personal/social events and how to control the objects of their physical environment. Thus the *expressive* is the entry point for movement in either the *transactional* or *poetic* directions. Such movement occurs as the more public conventions of form and message are mastered, and texts are decreasingly punctuated with upstage commentary.

Britton's taxonomy of language use, however, is far from static. Rather, his account is flexible in recognizing that individual texts frequently share a variety of characteristics simultaneously. It is most important, for instance, that we not ignore the expressive dimension of mature adult transactional and poetic texts. Although they are expressive in ways unlike the directness of unsophisticated texts, nonetheless the essential riches of voice, style and tone are present, an integration of sense and sensibility, of intellect and feeling, as opposed to the "neutral" anonymity of utterances produced solely at the command of others, bereft of any intentions on the part of the "speaker." In this sense schools are mistaken in promulgating the notion that it is the proper duty of education to wean children away from their expressive voices in order to assume the "objective" rhetoric of the disciplines. Such a program breeds dependent literacy—the opposite of the imaginative response Britton proposes as the cornerstone of learning.

Although Britton's essays weave continual variations on the central theme of how through language and social interaction we evolve increasingly more accurate maps of our worlds, they are divided here into three sections, each with a more specific focus. The essays in the first section, "Literature and the Shaping of Experience," span thirty years and point to Britton's central concern for literature as a fundamental way of knowing, of creating and organizing meaning in our lives. Literature is such an all-pervasive given in the development of

Britton's thinking that unwittingly it is rendered invisible at times when he concentrates on more immediately instrumental matters such as the participant role and transactional writing. In these essays, however, Britton stays fixed on the poem itself, shuttling back and forth between the primary satisfactions derived by a child's recognition of the developing sense of form and how this satisfaction grows into mature poetic creation and response. Throughout we see his profound faith in the emerging needs and capacities of children for the vision, energy and celebration of the poem and his good sense not to impose taste or standards, but rather to allow them to evolve naturally through shared enactment and reflection. In the final essay in this section we are presented with a broader theoretical picture of Britton's most recent thinking about literature and the spectator role in addition to a sketch of the development of one child's poetic writing. Through Britton's caring observations we begin to ascertain the magnitude of the tragedy that occurs when our schools, and especially English teachers, neglect this area where we discover and assert the values that are our humanity.

The essays in Section II, "Language and Intention," cover the wider range of language and how it works for us in its varying forms from speaking and listening to writing and reading. In each instance, Britton unequivocally concludes that language use in whatever form is only effective when it originates in the speaker's "determining tendency." We may not know in advance what we wish to say or write or what we will hear or read; however, our success depends in large part on our *intending* toward our own meaning, not someone else's. "The Speaker," "Words and a World," "Language and Representation" and "Talking" all point to the growing power enjoyed by the child because through language she is free to work on her representation of experience rather than always being forced to learn directly from the experience itself. Having broken free of the immediacy of events, when we return to them, we do so with the possibility of renewed control over them. Thus, the regulative function of language makes human conduct unique, and as talkers and writers we anticipate and adjust our theories about the world in order to keep adding to our shared social fabric.

"Writing to Learn and Learning to Write" presents Britton's most detailed account of the participant and spectator functions of language, and thus, although it lies firmly anchored at the center of the present volume, it could very well serve as a general introduction to his work. "A Reader's Expectations" carries over to reading the notion that our language mediated behavior is a continual anticipatory experiment— in simpler terms, in order to receive we must first give. "Notes on a Working Hypothesis about Writing" offers a succinct sketch of those elements that must be taken into consideration in any model of how writing works and is developed. Finally, "Shaping at the Point of Utterance" closes out the section with Britton freely speculating on how we create our meanings at precisely the moment when we are somehow forced to articulate them. Such a piece shows Britton on the edge of extending his own constructs, and further it leaves us with implications that the "at the point of utterance" phenomenon might have for a theory of invention, indeed for a truer account of the composing process in general.

In the essays of the final section, "Perspectives on the Profession," Britton reveals the connections between his thinking about language and behavior and the more immediate realities of schooling and public pressures, while offering a historical overview of his long career in education. "A Note on Teaching, Research and 'Development' " suggests that educational improvement will only result from a reciprocal dialogue between theory, research and practice. Such a model of change is analogous to how the young child uses language to build up better representations of the world: teachers must continually reconstrue their experience, not merely explain it away with ossified categories. In "Take It from — Where?" Britton struggles with the thorny question of accountability as he considers the role of behaviorial objectives in English teaching. This piece is of particular note, for it embodies Britton's mature *expressive* style in which we literally see his mind at work, making connections as he goes along, "fashioning a future" as he would free his own students to do. "How We Got Here" is Britton's personal record of the events and issues that have marked the teaching of English during the last half century. The emphasis on *we* reflects the fundamental collaborative approach to the profession that has characterized his creative teaching and research efforts throughout his distinguished career.

In the mid-seventies Britton served on the Bullock Committee, a British education commission which produced *A Language for Life*. Although he was one of the chief architects of this final document, in "Reflections on the Writing of the Bullock Report" Britton states his reservations regarding the enterprise, especially how official directives undercut the need for nurturing change from within. Britton's progressive stance has meant that he has not been without critics. In the two concluding essays he defends himself against those who on the one hand would take a narrow skills approach to literacy and on the other those who have attacked his conception of the spectator function of language as elevating the status of mere talk and gossip. "Language in the British Primary School" confronts the public/political issues arising from the implementation of the kind of language and learning policy that Britton and his colleagues have been advocating for so many years. The extent to which progressive ideas really have informed educational practices is in question, Britton contends, and certainly the recessionary social climate will tend to further drive a wedge between children's intentions and their satisfactions. His final plea for trust rather than surveillance, for keeping the evaluative function distinct from the teaching function needs to be continually reasserted.

"English Teaching: Retrospect and Prospect" was the James McAuley Memorial Lecture delivered at the Third International Conference on the Teaching of English held at Sydney, Australia, in 1980. Returning to the theme that literature, by giving us *an experience of order,* makes a future possible, Britton surveys the last five decades of our profession ending with a toast to English in the Eighties as being the Decade of the Teacher. Sanguine about the problems that need to be overcome if a dynamic holistic vision of English is ever to triumph, Britton remains optimistic. And it is precisely his style reflecting his quiet but intense efforts toward our common goals, his invitation to appropriate from him what we will in collaborative terms, that might renew our own dedication to the teaching of English—for Jimmy Britton, finally, belongs to us all.

I
Literature
and the
Shaping of Experience

1

Reading and Writing Poetry

I was reading some poems to a class of eight-year-olds. I read them James Stephens' poem beginning:

The wind stood up, and gave a shout;
He whistled on his fingers, and
Kicked the withered leaves about.

and then Walter de la Mare's poem about a night-watchman:

Two o' the morning by the clock,
And the stars a-shining clear!

and then Emily Dickinson's fragment:

The moon was but a chin of gold
    A night or two ago,
And now she turns her perfect face
    Upon the world below.

At this point a small boy, hugging himself like a cab-driver on a cold day, said, 'Please sir, will you read us a *warm* one!'

I think he was in dead earnest. There is a directness about young children's feeling relationships with the world around them that grown-ups have lost and can easily forget. It is part of the process of growing up to tone down our emotional responses by imposing an organized control upon them. We develop *habits* of response, and organize these habits into systems so that our long-term aims may not always be at the mercy of immediate emotional gratification. If we did not do so we should be adrift on a sea of emotion, prey of every emotional stimulus, and never in time for any appointment!

This is part of the price we pay for becoming responsible members of society. Young children have no such responsibility and may enjoy the freedom of direct and vivid feeling. We compensate ourselves, sometimes, by enjoying emotional experiences in a field in which there is no responsibility because no practical outcome is in-

Published in *Education* (Department of Education, New Zealand) 7 (2), 1958.

volved: that is to say in the arts—in poetry and drama, painting and music and the like. But there is a danger, as I. A. Richards has pointed out[1], first, that we may allow our systems of emotional response to become 'fixed', so that they grow less and less appropriate to the changing circumstances of our actual life; and secondly (more disastrous still) employ these inhibited and stereotyped responses when we read poetry or listen to music or look at pictures. This is to defeat the purposes of the arts altogether, and reduce what ought to be formative experiences to mere self-indulgence.

Poetry and Children

The danger point, Richards says, comes after the age of eleven. The first conclusion we should draw then is that young children should find it natural and easy to respond to real poetry—words that are aflame with the fire of imagination. Do not let us waste much of their time, therefore, over stories in verse that are more story than poetry, and comic verses which make them laugh without stirring their imaginations. They will like the stories and the humour, just as they like party games and mottoes out of crackers—but that can hardly justify us.

Of course, in every individual class we must experiment to discover what the children are able to enjoy. We can read the signs—the way they listen, the kind of comment they will sometimes offer: and we shall be guided also by the poems they will choose for themselves. If we aim at enjoyment, we can wait for understanding to follow, for that takes time (even a lifetime, on occasions). An emotional attachment to a poem establishes the necessary relationship—every poem that is a real experience requires to be penetrated, and the process of penetration is best achieved gradually; not by determined onslaught, but by a growing familiarity. Poetry is not to be regarded therefore as consumable stock ('Please sir, we *did* that one last year with Miss Jones!') but as something to be read and returned to. One aim would be that each child should build up his own repertoire of the poems he liked: and that the teacher should encourage him both by reading poems to the class and by making books available for him to browse in.

When a poem has been presented, I believe we ought to say nothing that appears to invite a final verdict. Children may be only too ready to turn their thumbs up or down, but the likely effect of inviting a verdict too early will be for the thumbs to go down. We ought rather to try and keep the doors open, to allow time for penetrating the poem.

It need hardly be said that a poem printed on a page is no more than a score: like a piece of music, it requires to be performed, and the teacher's ability to read a poem well is a major qualification. (Of course, we shall all avoid 'the poetry voice' for the simple reason that

that is, by definition, the way other people read poetry!) The rhythm of any line of verse is a balance between the underlying regular beat of the metre and the normal speech rhythm of the actual words used: I believe most of us err by giving too much to the underlying beat, and that we correct this error if we think more deliberately, as we read, of the sense and tone of the poem as a whole. Again, poetry is not drama, and many readers do not realize this. They project the poem as an actor speaks his lines—using a wide range of pitch. Poetry—lyric poetry in a broad sense—uses a narrow range of conventions because it never ceases to be essentially the voice of one man speaking his mind. In intimate quiet talk (however passionate) we tend to use a narrow range of pitch and this limitation does seem appropriately to suggest the narrow conventions of lyric poetry.

But a poem is more than a pattern of sounds in the air. One of the subtler means by which a poet communicates experience is by using movements of the vocal organs to reinforce his meaning—as echoes, so to speak, of the events and feelings involved. It is easy to highlight this device by quoting galloping lines in which the quick movements from consonant to consonant set the tongue itself galloping: but the process is more subtle and more widespread than this. I would sooner look for it in the constricted vocal movements that reinforce the sense of struggle in such a line as:

'And in this harsh world draw thy breath in
    pain'

or the smooth movement and open flow of breath in:

'. . . the isle is full of noises,
Sounds and sweet airs, that give delight, and
    hurt not.'

People accustomed to reading poetry aloud do not lose these effects when they read silently: the shadow movements accompanying silent reading are enough. But I suspect that inexperienced readers need to make the sounds with their own vocal organs and for this reason am a great believer in the chorus reading of poetry in school. Not as a performance—as a normal way of dealing with a poem, so that every child in the class is able to speak the words. But reading in chorus is not easy and nothing is more destructive of a poem than bad chorus reading. With the nine- and ten-year-olds I would take deliberate practice until they reached some competence; ensuring that they start together (for this, some such means as a count of 'one—two' seems inevitable), that they produce enough sound to take shape effectively (a perfunctory murmur cannot be articulated however strenuously the vocal organs perform), and that they do not drag by waiting upon each other. If after reasonable practice of this kind chorus reading does not become a pleasurable way of treating a poem, I should abandon it: and I should certainly not attempt it with a twelve- or thirteen-year-old class who have had no previous experience of it.

Some of the most valuable discussions of poems I have heard in school have been ones that made an indirect approach. They have been in fact discussions as to how a particular poem ought to be read. To arrive at a decision it was necessary to think about the experience of the poem, but to do so within a practical framework. And any conclusions were put to the test in a trial reading: thus judgment was based upon a further response to the poem as a whole—the soundest possible basis.

The process may be extended if, instead of chorus reading by the whole class, groups of children are asked to arrange orchestrated readings of the poem, readings in which the voices of individual speakers, alone or in combination, are used in the way a composer uses instruments in an orchestra. Again, this is not for the sake of a finished performance, and the object is defeated if the teacher allots the parts. It is, rather, an indirect means of studying the structure of a poem—the only way in which eleven- or twelve-year-olds could conceivably undertake such a study.

In the last analysis, a poem is a pattern, not of sounds or of movements, but of experience: it is *an* experience, a carefully organized, structured experience. To have the experience, the reader must build his own chain of responses and no one else can do it for him, however much they explain, question, discuss. It is a close-knit pattern: rhythm, rhyme and other sound effects, studied repetitions, cross-referring images, all combine to make it a seamless whole. It differs from prose in that it demands a special kind of attention—an awareness of the whole poem must accompany attention to each individual part. Thus it is that the experience of the poem is inseparable from the words, and that growing familiarity with the whole is the surest way of deepening response.

To consider very briefly this question of imagery will take us back to the point with which we started this section—the natural affinity between poetry and young children. The writer of a poem is not out to inform or instruct: he draws upon his experience not in order to pass on formulations about experience or facts about the world: what he does is to create fresh experience—something that is like life itself, though more orderly. For this reason a poet tends to use images or symbols rather than concepts. Both symbols and concepts are distillations of experience, but the process of abstraction from the context of life has been taken much further in the concept than it has in the symbol. To take a simple example, it is appropriate to bring a great deal more of our experience (the feelings that have accompanied past experiences, the associations that cling to those experiences) to bear upon the word 'blood' when the poet uses it as a symbol:

'Thy bones are marrowless, thy blood is cold.'

than it is when the textbook writer uses it as a concept:

'The normal temperature of the blood is 98.4 degrees Fahrenheit'.

It is many years before the growing child arrives at the stage of handling concepts with any ease. Piaget[2] states that roughly from the age of two to the age of eleven children's characteristic activity is that of make-believe play, and he calls this 'symbolic representation'. In play children work over their experiences, and their enactment is a symbol representing actual experience. By the age of eleven, Piaget says, a child is normally able to think in concepts.

Children's writing reflects this development. Much that they write at six or seven or eight is more like poetry than prose in that it is a gloss upon experience rather than a formulation of it. The six-year-old boy who scribbed over a page in brown crayon and then wrote under it:

'Exploring the rocks
  A place called Cromer
    I knocked the loose lumps of mud.'

was recalling past experience in order to enjoy it again. He was not concerned to present facts.

It is valuable for children to write in this way: recalling past events, sometimes to enjoy them, sometimes rearranging them to their liking where the actual was painful; combining experience with fantasy to produce exciting effects. And if we refrain from drawing too clear a distinction between what is poetry and what is prose in their reading, encourage them to exploit the binding power of repetition and avoid that of rhyme (which is a device beyond their control in the early stages), and allow freedom as to what they write and when they write, we shall find a good deal of poetry is being written in school. By the time they are ready to compile their own anthologies, they will be copying out some poems from books, and writing in others of their own composition.

We have so far taken it for granted that all this is worth while, that poetry is something in itself desirable. I should like now to enquire into that assumption, and to do so must make as it were a fresh start.

There is a sense in which we create the world we live in. Our experience reveals a world to us and we know no other world; yet experience differs from individual to individual. The same things may happen to two people but since the people are different they will interpret what happens differently: and it is *our interpretation* of our experience that builds a world for each of us.

It does not follow that there is no such thing as misinterpreting experience. We may build very badly and if we do we suffer for it—we imprison and isolate ourselves. I know people who live in a world in which anyone who is not an Englishman (I hope this sounds odd to you) is someone to mistrust; and others who live in a world in which professed altruism is either hypocrisy or delusion.

The process of creating our world is continuous in our waking hours and we interpret experience without being aware that we are doing so: we act, that is, upon assumptions without ever being aware that we have made them. But the process is intensified whenever we stand back and work over past experiences, whether in conversation, in writing, in acting or in painting, or in any other way. In doing these things we discover meaning. A seventeen-year-old schoolgirl, writing about her childhood, said:

> 'When I was thirteen I wrote a poem. I did so because I had read one by a young, amateur writer, and thought to myself, "I can do as well if not better than that." It is difficult to say whether my effort was good or bad; in retrospect it seems paltry, trite and pointless. But writing it altered my accumulated feelings about myself.'

If we can discover in what precise way poetry helps us to build our own worlds, we shall have fulfilled a major purpose of this article.

'If we can discover': it might seem merely coy to talk in this way, a sort of pedagogic euphemism, but I mean it literally. The process of drawing upon my experience of children and poetry, of sifting and arranging my ideas, in order to write this article is genuinely one of discovery. But the circumstances would have been very different if I had been writing a poem. The need to write this article is a very small part of the need for the journal *Education* to appear at intervals: which is a part of the need of teachers to pool their experiences and exchange ideas: which is a part of the general need for children to be educated at all—a need that can never be said to be finally satisfied.

A poem on the other hand can be written only in response to some inner need in the writer, and if it comes off at all, it satisfies that need. Poetry arises, indeed, when something needs to be said and the need is satisfied by the mere saying. (This is not true only of poetry, of course: it applies also to the few choice words you may use when you drop a spanner on your toe!)

Let me illustrate by referring to a few poems written in circumstances I happen to know. An eleven-year-old girl was up early one sunny morning and out in the garden before the rest of the household had stirred. There she found a dead thrush, in which she was very interested. She took it carefully indoors up to her mother's bedroom and asked if she might keep the wings for her natural history 'museum'. They agreed in the end that the specimen was in no fit state for further preservation, so the girl buried it and marked the grave with a cross on which she wrote 'Breac'—a Gaelic word meaning 'spotted' (Gaelic was something else she was interested in at the time). And later she closed the incident by writing this:

Death-Ode to Breac

He who once soared above the green woods,
The sun and wind on his speckled breast,
He who burst joyous into song,
May he now find peaceful rest.

Winging swiftly through the blue sky,
Under clouds like lamb's fleece,
O'er hill and valley, field and garden,
Breac, the songster, now rest in peace.

Some months later, the family left this house and this garden and went to live elsewhere. For a time the girl was absorbed in all that was new around her, but after a while she began to pine for the old garden, and in particular for one tree in it. She was noticeably miserable for some days and then she wrote another poem:

The Elm Tree

Oh! for the elm-tree at the bottom of the wood,
Basking gold in the evening sun,
The warm brown bark and sunlit leaves,
There I used to sit when the day was done.

I will never see that tree again,
Its branches safely bore me,
In the fork I would sit and gaze at the world,
But never again shall I see my tree.

There is nothing remarkable about the poem, but writing it seemed to satisfy something in the writer: a stage had been reached—the past had been dealt with in some way and she was ready again to live in the present.

I was in Crete for some months during the last war: Crete is a wonderful island and we enjoyed the life there tremendously until it worked up to a violent and unpleasant end. Those of us who came out safely arrived back in Alexandria and hung about there for some time.

One of my friends, a sober and level-headed barrister, wrote this before he was drafted to a new unit:

> Let not the end's dismay
> Oppress our gratitude for those times past
> Which brought to us great happiness.
> On these our thoughts
> Unto the last.
> And if that time seemed all too brief
> Let us not dim it with our grief.

Again, not remarkable as poetry, but it gave me great satisfaction at the
time, and must have been more satisfying still to its writer.

Writing these poems did not, of course, affect the material situation: the thrush remained dead, the tree was lost, and so on. But the
writing affected the writers: 'altered their accumulated feelings about
themselves', about their worlds.

Jean Piaget has described how a two-and-a-half year old girl was
once shocked by the sight of a plucked duck on the kitchen table. Some
days later he found her lying motionless on the sofa, arms pressed
against her body, legs bent. He asked her if she had a pain: 'No,' she
said, 'I'm the dead duck!'

The poems I have quoted, particularly the second and third of
them, show a similar situation: the writers' inner need was to come to
terms with disturbing events—to succeed in incorporating those
events in their created worlds. The need arose because their created
worlds were in danger of being disrupted. What the small child did in
her playing they did (in a more complex and comprehensive way) in
their poems.

But inner adjustment may be required for other reasons. We may
encounter some object, or person, or idea which makes special demands of us, calls for our homage. In paying homage we adjust our
world to include the powerful new phenomenon. W. H. Auden[3] has
said that a poem 'pays homage by naming' and points out the wide
variety of 'sacred objects' which may demand such homage, from a
pumping engine to a sweetheart! The need to pay homage may be a
strong one ('a passion of awe' Auden calls it) and the writing of the
poem satisfies the need. In 'Death Ode to Breac' homage was paid to a
dead thrush: many poems by young children celebrate the small creatures so important in their affections. This one was written by a nine-
year-old a few days ago:

To Lindy

> Little black dog with ginger paws,
> Butterfly ears and sharp little claws.

Chasing blackbirds, chasing balls,
Racing home when someone calls.

Happily snoozing in the chair,
Snuggling down without much air.
Squealing, smiling, when her friends come back;
Cleaning her coat of shiny black.

But poems of homage are more characteristic of adolescence. The need to love something more powerful than himself seems to be strong in many adolescents and their 'sacred objects' will often be vast, vague idealizations. In this poem by a seventeen-year-old girl it seems to me that the writer comes to terms with disturbing convictions about death and pays homage to an eternity more powerful than herself and more powerful than death:

Orion

I shall be starlight when I come to die,
Caught up forever, tucked in safe and cold,
Cold in the howling cold, without a tear
In all the reeling realms
To spill upon my sleeping starbright head.
The voiceless singing silence welcomes me;
The hound, wrought on the sky in stars
Shall bay to the moon
And hold me fast between his midnight paws.

In affirming that a poem is a form of words satisfying in itself, we might note that some critics believe the origins of poetry to lie in ritual magic, in the words that accompanied the mimetic rites by which primitive people hoped to assuage evil powers—drought or flood or tempest. The participants believed that these rites averted disaster: they were of course mistaken, but it is at least possible that the ceremonies resolved fears and hesitations in the men themselves and made them better husbandmen or hunters. There is no magic in poetry that psychologists will not one day explain, but we may still trace its descent from 'magic' in the curious modes of composition sometimes recorded by poets—how poems occur to them suddenly, sometimes even in dreams. (Blake believed he had only to write what the Divine Spirit revealed to him: Yeats accounted for some of his poems almost as mysteriously.) There is no doubt that experiences usually remain fallow—remembered or forgotten—for a period before they find expression in poetry. There has to be, as it were, an incubatory period. Their reappearance, perhaps with dramatic suddenness, after they seem to have been forgotten, is enough to make the process seem near-magical. Again, it is probably true that one effect of the regular beat of metrical language is to induce a mild kind of hypnosis in the reader, a lulling of the critical and logical aspects of the mind: and that by this means, and others, poets are able to make us *feel* the truth of some hypothesis which logical reasoning would refute.

Enough about witch-doctors. I suggested earlier that we create the worlds we live in and that misinterpretation might create for a man an isolated, a private world. The truth of the matter is that members of one society, with traditions in common and many experiences in common, tend to create for themselves worlds which are on the whole compatible. Much interpretation of experience is in fact a co-operative process: we share experiences (in conversation for instance) and so assist each other's interpretation. To this extent we build a common world belonging to our particular society, our pattern of culture.

And it is a changing world: as with the individual, so with the pattern of culture, new experiences make new demands. Today we must, if we are to preserve our world intact, come to terms with the fact of atomic power. At one level the adjustment must be made by scientists, politicians, men of affairs: but the heart of any pattern of culture lies in its attitudes, values, ideals, beliefs. Here the poet must play his part. As the child came to terms with her own anxieties in the poem she wrote, so the poet, first on his own behalf and then on behalf of us all, must try to resolve the conflict between existing values and the new threat. But the poet's achievement, should he succeed, cannot of itself change the pattern of culture. For that to happen, his adjustment—embodied in his poetry—must gain currency in society.

For the child, poetry is a primer in which he discovers our pattern of culture. Much we have until recently believed to be essential human nature, inherited by every human being, has been shown to belong to our particular (and widespread) pattern of culture— important ideals, for instance, regarding right and wrong. The child, in other words, must acquire these as he grows up. He learns, in the first instance, by living in his family, in the course of ordinary behaviour. But he learns also from poetry—beginning with nursery rhymes— since poetry embodies the values by which we live.

There is all the difference in the world between stating the values by which we live and embodying them. Moralists and philosophers might do the one, poets and artists do the other. In poetry the child does not understand the values, he lives them. The raw material of his own experience is shaped by the poem when he responds to it in much the same way as the raw material of the poet's experience took shape in writing the poem. The result is not new knowledge·of the world, but a new pattern of experience, an addition to his created world. Most children experience, for instance, the protective love of their parents. But when, say at seven or eight, they hear John Clare's *Song* their own experience is confirmed and given wider significance: they discover it as something that holds true outside their own homes, they begin to accept it as part of our way of living:

Song

O, wert thou in the storm,
  How I would shield thee:
To keep thee dry and warm,
  A camp I would build thee.

. . .

The rain should not wet thee,
  Nor thunderclap harm thee.
By thy side I would set me,
  To comfort and warm thee.

Again, man's relations with the animal world vary tremendously from one culture pattern to another. A child begins to absorb our complicated attitudes as he reads, say, Yeats' *To a Squirrel* or *Song of a Fool*, Robert Frost's *The Runaway*, Clifford Dyment's *Man and Beast*, or James Reeves' *Intruder*. Surprisingly early in childhood he begins to find his own anxieties—his fear of the dark or unknown, the horror and fascination for him of violence, his fears about death—reflected and resolved in the experiences poetry provides. And as he enters into these experiences he enters into our pattern of culture.

It is important that the child should create his own world in the light of these experiences: important for him and for our civilization. He may grow up to be a man who acts by and gives currency to stultifying, crude, or destructive values: he may grow up to be one who acts by and gives currency to the most sensitive adjustments to experience so far existing in our way of life. The difference is important, never more so than today.

References

1. I. A. Richards, *Principles of Literary Criticism*, Kegan Paul, 1934.
2. Jean Piaget, *Play, Dreams and Imitation in Childhood*, Heinemann, 1951.
3. W. H. Auden, *Making, Knowing and Judging*, Oxford University Press, 1956.

2

Words and the Imagination

Whitehead, in one of the chapters of his book *The Aims of Education*, shows that a child's need of language arises out of his attempts to explore the world around him. He gropes towards objects, grasps them, handles them: uses them, compares them with other objects: wants to *classify* them, ask questions about them; remember and consider them. The immense task of learning to speak is undertaken at an astoundingly early age: the language so acquired the child uses in further exploration and contemplation of the world around him.

We too often think of environment, the world around us, as something that awaits our contemplation, that "stays put." Nothing less true: the groping for objects and handling of them lead straight on to every kind of interaction between child and active environment. It is *experience* the child is groping for and seeking to interpret. In our attempts to penetrate to the meaning of experience we continue to use words as a primary instrument. This penetration in search of pattern, in search of significance, is a function, I suggest, of the imagination. (We are familiar with the workings of the imagination in the creative processes of art: this penetrative power bears the same stamp.)

This power—"imagination" if you will—works from an early stage, then, through the medium of language. Not, of course, at first written language: the pride of being the first means a child has of *recording* his impressions of experience must go to the visual arts. (The meaning of what is recorded may well be much enhanced, however, if we can hear also what the child says as he draws: adding words, that is, to the picture.)

The need to write follows at a later stage. By using words the child orders his responses to the world, arranges them, and in doing so reaps the benefit of grasping more of their meaning. But as responses grow more complex, they may sort themselves out only in written language. We write, often, in anticipation and in hope, and when we have written discover what it was we meant to say.

We know, as teachers of English, the penalty in a child of not

Published in *Athene* 6 (3), 1953.

being able to express himself in words at all. It is a kind of imprison-
ment, and his struggle to speak or write has the air of a painful and
strenuous bid to escape. The restriction, it often seems to us, is one of
experience itself, a poverty not only of words but of living.

What is concerned is no less than the making available of experience itself. We, as we live, must learn from experience, our own, first,
and other people's, second. But we do not learn from experience left in
the raw, unsifted, uninterpreted. Expression, in any form whatsoever,
is an interpretation of experience: we learn in the process of expression
itself and we learn also from experience made available, brought to
hand so to speak, by being expressed.

When we consider how important this process is to life itself, it is
no wonder that we recognize in the child a strong instinctual drive to
express himself imaginatively. The tendency amounts to a need and
those of us who have care of any of the arts in school find in that
need—in common—our challenge and our charter.

An interpretation of experience as I have been thinking of it is a
penetration of experience: it is not the mere purveying of a distilled
essence, or a key formula, or a mathematical solution. There is something in it of a reconstruction of events—and yet an ordered reconstruction. The artist's interpretation of experience is concrete; sensuous,
emotional: yet it is not a mere re-enactment either—it is a work of the
creative imagination.

As far as words are concerned, it is in poetry above all that the
penetrative and constructive powers of the imagination find expression. Poetry, said Professor Garrod, "deals not with things as they are,
but with things *as they matter.*" To read a poem, based—as a poem
must be—upon experience, is not the same thing as to go through that
experience oneself: it is rather that the reader takes the particular path
into apprehension of the real which the poet took (or as near to that as
the words of the poem working upon the experience of the reader can
achieve). The poet's interpretation of experience, since words have
meaning, or represent concepts, is concrete, sensuous, emotional and
intellectual. As a user of words the poet has a greater power to interpret experience since he exploits all the resources of words, while the
prose writer uses only some of them. Poetry, for these reasons, will
occupy a central position in the English teaching at most schools. It
will be both written and read.

We share with teachers of art a genuine delight in the products of
the child's imagination: his way of using words "freshly," without the
dullness that verbal facility can bring. If he can be steered clear of the
trap—it is widely recognized as such—of imitating the rhymed verses
of his elders, the child can write words which are poetry by virtue of
their truth to the imagination, to the inner eye and the inner ear. We do
not want to be sentimental over this, and there is no need to be: the

child and the poet take pleasure both in the experience embodied and in the words that embody it. There is no difference save that the experience, and—to a lesser degree—the vocabulary, bear in the child's case the appropriate restrictions. It is precisely because he retains a sense of the "new-foundness," the freshness, and so the delight, of words that the poet is the kind of artist he is.

But we suspect we must go further than this. We suspect there are stages in a child's development when, both in what he reads and what he writes, he needs to escape for a time from the conflicts of actual experience and *take refuge in* imagined experience; and that for this purpose the more familiar and accessible, and the more docile, the imagined experience, the better it suits his need for peace and protectedness. We are thinking of course particularly of the adolescent, and particularly of his rejection of powerful original emotional poetry in favour of a rather sentimental kind of poetry which deals in conventional feelings and conventional situations. He finds the conventional situation, both in life and in art, useful to him since it enables him to respond to strong and disturbing feelings arising within him, and yet keep his response within strict bounds. The stock situation acts rather as a rein than as a spur. The unfamiliar stimulus of an original and powerful work of art, on the other hand, threatens the self-imposed bounds, and is often rejected for this reason. As Jenkinson points out in his survey *What Do Boys and Girls Read?* children read for two reasons: they read not only because they are growing up, but also because of the *difficulties of growing up.*

We record this simply to advocate tolerance for what may be judged aberrant tastes. Growth is often assumed to be something like the turning of the sunflower towards the sun: it is no denial of the sun's virtues to admit the possibility of the need occasionally for a little shade! Man is a complex creature and some stages of his life-history are more complicated than others. If the adolescent does not seem to know what he wants for long, let us not be too sure that we know better than he does. The destination we may see clearly enough, but the route by which it is reached may be more devious, and more variable, than our assumptions about it have been.

The destination is certainly clear to this extent: a cultural education must aim at teaching a child to supersede the stock situation and the conventional feeling in what he reads: that art may so come, in time, to enrich experience.

And the final destination aimed at by teachers of poetry is that rare and happy state of being able and accustomed, as an adult, to turn to genuine poetry as a means of continued growth throughout life. In poetry more than in any other art, I venture rashly to say in conclusion, creative effort is required—sometimes of a high order—for the mere entering into what the artist seeks to communicate. This—rashly again—seems to me to be connected with the fact that poetry uses words and words are able to treat experience with an explicitness that is not found in any other medium.

If this sounds a braggart note to end on, perhaps readers will forgive me: it needs some conviction—and co-operation—to enable teachers of a relatively unpatronized art to persevere in their efforts!

3

Poetry and Our Pattern of Culture

Statements about the way people ought to behave in our society must to some extent be responsible for the way they do in fact behave. Such statements exist in the statutes of English law on the one hand and in school rules, club rules, the rules of Association football on the other. But I believe most of us for most of the time pick and choose our ways of behaving with no reference whatsoever to any such statements.

The guardian angel who brought us up short from time to time with the question, 'Why did you do that?' would surely get a bewildering variety of answers—if, with benefit of school-teaching experience, we can envisage such an unpleasant procedure. 'Because I felt like it' or 'Because I simply had to'; 'Because I love him'—or envy or pity or hate or despise; 'Because I'm in a hurry' or in a rage or in a dream. 'Because it was my duty' would be a rare answer, I think, and 'Because I *felt* I ought to' much more frequent. Many of our ways of behaving relate back, in other words, to ways of feeling.

No doubt our 'pattern of culture' includes many modes of behaviour that cool reason, deliberation, prudence or simply external authority dictate but I am not concerned with them here. Poetry is half my subject and it is not primarily in the area of culture determined by reason that poetry exercises its influence. Putting it very simply, I am not concerned here with the thousand ways in which *knowledge* derived from precept and deduction must determine our conduct, but with the thousand and one ways in which our conduct is determined by feeling and intuition.

Let us be clear about one thing to start with: such ways of behaving can only be learnt from experience and experience which is often painful. They are not something we inherit at birth as members of the human species. Ruth Benedict's *Patterns of Culture* brings out this point very clearly: much that we have taken for granted for generations

First published in *Presenting Poetry*, Thomas Blackburn (ed.), 1966. London: Methuen for the University of London Institute of Education.

as simply a part of 'human nature' proves to belong to our own culture and is not necessarily found in other cultures. (The culture we call Western civilization has become so widespread that those of us who live within it fail to realize what different modes of feeling and behaving, what different values and attitudes, there are in other patterns of culture.)

Before going on to ask how we learn such ways of behaving I want to look briefly at the relation between these ways of behaving derived from feeling and those other intellectually formulated ways which are based on knowledge derived from precept and deduction. The crux of the relationship may be suggested by pointing out that working by rule is more effective in problems circumscribed by the textbook than it is in the uncircumscribed problems of daily life. Ideas, concepts, abstractions, unlike concrete objects, may be easier to define than they are to recognize. It is one thing, for example, to have embraced a clearly defined educational aim, and another thing to decide which particular course of action open to you at a given moment in the class room is most likely to further that aim. Again, life frequently seems to offer us what is a choice between failure and failure, between evil and evil, or at best between one curate's egg and another.

This is not an argument against reasoning and the application of all the knowledge we have; it is rather an attempt to explain why feeling enters in at all, and I can only give an answer in the crudest terms: that for most of our moment-by-moment choices reasoning is too *slow*. Because of the many-sidedness of situations there is always the danger that we shall ignore essential components, and so arrive at a snap decision that is of little value. Analysis, the disentanglement of the threads, may give place then to a more effective method of selection which I can only call a kind of empathy, a way of *feeling into* the situation; global, syncretic rather than analytic. ('Because I felt I ought to' is probably a better description of what actually went on than 'Because it was my duty'.) Perhaps D. H. Lawrence means something of this sort when he has Lady Chatterley say, 'It is the way our sympathy flows and recoils that really determines our lives.'

It is important for what I want to say about poetry to notice at all events that there is a gap between the beliefs, values, and ways of behaving of our society as they are codified or formulated, and our behaviour as it expresses itself through our everyday actions. It is the difference between 'justice' and the actions of a just man. It could make sense of, 'I felt I ought to, although I knew it was my duty not to,' which is otherwise arrant nonsense.

Since the values of our pattern of culture are expressed in these two different forms there are two distinct learning tasks for the child. Rules, precepts, prohibitions come very early into his life. Attitudes and ways of feeling he begins to acquire even earlier. These potential attitudes and ways of behaviour are developed by every experience he undergoes and by a kind of 'creative' imitation or improvisation. Much of this improvisation takes the form of play—trial without the possibility of error—since the infant has four or five years of comparative irresponsibility accorded to him in which to practise responsibility against the day that it is expected of him. To improvise in the behaviour of mothers and fathers, doctors and nurses, brides and mourners, is to practise the art of associating feelings with situations and of allowing action and decision to spring from those feelings. Not all of it is play, of course, and life-long attitudes to the most important aspects of experiences have their foundations in the feeling-relations entered into in the day-to-day life of the family.

But poetry, in common with all literature, is as much a rehearsal of experience as is make-believe play. (Here is trial without the possibility of error for all of us.) Patterns of feeling-experiences in the family are found again in a wider context—in poems and stories that are about *anybody's* mother or father or sister: the kind of protectiveness for example that a child has known in his own home he finds now in lullabies that don't belong just to him. 'When the bough breaks the cradle will fall, And down will come baby, cradle and all.' He also finds in such lullabies an expression of his deepest fears and anxieties. He is in fact responding to what is an embodiment of part of our pattern of culture.

Stories or poems about witches and monsters and giants have their function too: as play may do, they allow the expression of and so give shape to feelings that enter into family relationships, surely enough, but may not be given free expression there. I would not explain this as a matter of 'purging' or getting rid of forbidden emotions. To be capable of these feelings and yet to control them, that is the object, and it seems to me that to express them in play or in response to a poem is a way of organizing them and so bringing them under control. The resulting behaviour is one step nearer to that useful abstraction, the mature adult.

But I want to examine in greater detail the particular role that poetry of a certain kind can play in relation to our pattern of culture. 'The nucleus of every poem worthy of the name', says Robert Graves,[1] 'is rhythmically formed in the poet's mind, during a trance-like suspension of his normal habits of thought, by the supra-logical reconciliation of conflicting emotional ideas. The poet learns to induce this trance in self-protection whenever he feels unable to resolve an emotional conflict by simple logic.' I would not accept that 'every poem worthy of the name' is of this kind or created in this way but it is this poetry of conflict and tension that I want to consider. I. A. Richards called it 'poetry of contrary impulses' and believed that its power lay (as I believe the virtue of a right choice of action lies) in its *inclusiveness*, a certain fullness of response to theme and situation. Of the many-sidedness of a situation, the stresses, the irreconcilable demands, as much as possible would be represented in the poem. Cleanth Brooks,[2] quoting this point of Richards's, adds as his comment that he 'will regard as acceptable any poem whose unifying attitude is one which really achieves unity, but which unifies not by ignoring but by taking into account the complexities and apparent contradictions of the situation concerned'.

Let me relate these ideas prosaically with mundane affairs. The data we take forward to any new experience is a set of expectations derived from the whole of our past experience: we carry with us as it were a world schema, a representation of the world as we have found it to be. The new experience is there to be incorporated; if it proves not too unlike our expectations we can adjust our world picture to incorporate it easily enough as we actually participate in the new experience. But if it is particularly unlike our expectations or touches off some inner anxiety we cannot do this. Since events don't wait for us, we must participate as best we can, but afterwards we are left in a state of mind that can only be described as a kind of indigestion. We need then to go back over the experience, represented in some way, and come to terms with it. The usual course for most of us will be to *talk* about it—representing it and working upon it in speech—and the need to do so may continue a long time before we succeed in coming to terms. But we may write about it, and if our writing succeeds then it will have some of the poetic qualities described by Robert Graves.

'A poem', to quote Cleanth Brooks[3] again, 'does not deal primarily with ideas and events but rather with the way in which a human being may come to terms with ideas and events.' For me, a poem of the kind I have described *is* the way a human being has come to terms with ideas and events. I believe children, and ordinary men and women, and poets are all capable of writing in this way, and that what each will write is valid in so far as it achieves for the writer this process of coming to terms. I regard the following as a valid example of the kind of writing we are considering: it is a six-year-old child with a problem on her hands:

'There was a child of a witch who was ugly. He had pointed ears thin legs and was born in a cave. He flew in the air holding on nothing just playing games.

When he saw ordinary girls and boys he hit them with his broom stick. A cat came along. He arched his back at the girls and boys and made them run away. When they had gone far away the cat meeowed softly at the witch child. The cat loved the child. The child loved the cat the cat was the onlee thing the child loved in the world.'

In so far as the needs of a writer are our own needs, what he has
written can help us to come to terms with our own disturbing experiences. That this is not an infrequent happening may be accounted for
by the existence of what Coleridge called 'the all-in-each of every
man'. And we can bear it out as teachers: look beneath the surface of
the poems that children take to at various stages of their development
and—discounting the unserious poems that are liked for other
reasons—you are likely to find some manifestation of the basic irrecon-
cilables of growing up: the need to conform at war with the desire to
rebel; the need to be adventurous at war with the need for security; the
need to grow up at war with the need to be fussed over; the need to
love at odds with the law of the jungle; the need for privacy in conflict
with the desire to be the life and soul of the party; the need to adore at
odds with the wish to overpower.

Although what the poet writes and what the child writes may be
equally valid, it is still true that what the poet writes is likely to be
more influential, that is, effective for a greater number of readers.
Moreover, as an adult member of society the poet resolves his conflicts
in a way that is appropriate to our pattern of culture. Indeed, it is out of
such adjustments that the pattern itself has been created. The attitudes, ways of feeling and ways of behaving we set out to consider
are the quintessence of the adjustments made by artists of all kinds at
all periods in the history of our civilization.

In the many-sidedness of situations we have observed a kind of
polarity, a two-sidedness (a two-sidedness which is perhaps finally
expressed in the conflict between a desire for life and the need to
acknowledge the fact of death).

The language of poetry, it seems to me, differs most from the
language of prose statement in the power it possesses to represent,
indeed to recreate, this two-sidedness. It does so in many ways—by its
ambiguous use of words and syntax, by using rhythm and the corporeal
qualities of words to give a sense that may be at variance with the
paraphrasable meaning; by using images which may themselves bring
contrary impulses into play. What I want to illustrate is no single one
of these but a strategy of poetry to which they may all contribute at
times.

When we read a passage of informative prose—a letter, for example, telling us about a friend's visit—we may read it and put it aside.
We have its message. We may not remember any of the words, but we
know what was conveyed. Our knowledge is not in any order, as the
letter was; it no longer has a beginning and an end.

It is wrong to suppose that a poem (of the sort we are considering)
does not have a meaning of this kind, though it may be much more
complex and difficult to come at than it is in prose statement. A major

difference between such poetry and prose lies in the fact that in the poem this meaning is not the sole end and object of the communication (as it was with the letter) but a bare beginning. Indeed you cannot begin to read the poem in the way such a poem must be read until you have this meaning there in your mind. For it is the constant interplay between the first acquired meaning and each significant detail of the words of the poem that gives such poetry its peculiar power to express two-sidedness.

My illustration is a poem by Emily Dickinson.

Ample make this bed,
Make this bed with awe;
In it wait till judgement break
Excellent and fair.

Be its mattress straight,
Be its pillow round;
Let no sunrise' yellow noise
Interrupt this ground.

Though this is quite clearly a poem about death, I suggest that its first-communicated, and paraphrasable meaning is a description of a child being put to bed. (That it is so clearly about death—in the last line—means that the tension is already set up between two conflicting attitudes, even before we move back to the detail with the 'sense' in mind.) It is not, of course, an explicit description: had 'good night' for example been actually *spoken* to the child the double meaning could hardly have been sustained. 'Good night' is not directly stated, it is suggested by the wishes that, in the second stanza, take the place of the instructions in the first.

Be its mattress straight,
Be its pillow round

The child is tucked up for the night, until the morning; tucked up in bed, whatever she may be at other times, she is 'excellent and fair'. Good night is said, and the household warned not to disturb her.

But the detail pulls in another direction. The bed is made 'with awe'; the first dire note. It is 'judgement' and not next morning that is to break, and once that fusion between judgement and dawn has taken place, then the bright sun of the next morning, since it will not now awake the child (or person) into temporal life but death, must be given some other form. It is given the form of 'yellow noise', the noise—or even the sudden light of an opening door—that, in the first meaning, might have awakened the sleeping child in the night. 'Interrupt' plays a startlingly different role in each of the two meanings: with reference to the sleeping child it has the ordinary sense, of disturbing 'her sleep';

with reference to the dead child it harks back to its Latin origin and means 'break into'. And the word 'ground'—contributing to the second meaning only—sends us scurrying back to reinterpret the whole poem.

If the poem works for you as it does for me (and for quite young children, as I have found) then it provides a resolution between two otherwise distinct attitudes, What we feel for the child at her bedtime we are prevailed upon to feel about someone dead and in a grave.

The reader who reconciles the love of life with the acknowledgement of death in such terms as these acquires a way of feeling that is part of our pattern of culture; and a way of feeling that will affect his ways of behaving.

We need to remind ourselves here that a pattern of culture is not something to be passed on from generation to generation without change. Society must come to terms with new experiences no less than individuals. And that is why a poet of the past, however much he may have contributed to our inheritance, is no substitute for a living poet.

Again, it is not enough that poets and other artists should make sensitive adjustments to the experiences of our day and age. These will not become part of our pattern of culture until, by adopting them in response, we give them currency. My stock example of this is the need of our day and age to come to terms with the existence of the atomic bomb, and I am thinking not of policies or of laws and regulations, but of ways of feeling and behaving.

The responsibility upon us as teachers to watch over and guide the attitudes of our children is probably heavier than it has ever been. Mass media are powerfully at work in precisely the same fields of operation as the poets. They too offer to reconcile the irreconcilable; but too often the reconciliation they provide is false because they are ignorant of the real conflict. Kathleen Nott,[4] looking at poetry and mass media side by side, has put her view very strongly.

> 'I think that very few people will disagree with me when I say we live in a world of mass media, mass communication, propaganda, in other words of downright lies. And I cannot think of anything else among verbal media which by its very nature repudiates this lying or grossly inaccurate use of language, in the way poetry does . . . It is a matter of the individual voice doing its utmost to say precisely what it feels at any given moment.'

I do not disagree with this comment upon today, but I have in conclusion one long-term reservation to make. I believe that new 'individual voices' will eventually be heard speaking in the mass media themselves; and when they do they may powerfully affect, unify and extend our pattern of culture because they are likely to gain wide currency quickly. Valuable things have to begin somewhere, and when they do they are often valuable in new ways—which means that some of us may not recognize them when they come.

References

1. *The Common Asphodel,* Hamish Hamilton, 1949, p. 1.
2. *The Well Wrought Urn,* Dobson, 1949 and University Paperbacks, 1966, p. 228.
3. op. cit., p. 229.
4. *Art, Science and Education,* a conference report published by the Joint Council for Education Through Art, 1958, p. 109.

4

Response to Literature

Men make some things to serve a purpose, other things simply to
please themselves. Literature is a construct of the latter kind, and the
proper response to it is therefore (in D. W. Harding's words) to 'share
in the author's satisfaction that it was as it was and not otherwise'.
Literature is a construct in language, and language is of all the symbolic systems or modes of representation the most *explicit*, the best
fitted, for example, to present a running commentary upon experience.
It follows that much of the satisfaction in most literature comes from a
contemplation of the form given to events, a characteristic that distinguishes a work of literature from a sculpture or piece of music, where
other forms are contemplated. A novel, in Susanne Langer's terms, is 'a
virtual experience'. The satisfaction in which a reader shares, therefore, must have something in common with the satisfaction he feels,
not so much in having an experience as in looking back at an experience he has had; it is as though he were to look back at an experience
he has *not* had.

Clearly a naïve reader may share a satisfaction in circumstances
which would only infuriate or at least disappoint a more sophisticated
reader. Is this naïve response different in kind from that we desire for
literature, or merely different in intensity of feeling or complexity or
comprehensiveness or verisimilitude? In other words, are such responses (and children must make many of them) the bad currency we
seek to drive out, or are they the tender shoots that must be fostered if
there is to be a flower at all? Kate Friedlander,[1] a Freudian psychologist, noticed the tremendous satisfaction young children derive from
reading stories related to an Oedipus situation (the fatherless boy
proves his manhood in *Treasure Island*, the orphan girl has a series
of substitute mothers in *Heidi*, and so on), but she sharply distinguishes
this satisfaction from 'a literary response', which she seems to feel must
somehow have to do with art rather than life. I am sure she is wrong;
these responses are unsophisticated in the sense that they might be
equally as appropriate to a story of less merit as to *Treasure Island*, but

Published in *Response to Literature*, James Squire (ed.), National Council of
Teachers of English, 1968. Reprinted by permission.

they are the stuff from which, with refinement and development, literary responses are made. Again, at quite a different level, teachers using the 'practical criticism' method sometimes introduced passages of literature paired with sentimental or otherwise second-rate writing, inviting comment leading to a verdict. Is not this an attempt to drive out bad currency? If, as I believe, satisfaction with the second-rate differs in degree but not in kind from the higher satisfaction, teachers should surely be concerned to *open* doors; as the pupils advance, other doors will close behind them with no need for the teacher to intervene.

Our aim, then, should be to refine and develop responses the children are already making—to fairy stories, folk songs, pop songs, television serials, their own game-rhymes, and so on. Development can best be described as an increasing sense of form. In literature, I have suggested, this means principally a sense of the pattern of events, and this, however rudimentarily, children certainly feel in the stories that satisfy them. (A three-year-old referred to Cinderella as, 'A big sad book about two ugly sisters and a girl they were ugly to.') Progress lies in perceiving gradually more complex patterns of events, in picking up clues more widely separated and more diverse in character, and in finding satisfaction in patterns of events less directly related to their expectations and, more particularly, their desires; at the same time, it lies in also perceiving the form of the varying relationships between elements in the story and reality, as increasingly they come to know that commodity.

But the forms of language itself—its words with their meanings and associations, its syntax, its sounds and rhythms, its images—these contribute to the total form, not as fringe benefits but as inseparable elements of a single effect. 'An increasing sense of form' must be taken to mean an extension of responses to include these forms, or perhaps an integration of earlier responses to some of them into a total and inclusive response.

Our sense of literary form increases as we find satisfaction in a greater range and diversity of works, and particularly as we find satisfaction in works which, by their complexity or the subtlety of their distinctions, their scope or their unexpectedness, make greater and greater demands upon us. Our sense of form increases as our frame of reference of reality grows with experience, primary and secondary, of the world we live in. A sense of literary form must grow thus, from within; it is the legacy of past satisfactions. It may become articulate, finding expression in comment and criticism, but equally it may not; and this, as pedants, we find very difficult to admit. There are certainly situations in the classroom where receptive listening and a following silence are more eloquent testimony of satisfaction than any comment could be.

It is probably true that the responses of most adult readers are sharpened (and perhaps more fully integrated with their previous experiences) if they are in some measure formulated, so that they become aware of the nature of the processes that have led to satisfaction. But it is certainly not true for children under the age of eleven or so, children who have not yet passed through what Piaget has called the stage of 'concrete operations'. Here their responses to literature may indeed be lively, discriminating, and complex, but it will be no help to them to attempt to formulate those responses. There is ample scope for talk, of course, and value in it; but it will be talk about the people and events of literature and not about forms, conventions, devices, techniques. We should be more afraid of introducing such matters too early than too late.

It is equally clear that to be made aware of the processes that have led to the satisfaction of *another* reader—a teacher, say, or a critic—can have value only in so far as the knowledge helps us formulate our own processes, helps us, that is, become aware of the form of a response we have already made or are capable of making. A critical statement is a discursive form and quite different in organization from the 'presentational symbols' or 'expressive forms' of literature; an understanding of the one cannot substitute for a response to the other. I take this to be the reader's counterpart of what Robert Frost said of the writer: 'You cannot worry a poem into existence, though you may work upon it once it is in being.' The author's satisfaction in his work is something he *feels* and not something that can be *proved* right or wrong. The principle of organization of a critical statement is cognitive; that of a work of literature is, in the final analysis, affective.

The point at which critical statements can be of help to a student is therefore a difficult one to determine. It is even more important, however, to consider the manner in which such help is offered. The voice of the critic must not be allowed to seem the voice of authority; more harm has probably been done to the cause of literature by this means than by any other. It is all too easy for the immature student, feeling that his own responses are unacceptable, to disown them and profess instead the opinions of respected critics. And to many teachers, with their eyes on what may rightly go on in other parts of the curriculum, this looks like good teaching. It may of course be the best kind of preparation for an ill-conceived examination, and this may be the real root of the trouble.

To have children take over from their teachers an analysis of a work of literature which their teachers in turn have taken over from the critics or their English professors—this is not a short cut to literary sophistication; it is a short circuit that destroys the whole system. A response to a work of literature is, after all, an interaction between the work and the reader—not a free interaction, of course, but even the most disciplined responses of two different persons must reflect something of their individual differences. Further, while Shakespeare may continue supreme and Samuel Rogers forgotten, some very general differences of opinion must be expected even among the initiated: there will probably always be respected critics who judge *Silas Marner* to be a bad novel and other critics, equally respected, who regard it highly.

Perhaps the meaning of a work of literature may be compared (as most other things have been) to the ripples that move out from a stone thrown into water; what happens to them depends to some extent upon the configuration of the pond. To me, Blake's poem 'Never Seek to Tell Thy Love' has some relevance to the arguments I put forward earlier concerning the difference between a critical statement and a response; I do not expect the poem to suggest that to another reader, unless perhaps his interest in language resembles my own.

How then do we encourage the improved response, the developed sense of form?

A girl of eight was asked what sort of things she liked reading. 'Well,' she said, 'there's *Treasure Island*—that's a bloody one for when I'm feeling boyish. And there's *Little Men*—a sort of half-way one.' 'Don't you ever feel girlish?' she was asked. 'Yes, when I'm tired. Then I read *The Smallest Dormouse*.'

We must expect, and encourage, reading to go on for various purposes at various levels and not concern ourselves solely with performance at maximum effort. 'Reading for enjoyment' (to pick up an ancient controversy) will certainly be an apt description of the lower levels of effort but is probably misleading when applied to the most demanding kind of reading. Satisfaction, however, the appropriate satisfaction we have repeatedly referred to, must be there in the end, and no examination or other external incentive can take its place; reading without satisfaction is like the desperate attempts we make to keep a car going when it has run out of petrol.

That a student should read *more books* with satisfaction may be set down as one objective; as a second, he should read books with *more satisfaction*. We need to foster, in other words, wide reading side by side with close reading. The importance of freedom of choice is obvious enough in the first situation, less recognized in the second, since close reading is usually taken to mean class teaching. But choice is no less desirable in the classroom, and students should whenever possible choose what is studied by the class as a whole or, better still, by groups on their own with occasional help from the teacher.

The problems lie, then, not in knowing what to do but in getting enough suitable books sufficiently accessible. Paperbacks have made things much easier; local prescriptions and proscriptions that have militated against spending money in this way are on the decline in some areas, still need vigorous attack in others. When other attempts have failed, boys and girls themselves have sometimes provided a class library by pooling paperbacks, say for a term at a stretch. Such a collection may need supplementing to meet the needs of the best readers, who are likely to contribute the most rewarding books and find few of comparable value in return.

Close reading and wide reading should not be thought of as quite separate activities. Active response to a work of literature invokes what might be called an unspoken monologue of responses—a fabric of comment, speculation, relevant autobiography. It is natural for something which one member of the class has read to be brought before the rest of them at his suggestion as the object of a closer scrutiny. (It is always preferable of course that a passage studied should in some way be related to the whole book.) Talk in class should arise from, and further stimulate, the individual monologues of response.

It is in the context of this talk that views of the critic or teacher can best be handled if they are to be useful at all. Clearly, for advanced college-preparatory pupils they can be valuable. As part of the to and fro of discussion critical judgements may be accepted for the help they offer; if the discussion is as open as it should be, they will frequently be disputed and sometimes rejected by individual students. The attitudes engendered by the mode and tone of discussion carry forward and influence the reading of both literature and criticism.

In all I have said so far I have accepted the terms of my commission as they would be generally understood. By 'literature' I have therefore meant the body of works represented in literature syllabuses, studied in university schools of English, and the like. However, before finishing my task I should like very briefly to point to an unorthodox way of defining literature which has the advantage of placing it among linguistic activities generally.

I would go back to my opening paragraph and define literature as a particular kind of utterance—an utterance that a writer has 'constructed' not for use but for his own satisfaction.

Sapir[2] pointed out long ago that man, unlike the zoological animals, does not handle reality by direct and *ad hoc* means but via a symbolic representation of the world as he has experienced it. Given this, two courses are open to a man: he may operate in the real world by means of his representation, or he may operate *directly upon the representation itself*—improvising upon it in any way that pleases him (that allays his anxieties, for example, or sweetens his disappointments, or whets his appetite, or flatters his ego).

We all use language in both these ways, to get things done in the outer world and to manipulate the inner world. Action and decision belong to the former use; freedom from them in the latter enables us to attend to other things—to the forms of language, the patterns of events, the feelings. We take up as it were the role of spectators: spectators of our own past lives, our imagined futures, other men's lives, impossible events. When we *speak* this language, the nearest name I can give it is 'gossip'; when we *write* it, it is literature.

By this definition, then, literature is not simply something that other people have done. What a child writes is of the same order as what the poet or novelist writes and valid for the same reasons. What are the reasons? Why do men improvise upon their representations of the world? Basically because we never cease to long for more lives than the one we have; in the role of spectator we can participate in an infinite number.

References

1. Kate Friedlander, 'Children's books and their function in latency and puberty,' *New Era*, volume 39, 1958.
2. Edward Sapir, *Language*, Harcourt Brace, 1921.

5

The Role of Fantasy

Sometimes, as I am on the point of going to sleep, the image of a hideous face comes to float above my pillow. It may be a face that threatens hideously or one that is itself hideously mutilated—but I suspect there is, deep enough within me, a common origin for the two versions. Usually—or perhaps I should say in the cases that I can recall—I am enough awake to have to deal with this apparition: and I do that best by wakening further to summon the image of some other face, a familiar and benign one. These two acts of my imagination have a good deal in common, no doubt, yet originate quite differently, for one is voluntary, the other involuntary. In our waking hours, up and about, the bidden and the unbidden images are likely, I believe, to be less clearly differentiated since they will arise, directly or indirectly, in closer association with whatever occupies our attention.

Both deliberately and despite ourselves, then, we are pro-liferators of images. Even in the process of attending to what is before our eyes, we generate images of what we expect to see. As, for example, we try to 'make out' a mysterious object in the distance, we are likely to perceive it as more like the object we took it for than its actual features might justify: thus, at times, we shall change our 'recognition'—what we took to be a bear we shall now recognize as a bush, what we took to be a mountain peak we shall now recognize as a cloud formation. Though we have taken a special case as illustration, it is likely that all perceiving involves the generating of visual expectations and their matching with what our sight indicates. In other words, it requires an act of the imagination to construct any situation in which we actually find ourselves. A. A. Milne has illustrated this unfamiliar truth in his poem 'Nursery Chairs' from *When We Were Very Young*. In each of the first three stanzas, he has the three-year-old imagining (with the aid of a chair) that he is an Amazonian explorer, or a lion in a cage, or a sailor on the high seas; and for the final stanza:

Published in *English in Education* 5 (3), Winter, 1971.

Whenever I sit in a high chair
For breakfast or dinner or tea
I try to pretend that it's *my* chair,
And that I am a baby of three.

Nowadays, when I dream in my sleep, I usually dream of people talking, and often remember what they have said. It is all very reasonable. Very occasionally, however, silent images build up into a frightening situation, sometimes of falling or leaping into space, but more often of having to get somewhere on foot, knowing that I am under dire threat if I am not there in time, and experiencing (as Beckett's old men do) extraordinary physical difficulty in making any progress at all. Obviously I cannot generalize from this difference between the commonplace and wordy and the silent and frightening among dreams: but it is true of my own experience and illustrates a point I want to make.

Our concern here is with fantasy themes in children's reading. It was important therefore to remember at the outset that language is only one way of representing to ourselves both the actual world and unreal, fantastic worlds; and that other means, such as the visual image, antedate the use of words and continue to operate both in association with words and independently. Putting experiences into words is a process of *ordering* them in a particular way, imposing on the data, in fact, some effects of the organization inherent in language itself. (Language, as the linguists tell us, is *rule-governed* behaviour.) My description, for example, of the kind of walking paralysis that afflicts me in my dreams is a far more orderly expression of a state of affairs than anything that enters the dream.

To speak is to 'articulate', over a wide range of that word's meanings; both to joint and to join; to provide with a framework; to knit, perhaps, or to weave—and the web, as Robert Graves has suggested, is a *cool* one—a means of lessening the intensity of experience:

Children are dumb to say how hot the day is,
How hot the scent is of the summer rose,
How dreadful the black wastes of evening sky,
How dreadful the tall soldiers drumming by.

But we have speech to chill the angry day,
And speech, to dull the rose's cruel scent.
We spell away the overhanging night,
We spell away the soldiers and the fright.

There's a cool web of language winds us in . . .

It has often enough been claimed, with justification, that by the use of language we construct the world of ideas. We need to note for our present purposes that as soon as we bring words into our reflection of experience, the *image* takes one step towards the *idea*.

Let us begin to define the area of our concern here by saying that we shall take fantasy to mean the handling of images *as play*—a statement that will need to be explained, extended, perhaps modified in the course of our consideration. As human beings we proliferate images; and to varying degrees, by various means and to various ends, we work upon them, manipulate them further. How for our present purpose do we sort these many variables? To begin with the very broad distinctions, adaptive behaviour—recognized throughout the evolutionary scale as the purposive activity by which organisms survive and prosper in relation to their environment—may in human beings be distinguished from behaviour which supersedes the demands of the here and now, the immediate environment. Certainly a young child's curiosity may seem to direct him into activities in which he seeks to use and control the objects around him—adaptive behaviour—but then to go a stage further where he seems to explore *for the sake of finding out,* for the sake of *knowing.* One cannot divorce this function of the human mind from the existence of language; language which so manifestly assists adaptive behaviour brings also this new possibility, that of storing the outcomes of experience and of other people's experience with scant regard for their immediate adaptive value. To adaptive behaviour, then, we add this that has been called 'reflective behaviour'. The small boy whose chances of controlling an automobile are still at least a dozen years away may nevertheless treasure a great deal of knowledge about how automobiles work.

The organization to which images are submitted for reflective purposes—to arrive in other words at knowledge—is the kind of organization that psychologists and philosophers are most familiar with. We have already referred to it in speaking of language, of 'articulation', of 'ideas', though of course a great deal more could be said. Words provide us with the means of classifying phenomena at different levels of generality; and of abstracting aspects of phenomena and creating superordinate abstract categories; and of systematically relating those abstractions into theories about the universe or any part of our experience of it. All these processes continue, of course, to be capable of serving practical ends, capable of entering into adaptive behaviour (as witness the technical devices in daily use whose origins lie in a scientific curiosity about the nature of matter); but they are by no means restricted to such purposes, and that being so they account for a wide range of human preoccupations we can roughly call 'reflective'.

So much has been known for so long about the laws of knowing, about the cognitive mode of organization, that it has sometimes been taken as the only form of organization that images (or whatever else we might decide to call the fundamental acts of the human mind) could enter into. Let us clear our ground by agreeing, in crude terms, that from *images* by organization of this cognitive kind come *ideas:* and that language in its characteristic and ordinary uses is the principal means by which the organizing is carried out. But is that the whole story?

Susan Isaacs,[1] in writing of the intellectual development of young children, seems inclined to accept the view that order comes out of *disorder* as a child comes to master cognitive processes:

> I consider it very important that we should not blur the distinction between thought and fantasy in our theories of intellectual growth . . . The egocentrism of the little child is strictly an affair of feeling and fantasy, not of thought. He is egocentric in so far as he has not yet learned to think. But as experience comes to him, and noetic synthesis grows, true relational thought emerges more and more out of the matrix of feeling and fantasy. . . . But the essential characteristic of egocentric ways of dealing with reality is surely that they *have* no "structure". It is not that one kind of structure gives place to another; it is rather that there is a progressive penetration of feeling and fantasy by experience, a progressive ordering by relational thought of the child's responses to the world.

What we are asking here is whether feeling and fantasy, at the stage of a child's development Susan Isaacs is describing, may not in fact represent, at least in embryonic form, some other kind of organization of his mental activity, an organization on a different principle from that of the cognitive; secondly, whether such an organization, if it exists, could appropriately be associated with 'play' in the way we have suggested; and finally how activities in play would relate to the two broad categories we have referred to, adaptive and reflective.

Play, as we mean it, is a voluntary activity: it occupies because in itself it *preoccupies,* and not for any reason outside itself—not, for example, as the direct legacy of any other kind of activity. Secondly, in so far as play takes up images of the actual world, it does so in a context and a mode of organization which indicates a comparatively low level of concern for their verisimilitude, their resemblance to things in the actual world. For this reason simulation exercises and the 'games' currently popular as a mode of teaching are not in our sense play activities. Putting this more generally, to the images we generate we attach varying degrees of credence: in our attempts to make out whether what we are looking at is a mountain peak or a cloud formation we shall generate visual expectations in close relation to what we believe to exist; in play we abandon such claims: the credibility of what we pretend in make-believe play is not likely to be a determining criterion: in our ordinary daydreaming (and we count this as a kind of play) we are not primarily concerned with the likelihood of fulfilment.

To say this is to draw a distinction between, on the one hand, play and on the other, the adaptive and reflective activities that create for each of us a shared world—the 'actual' world as we know it, that is to say, as we have represented it to ourselves in the course of such adaptive and reflective activities. In play we improvise upon the representation for reasons other than that of improving its truth to the facts of our experience. And freed from this necessity, we seem able in some sense to *be more ourselves*. This general distinction between the familiar kind of organization that belongs to adaptive and reflective behaviour (cognitive organization) and the postulated other kind of organization we are now looking for in play activities is one that has already been made elsewhere in terms of 'participant' and 'spectator' roles. Here I must take that as read, and yet rely on it to support two points I need to make. First, to suggest that the arts (including literature) represent a highly organized activity within the general area of 'play': all we have said earlier about playing might be applied to the practice of the arts, and the alternative kind of organization we are looking for is 'art-like'—occurs indeed in its most perfected version in a work of art. (To say that is of course merely to *begin* to understand the nature of the organization.) The claim is important in our present context, for, if it is true, a child's daydreaming and the stories he reads—stories such as *Alice in Wonderland*—are birds of a feather.

The second claim that arises from previous thinking about participant and spectator roles is the claim that spectator role activity is primarily *assimilative* in function. Freed from the demands made upon us as participants in the world's affairs, we are able to take more fully into account *our experience as a whole*. To put the same point rather differently, even where a poet may focus narrowly upon some tiny particular such as a snow flake, yet it is with the *whole of himself* that he looks. This item of his experience becomes as it were a small peephole through which we can see a great deal of his personality. A concern with the world-as-I-have-known-it, with my total world representation, is essentially an assimilative activity—a digestive activity, if the crude figure can be accepted. Play, then, is an activity which is not adaptive or reflective in function, but assimilative.

Daydreams, make-believe play, a child's storytelling, *Alice in Wonderland*, *Treasure Island*, and the rest—these are all play activities just as they are all activities in the spectator role. Seeing them as play, however, makes it possible, I believe, to move on to a further important distinction. We have suggested that play loses its essential characteristic when it submits the necessity of truth to the facts of experience. But we must note now that there is another necessity that may encroach upon it, one that I can only call an inner necessity. What was idle daydreaming on the part of a given individual may, from inner need, become obsessional: the images of play may be called upon to meet inner demands which become so urgent that those images are no longer freely manipulated, or a matter of choice. 'Escapism' is a word I have always found it difficult to use or understand: it must be a part of the assimilative function of play that we are able, in play, to improvise freely upon events in the actual world and in doing so enable ourselves to go back and meet the demands of real life more adequately: here is a kind of escape, but a fruitful one. On the other hand, the play images of a Walter Mitty may become a systematic means of avoiding the demands of real life and lessening the possibility of adequate response: and this perhaps is what 'escapism' should mean. When this happens we can only infer the existence of inner psychic demands powerful enough to rob play-like activities of the freedom that makes them genuinely 'playful'.

I heard in New England, only a week ago, of an eighteen-year-old girl who is wandering alone from picnic-site to picnic-site in the woods of Vermont, and calling herself 'the White Rabbit'. When my friend's young children asked what her 'real name' was, and why she had taken this other name, she grew very distressed. The experience of *Alice in Wonderland* must for that girl be very different from the eagerly appropriate delights and horrors, loves and fears, that generations of children have moved freely into and out of in reading the book.

I want to see play, then, as an area of free activity lying between the world of shared and verifiable experience and the world of inner necessity—a 'third area', as Donald Winnicott has called it. The essential purpose of activity in this area for the individual will be to relate for himself inner necessity with the demands of the external world. The more the images that clothe inner instinctual needs enter into the play activity, directly or indirectly, and the more they engage and relate to images from the world of shared experience, the more effectively, it seems to me, is the activity achieving its assimilative function. In the range of activities that come into the category of play as we have defined it, some will take up more of the demands of the inner world and are likely for that reason to include features that are inconsistent with our everyday notions of reality. It is activities towards that end of the scale that we shall most readily, and rightly, call 'fantasy', whether they are children's own creations or the stories they read.

My intention in this exploratory article has been to link ideas already familiar to me with the suggestions put forward by Donald Winnicott in his recent book *Playing and Reality*,[2] published soon after he died. That my task (like so many others in this area of thinking) is far from complete will be clear from a reading of the following brief quotations from that book:

'I have tried to draw attention to the importance both in theory and in practice of a third area, that of play, which expands into creative living and into the whole cultural life of man. This third area has been contrasted with inner or personal psychic reality and with the actual world in which the individual lives, which can be objectively perceived. I have located this important area of *experience* in the potential space between the individual and the environment, that which initially both joins and separates the baby and the mother when the mother's love, displayed or made manifest as human reliability, does in fact give the baby a sense of trust or of confidence in the environmental factor.

Attention is drawn to the fact that this potential space is a highly variable factor (from individual to individual) whereas the two other locations—personal or psychic reality and the actual world—are relatively constant, one being biologically determined and the other being common property.'

'Cultural experience begins with creative living first manifested in play.'

'In using the word culture I am thinking of the inherited tradition. I am thinking of something that is in the common pool of humanity, into which individuals and groups of people may contribute, and from which we may all draw if we have somewhere to put what we find.'[3]

Culture, the common pool of humanity, offers the young child witches and fairy godmothers, symbols which may embody and work upon the hate and love that are part of a close, dependent relationship: he will read of witches and tell stories of his own that arise directly from his needs. In doing so, he performs an assimilative task, working towards a more harmonious relationship between inner needs and external demands. Culture offers him, at a later stage perhaps, *Alice in Wonderland,* which among many other matters must certainly be concerned, if covertly, with *scale*—with bigness and littleness—and so with the difficulties a small comparatively powerless creature may feel in facing the demands of a world of full-grown, powerful adults.

If the Freudian view is right, there will be children whose ability to operate in the 'third area' has been so severely restricted in infancy that we as teachers can do little to help them. For the rest, it is important that we should recognize their need to 'play', understand as fully as we can the nature and the value of such activity, and provide the cultural material on which it may flourish.

References

1. Susan Isaacs, *Intellectual Growth in Young Children,* Routledge and Kegan Paul, 1930, p. 107.
2. D. W. Winnicott, *Playing and Reality,* Travistock Publications, 1971.
3. *Playing and Reality,* pp. 102–3, 100, 99.

6

Spectator Role and the Beginnings of Writing

In Search of a Theory

Literary and Nonliterary Discourse

·Works of literature constitute a form of discourse: We have theories of GENRE to distinguish among works of literature, but no satisfactory theory to account for what is common to all such works and in what general ways they differ from nonliterary discourse. The 1958 interdisciplinary symposium on "Style in Language" at Indiana University attempted to make such a distinction, but the only consensus that seemed to emerge was the low-level generalization that literary discourse is "noncasual discourse." Moreover, in summing up that symposium, George Miller remarked, "I gradually learned to understand a little of what the linguist has on his mind when he begins to talk; his verbal behavior during these past days has not puzzled me quite the way it once would have. But the critics have some mystic entity called a "poem" or "literature," whose existence I must take on faith and whose defining properties still confuse me. (The fact that they cannot agree amongst themselves on what a poem is adds to the mystery.) [Sebeok, 1960, p. 387]."

Since a great deal of (mostly unpublished) writing by nonprofessionals, by children in school and students in college, takes on forms that are clearly related to literary forms, it seems appropriate that any study of the psychology of writing should attempt to deal with this problem; and that the theory adumbrated should seek both to relate the artlike writings to literary works of art, and to distinguish between them.

One of the most important contributors to the Indiana symposium was Roman Jakobson who put forward his model of the 'constitutive factors' in a speech situation:

Published in *What Writers Know*, Martin Nystrand (ed.), Academic Press, 1982.

	Context	
Addressor	Message	Addressee
	Contact	
	Code	

and the functions assignable to an utterance or part utterance in accordance with the factor on which it focuses:

	Referential	
Emotive (or	Poetic	Conative
Expressive)	Phatic	
	Metalingual	

He made it clear that a verbal message was very unlikely to be fulfilling one function only, but that in taking account of the various functions liable to be copresent we might expect to find them hierarchically ordered, one function being **dominant**. "The verbal structure," he added, "depends primarily on the dominant function [Sebeok, 1960, p. 353]."

I want to accept as starting point his view that the poetic function (in the broad sense of 'poetic,' equivalent to the verbal arts) may be defined as a "focus on the message for its own sake," and to agree in principle that the poetic function may be either dominant or merely accessory. But Jakobson goes on to say:

> Any attempt to reduce the sphere of poetic function to poetry or to confine poetry to poetic function would be a delusive oversimplification. Poetic function is not the sole function of verbal art but only its dominant, determining function, whereas in all other verbal activities it acts as a subsidiary, accessory constituent [Sebeok, 1960, p. 356].

Any linguistic choice made on the sole grounds that "it sounds better that way" would seem to exemplify Jakobson's conception of the poetic function in an accessory role. Yet it seems to me that the urgent necessity is to characterize the structure and status of verbal messages in which the poetic function is dominant, that is, to find ways of distinguishing poetic from nonpoetic discourse. Jakobson's model itself might even suggest a dichotomy of this kind, a dominant focus on the message itself for its own sake being in contrast with a message dominantly focused on something beyond or outside itself.

Susanne Langer (1953) recognizes such a dichotomy when she comments on the switch required when readers or listeners turn their attention from nonliterary to literary discourse. An "illusion of life," she says, is the primary illusion of all poetic art. It is at least tentatively established by the very first sentence, which has to switch the reader's or hearer's attitude from conversational interest to literary interest, i.e., from actuality to fiction. We make this shift with great ease, and much more often than we realize, even in the midst of conversation; one has only to say "You know about the two Scotchmen, who . . ." to make everybody in earshot suspend the actual conversation and attend to "the" two Scots and "their" absurdities. Jokes are a special literary form to which people will attend on the spur of the moment [1953 p. 213].

And, speaking of Blake's poem *Tyger*, she comments, "The vision of such a tiger is a virtual experience, built up from the first line of the poem to the last. But nothing can be built up unless the very first words of the poem EFFECT THE BREAK WITH THE READER'S ACTUAL ENVIRONMENT [p. 214, emphasis added]."

In *The Reader, the Text, the Poem*, Louise Rosenblatt (1978) makes a broad distinction between two types of reading process, **efferent** and **aesthetic.** In efferent reading the reader's concern is with what he takes away from the reading (hence "efferent" from *effero* [I carry away]). In aesthetic reading, in contrast, "the reader's primary concern is with what happens DURING the actual reading event. . . . The reader's attention is centered directly on what he is living through during his relationship with that particular text [1978, pp 24–25]." She is careful to point out that this is no hard and fast division but rather a continuum between two poles. Thus, "given the assumption that the text offers a potentially meaningful set of linguistic symbols, the reader is faced with the adoption of either a predominantly efferent or a predominantly aesthetic stance [1978, p. 78]." We shall return to this matter of the relation between a reader's and a writer's options.

Support for a general distinction between literary and nonliterary discourse comes also from a linguist's work in stylistics. Widdowson (1975) claims that what is crucial to the character of literature is that "the language of a literary work should be fashioned into patterns over and above those required by the actual language system [1975, p. 47]." I shall return to consider this claim in a later section.

Spectator and Participant Roles

As we have noted, many of the features we find in poetic discourse (the language of literature) we find also widely distributed in many other forms of discourse. A mere study of the distribution of such features will not, I believe, add up to an adequate description of the verbal structure of a message in which the poetic function is dominant. We have no difficulty in practice in recognizing the difference between a novel with a political purpose and a piece of political rhetoric or persuasive discourse. What are the factors that shape the literary work as a whole?

The theory I want to pursue is one that I first put forward many years ago (Britton, 1963), in what seems to me now a crude form. My purpose then was to find common ground between much of the writing children do in school and the literature they read. I was concerned that, unlike the arts of painting and music, literature, as far as schools and universities were concerned, was not something that students DO, but always something that other people HAVE DONE. To bridge this gap, I looked for what seemed to be the informal spoken counterparts of written literature—not the anecdote as such, I decided (Langer's tale of the two Scotsmen)—but the kind of gossip about events that most of us take part in daily. To quote from that account, "The distinction that matters . . . is not whether the events recounted are true or fictional, but whether we recount them (or listen to them) as spectators or participants: and whenever we play the role of spectator of human affairs I suggest we are in the position of literature [Britton, 1963, p. 37]." The roles of spectator and participant were differentiated in this way:

When we talk about our own affairs, clearly we can do so either as participant or as spectator. If I describe what has happened to me in order to get my hearer to do something for me, or even to change his opinion about me, then I remain a participant in my own affairs and invite him to become one. If, on the other hand, I merely want to interest him, so that he savours with me the joys and sorrows and surprises of my past experiences and appreciates with me the intricate patterns of events, then not only do I invite him to be a spectator, but I am myself a spectator of my own experience. . . . I don't think it is far-fetched to think of myself talking not about my own past, but about my future, and, again, doing so in either of the two roles. As participant I should be planning, and asking my listener to participate by helping or advising or just 'giving me the necessary permission'. As spectator I should be day-dreaming, and inviting my listener to share in that kind of pleasure [Britton, 1963, p. 39].

To complete the account, I then made reference to taking up the role of spectator of imagined experiences in fantasy or fiction.

Three years later I prepared an advance paper for discussion at the Anglo-American Seminar at Dartmouth, a paper on "Response to Literature" (Britton, 1968), and as a brief postscript to that document, I referred to the "unorthodox view of literature" that characterized it as a written form of language in the role of spectator and so related it to the spoken form, gossip about events. The paper was discussed by a study group under the chairmanship of the British psychologist, D. W. Harding. It was not until the first meeting of the study group was over that he asked me whether I knew his own papers putting forward a similar view; and that evening, in Dartmouth College Library, I read for the first time "The Role of the Onlooker" (Harding, 1937) and "Psychological Processes in the Reading of Fiction" (Harding, 1962). There I found a fully and carefully argued case for distinguishing the role of an onlooker from that of a participant in events and for relating gossip to literature as activities in the former role.

The final report of that study group was prepared by Harding and included this comment:

> Though central attention should be given to literature in the ordinary sense, it is impossible to separate response to literature sharply from response to other stories, films, or television plays, or from children's own personal writing or spoken narrative. In all of these the student contemplates represented events in the role of a spectator, not for the sake of active intervention. But since his response includes in some degree accepting or rejecting the values and emotional attitudes which the narration implicitly offers, it will influence, perhaps greatly influence, his future appraisals of behavior and feeling [Harding, 1968, p. 11].

D. W. Harding

In the two articles I have referred to, Harding explored the relationship between three processes that seemed to him to have much in common: (a) watching events without taking part in them; (b) exchanging gossip—informal recounting or description of events; and (c) reading (or writing) fiction. An understanding of the first of these, that of being literally in the role of spectator, is essential to an understanding of his view of the other two. An onlooker, he says, (a) ATTENDS (and this will range from "a passing glance" to a "fascinated absorption") and (b) EVALUATES (within a range from "an attitude of faint liking or disliking, hardly above indifference" to one of "strong, perhaps intensely emotional" response). What we attend to, he suggests, reflects our interests (if we take interest to mean "an enduring disposition to respond, in whatever way, to some class of objects or events"); how we evaluate reflects our sentiments, if we take a sentiment to be "an enduring disposition to evaluate some object or class of objects in a particular way [Harding, 1972, p. 134]."

A major aspect of a spectator's response to the events he witnesses will be a concern for the people involved and an interest in the way they react, but there is likely to be present also an interest in and evaluation of the pattern events take, with a sense that what is happening here might one day happen to him. Both aspects are, in a broad sense, learning experiences: As spectators we not only reflect our interests and sentiments but also modify and extend them. "In ways of this kind," Harding writes,

> the events at which we are "mere onlookers" come to have, cumulatively, a deep and extensive influence on our systems of value. They may in certain ways be even more formative than events in which we take part. Detached and distanced evaluation is sometimes sharper for avoiding the blurrings and bufferings that participant action brings, and the spectator often sees the event in a broader context than the participant can tolerate. To obliterate the effects on a man of the occasions on which he was only an onlooker would be profoundly to change his outlook and values [1962, p. 136].

To be one of a number of spectators is to take part in a mutual challenging and sanctioning of each other's evaluations. "Everything we look on at is tacitly and unintentionally treated as an object lesson by our fellow spectators; speech and gesture, smiles, nudges, clicks, tuts and glances are constantly at work to sanction or correct the feelings we have as spectators [Harding, 1937, p. 253]."

This aspect of a spectator's experience is sharply emphasized when we turn to the second of the three processes I have listed, that of deliberately taking up the role of spectator of represented or recounted experiences, as for example when we go home in the evening and chat about the day's events. We HAVE BEEN participants but are so no longer; taking up the role of spectator, we invite our listener to do the same. Harding goes so far as to imply that this familiar habit is something we indulge in for the purpose of testing out our modes of evaluating; having, in fact, our value systems sanctioned or modified by others whose values, in general, we reckon to share. We do not recount everything that happens to us: What we select constitutes a first level of evaluation. But it is as we recount the events in a manner designed to arouse in our listeners attitudes towards them that chime with our own that we more specifically invite corroboration of our ways of evaluating. On this basis, I think it is no distortion of Harding's account to suggest that as participants we APPLY our value systems, but as spectators we GENERATE AND REFINE the system itself. In applying our value systems we shall inevitably be constrained by self-interest, by concern for the outcome of the event we are participating in; as spectators we are freed of that constraint.

Harding goes on to suggest that what takes place informally in chat about events is in essence similar to what is achieved by a work of fiction or drama. "True or fictional, all these forms of narrative invite us to be onlookers joining in the evaluation of some possibility of experience [1962, p. 138]."

The London Writing Research Project

At the time of the Dartmouth Seminar my colleagues and I at the University of London Institute of Education were beginning to plan the Schools Council Project on the written language of 11- to 18-year-olds. Our first and major task was to devise modes of analysis of children's writings by means of which the development of writing abilities might be documented. We envisaged a multidimensional analysis and worked on what seemed to us two of the essential dimensions. The first resulted in a set of categories we called "sense of audience" (Who is the writing for?) and the second in a set of function categories (What is the writing for?). These are fully described in *The Development of Writing Abilities, 11–18* (Britton, Burgess, Martin, McLeod, & Rosen, 1975) and for my present purpose I need only indicate how the spectator–participant distinction was taken up and developed as the basis of the function category set.

To relate gossip to literature is not only to show a similarity in that they are both utterances in the spectator role, but also to indicate a difference. The formal and informal ends of the spectrum have very different potentials. One of the important ways in which we frame an evaluation and communicate it is by giving a particular shape to the events in narrating them; at the formal end of the scale all the resources of literary art, all the linguistic and conceptual forms that a literary artist molds into a unity, are at the service of that shaping and sharing.

Clearly, an account given of an experience in a letter to an intimate friend might also be placed at the informal end of the scale, in contrast perhaps to the same event narrated by the same writer as part of a short story or a published autobiography. (Dr. Johnson wrote a letter from the Hebrides to a friend in which he said, "When we were taken upstairs, a dirty fellow bounced out of the bed on which one of us was to lie"; this appears in his *Journal* as "Out of one of the couches on which we were to repose there started up at our entrance a man black as a Cyclops from the forge"—more of a parody of the point I am making than an illustration, I think!)

The informality of a chat or a personal letter is certainly in part a reflection of a relaxed relationship between the communicating parties—closeness rather than distance, warmth rather than coldness. Perhaps influenced also by Moffett's model of kinds of discourse in which he sees the I–you rhetorical relationship and the I–it referential relationship as intimately connected (Moffett, 1968, p. 33), we came to identify the informal end of this continuum with expressive language as Sapir (1961, p. 10) has defined it; further, to see that the "unshaped," loosely structured end of the spectator role continuum merged into the informal pole of language in the role of participant.

This gave us three major categories of function: transactional, expressive, and poetic. **Transactional** is the form of discourse that most fully meets the demands of a participant in events (using language to get things done, to carry out a verbal transaction). **Expressive** is the form of discourse in which the distinction between participant and spectator is a shadowy one. And **poetic** discourse is the form that most fully meets the demands associated with the role of spectator—demands that are met, we suggested, by MAKING something with language rather than DOING something with it.

Though our principal source for the term "expressive" was Edward Sapir, we found it was one widely used by other linguists. Jakobson labeled the function arising from a focus on the addressor either "emotive" or "expressive" and saw it as offering "a direct expression of the speaker's attitude towards what he is speaking about [Sebeok, 1960, p. 354]"; a point that Dell Hymes later glossed: "A sender cannot help but express attitudes towards each of the other factors in a speech event, his audience, the style of the message, the code he is using, the channel he is using, his topic, the scene of the communication [1968, p. 106]." Labov (1966, p. 13) characterizes the expressive function as "the role of language as self-identification," and it is this aspect that Gusdorf elaborates: "The relation to others is only meaningful insofar as it reveals that personal identity within the person who is himself speaking. To communicate, man *expresses* himself, i.e. he actualizes himself, he creates from his own substance [1965, p. 69]." Thus the expressive function in our model is not simply the informal end of two scales, the neutral point between participant and spectator role language, but has its own positive function to perform—a function that profits from the indeterminacy between carrying out a verbal transaction and constructing a verbal object to be shared. The positive function of expressive speech is, in simple terms, to make the most of being with somebody, that is, to enjoy their company, to make their presence fruitful—a process that can profit from exploring with them both the inner and outer aspects of experience.

But in expressive writing the presence, the "togetherness" is simulated: The writer invokes the presence of the reader as he writes; the reader invokes the presence of the writer as he reads. Thus a working definition of expressive writing would be "writing that assumes an interest in the writer as well as in what he has to say about the world." We might add that it would be foolish to underestimate the importance of expressive speech or writing as means of influencing people and events. Advertisers and propagandists are only too ready to exploit its effectiveness.

Our description of expressive writing thus distinguished it from a verbal transaction on the one hand and a verbal object on the other. The verbal transaction and the verbal object are communicative rather than expressive, being in both cases language in the public domain; yet they communicate in very different ways. Expressive and referential strands, as Sapir explains, intermingle in all discourse, but the degree to which the former predominates is criterial in distinguishing expressive from transactional discourse. The change from expression to communication on the poetic side is brought about by an increasing degree of organization—organization into a single complex verbal symbol.

H. G. Widdowson

It is this last distinction that is illuminated by the work in stylistics of Widdowson (1975). He cites from literature examples of nongrammatical expressions that are nevertheless interpretable, finds such expressions in nonliterary texts, but concludes that they occur randomly in nonliterary writing, "whereas in literature they figure as part of a pattern which characterizes the literary work as a separate and self-contained whole [p. 36]." Interpretation of these expressions that violate the grammatical code relies on viewing them in the light of the context; and he goes on to show that this is also true of most metaphorical expressions (which again occur randomly in ordinary discourse but as part of a total pattern in a work of literature). Context, however, in ordinary language will include aspects of the social situation in which the utterance takes place and remarks that have gone before; whereas in literature context consists of the verbal fabric alone. Widdowson identifies patterns of three kinds to be found in literary works: phonological (metre and verse form are obvious examples), syntactical (parallel structures, for example, can invest an item with meaning which is, so to speak, by halo effect from other items in the series), and patterns formed by semantic links between individual lexical items. "At the heart of literary discourse," he concludes, "is the struggle to devise patterns of language which will bestow upon the linguistic items concerned just those values which convey the individual writer's personal vision [1975, p. 42]."

He goes on to suggest that the effect of the patterning over and above the patterns of the language code is "to create acts of communication which are self-contained units, independent of a social context and expressive of a reality other than that which is sanctioned by convention. In other words, I want to suggest that although literature need not be deviant as text it must of its nature be deviant as discourse [1975, p. 47]." This he achieves principally by pointing out that normal discourse features a sender of a message who is at the same time the addressor, and a receiver of a message who is also the addressee, whereas in literary discourse the author, as sender, is distinguished from the addressor, and the reader, as receiver, from the addressee.

Striking examples of this disjunction illustrate his point ("I am the enemy you killed, my friend" from Owen; "With how sad steps, O moon" from Sidney), but he goes on to indicate that this modified relationship holds in general for works of literature. An addressor thus fuses meanings associated with a grammatical first person with those associated with a third, an addressee those of the second and third persons. This account of a systematic modification of the grammatical code he completes by showing how third person and first person are fused when in fiction a narrator describes the experiences of a third person sometimes in terms of what might have been observed, sometimes in terms of inner events that only the experiencer could know. On these grounds he concludes: "It would appear then that in literary discourse we do not have a sender addressing a message directly to a receiver, as is normally the case. Instead we have a communication situation within a communication situation and a message whose meaning is self-contained and not dependent on who sends it and who receives it [p. 50]."

In defending this view against likely objections, he makes two interesting points that are relevant to my theme. In many literary works, particularly perhaps in lyric poems, it is evident that the "I" of the work is the writer himself. In arguing that "it is not the writer as message sender, the craftsman, the 'maker' that the 'I' refers to but to the inner self that the writer is objectifying, and the very act of objectifying involves detaching this self and observing it as if it were a third person entity [1975, p. 53]," Widdowson sketches out, somewhat loosely, three forms of discourse in terms of the role of the "I": (a) In diaries and personal letters there is no distinction between sender and addressor: The writer may reveal his inner thoughts and feelings, and in doing so he takes responsibility—his readers may assume that he is "telling the truth." (b) In all other forms of nonliterary language, the writer, as sender and addressor, adopts a recognized social role and what he says and how he says it are determined by that role: "he is not at liberty to express his own individual sentiments at will. . . . [H]is addressee will be concerned with what he has to say in his role and not with his private and individual thoughts [p. 52]."; (c) literary discourse, where the sender and addressor are disjoined, is concerned with the private thoughts and feelings of the writer, but in "bringing them out of hiding" he objectifies them and may explore them through the creation of personae, so that "we cannot assume that when a literary writer uses the first person he is describing his own experiences or making a confession." The literary writer, in fact, aware of the convention that distinguishes sender from addressor, is "relieved from any social responsibility for what he says in the first person [p. 53]." (Love letters, he notes, count as evidence in a court of law, love poems don't!)

This analysis provides an interesting gloss on the three major function categories in our model: expressive, transactional, and poetic.

The second objection Widdowson anticipates relates to the familiar problem of "the novel with a message." Our claim that a literary work was a verbal object and not a verbal transaction was objected to on just these grounds, and we argued in reply that a poetic work achieved its effect indirectly, via the poetic construct taken as a whole. Widdowson's claim that a literary work is a self-contained unit independent of a social context risks the same kind of objection: His answer is

> that it may indeed be the purpose of a writer to stir the social conscience but he does not do so by addressing himself directly to those whose consciences he wishes to stir. He expresses a certain reality, a personal vision, and the reader, as an *observer* of this reality, might then feel constrained to act in a certain way. But he is not directed to act by the writer (1975, p. 53).

Widdowson then develops a point that will be familiar to readers of Jakobson (1971, e.g., p. 704); he explores the way paradigmatic relationships invade the area of syntagmatic relationships in poetic discourse, and illustrates this at the level of phonemes and the grammatical level of words and phrases. Phonological distinctions that by the normal language code exist as a range from which **selection** is made (the story for example is about a cat and not about a hat, a bat or a mat) invade the syntagmatic relationship, the process of **combination** in a literary work, as for example when a poet chooses "bright" in preference to "shining" because that word fits into the sound pattern, including perhaps both rhythm and rhyme, of his poem. More germane to his principal argument is Widdowson's example of a series of verbal groups any one of which might have served to complete a sentence in a T. S. Eliot poem. Widdowson then shows how Eliot in fact does not SELECT, but COMBINES: "Words strain/Crack and sometimes break . . ." etc. This strategy, Widdowson notes, reflects the writer's struggle to resolve ambiguities and allows him to invite the reader to take part in that process. By such means works of literature communicate "an individual awareness of a reality other than that which is given general social sanction but nevertheless related to it [1971, p. 70]."

Contextualization

One of the important ways in which we may characterize the difference between transactional and poetic discourse is by reference to the way a reader grasps the message. If what a writer does when he draws from all he knows and selectively sets down what he wants to communicate is described as 'decontextualization', then the complementary process on the part of a reader is to 'contextualize', interpreting the writer's meaning by building it into his existing knowledge and experience. We have suggested (Britton *et al.*, 1975, pp. 85–86) that in reading a piece of transactional discourse we contextualize the material in piecemeal fashion; passing over what is familiar, rejecting what is incomprehensible to us or perceived as inconsistent with our own thinking, accepting in piecemeal fashion what seems to us interesting, building our own connections between these fragments and our existing knowledge (which is open to modification, of course, in the process). With poetic discourse, on the other hand (and much of what Widdowson has said will support this difference), we apply our own knowledge and experience to the reconstruction of the writer's verbal object, and until we have done this, until we have the sense of a completed whole, a single unique symbol, we are in no position to reexamine our own thoughts and feelings in the light of the author's work. This we have called **global contextualization.** I think our response to a novel with a message may sometimes be a deliberate reexamination of the kind this suggests, but I have come to believe that in most cases global contextualization is a process that goes on over time and one we may not even be conscious of. We are constantly learning from our own first-hand experiences and mostly, because of the wideranging and diffuse nature of the process, without being aware that we are doing so. I am inclined to think that our response to a work of literature is like that.

We do of course contextualize in piecemeal fashion while reading works of literature: We pick up clues as to what life is like in places we have never visited, what it was like at times before we were born. But this is quite subsidiary, for most of us, to the main effects of literature; and it has its risks, since the verbal object, as Widdowson shows, deals with a reality "other than that which is given social sanction." There may be pygmies in the Australian rain forests the novelist describes, but that is no guarantee that they exist in fact. Nevertheless, for historians or sociologists, say, to study literature for the information they can glean is of course a legitimate option; they will be employing a process of piecemeal contextualization where what the author offered was a work to be contextualized globally. Louise Rosenblatt (1978), as we have mentioned, has paid close attention to this matter of the reader's options and raised some important issues. In defining a literary work of art as "what happens when a reader and a text come together [p. 12]," she is I think loading the dice in the reader's favor, but the weight has for so long been on the author's side that this is understandable. There are of course anomalies, as when a text produced by an author as propaganda survives when its injunctions are no longer appropriate, and survives as a piece of literature; or when an informative text (Gibbons *Decline and Fall* is the stock example) survives when much of its information has been superseded and even discredited, to be read now not as information but for the unique and individual qualities typical of a work of literature.

There are anomalies, but without wishing in any way to infringe on the reader's freedom to choose, I do suggest that in the vast majority of cases the general conventions chosen by the writer—whether to produce expressive, transactional, or poetic discourse—are in fact the conventions by which the reader chooses to interpret.

Young Fluent Writers

L. S. Vygotsky

I have known a number of children who by the age of 5 or 6 had taught themselves to write. In each case it was stories that they wrote, and usually the stories were made up into little books, with pictures as well as writing. I take it as some evidence of the extraordinary ability human beings have of succeeding in doing what they want to do. One of these young children, under the age of 4, began by producing a little book with "pretend writing" in it—and surely, just as we pretend to BE someone we want to be, so we pretend to DO something we want to do. Some 20 months later the scribbled lines had given place to a decipherable story. Evidence of this kind is too often ignored, and it takes a Vygotsky, speaking across the decades since his death, to observe that the attempt to teach writing as a motor skill is mistaken (Vygotsky, 1978, p. 117); that psychology has conceived of it as a motor skill and "paid remarkably little attention to the question of written language as such, that is, a particular system of symbols and signs whose mastery heralds a critical turning-point in the entire cultural development of the child [p. 106]." It was his view that make-believe play, drawing and writing should be seen as "different moments in an essentially unified process of development of written language [p. 116]." And this he contrasted with what he found in schools: "Instead of being founded on the needs of children as they naturally develop and on their own activity, writing is given to them from without, from the teacher's hands [p. 105]."

I suggest that the 4-year-old I have referred to made what Vygotsky calls "a basic discovery—namely that one can draw not only things but also speech [1978, p. 115]." Since pictorial representation is first-order symbolism and writing is second-order symbolism (designating words that are in turn signs for things and relationships), Vygotsky saw this discovery as a key point in the development of writing in a child; yet he recognized there was little understanding of how the shift takes place, since the necessary research had not been done (p. 115).

Outline for a Case Study

My records on the development of Clare, the 4-year-old whose pretend writing I have referred to, may illustrate some of the points Vygotsky has made in his account of "the developmental history of written language."

(1) Her conversational speech was quite well developed by the time she was 2 years old. Much of her talk was playful (seeing me at the washbasin, *What have you got off, Daddy?*—at 2:3) and she used made-up forms freely (*I'm spoonfuling it in, I'm see-if-ing it will go through, smuttered in your eyes*—for uncombed hair—all at 2:7). Her curiosity about language was in evidence early (*When it's one girl you say "girl" and when it's two three four girls you say "girl s." Why when it's two three four childs you say "child ren"?*—at 2:10; *"Fairy girl with curly hair," that makes a rhyme, doesn't it?*—at 2:11; on hearing something described as 'delicious,' *Is delicious nicer than lovely?*—at 3:1).

(2) Extended make-believe play, involving her toy animals in family roles, was established by the time she was 3. Storytelling developed from it, the animals becoming the audience. The toy animals (she was given dolls from time to time but they were never adopted into the family) seem to have sustained a key role. They were the *dramatis personae* of her make-believe play, the subject of the stories she told, of her drawings, and later of the stories she wrote. Vygotsky's point that in make-believe play the plaything is free to take on a meaning that does not rely on perceptual resemblance is amusingly illustrated by the fact that when Clare enacted a queen's wedding, the least suitable of the animals—a scraggy, loose-knit dog—was chosen for the role of queen!

(3) Her earliest recognizable drawings came just before she was 2 and though they are clearly attempts at human figures, the talk that always accompanied the drawing was often in anthropomorphic terms (*the mummy bird, the daddy bird*). A picture drawn in colored chalks at 3:5 shows a large figure of a girl on the left-hand side and a house on the right. Her commentary as she drew explained: *The girl is carrying a yellow handbag and she has a brown furry dog on a lead. Her feet are walking along. . . . I have put a car outside the house. I am putting blue sky, now I am putting in the sunshine.* (Here the diagonal blue strokes that had indicated the sky were interspersed with yellow ones.) *She's got a tricycle with blue wheels and a chain. Mrs. Jones across the road has yellow and brown on her windows. I shall put yellow and red on mine.*

It is an important part of Vygotsky's thesis that a young child's drawing is "graphic speech," dependent on verbal speech: The child draws, that is to say, from the memory of what he knows rather than from what he presently observes; and that what he knows has been processed in speech and is further processed in the speech that accompanies the drawing. The space in Clare's picture is well filled, but not in terms of topographical representation: The girl and the house are upright; the car is drawn vertically standing on its head; the dog vertically sitting on its tail; and the tricycle has its frame, wheels and chain spread out, looking more like an assembly kit.

(4) What circumstances could be supposed to facilitate the process that Vygotsky calls the move from drawing objects to drawing speech? Imitating the general pattern of writing behavior, Clare at the age of 3:6 produced parallel horizontal lines of cursive scribble, saying that she was *doing grownup's kind of writing.* At 3:11 she produced the little story book I have described with similar lines of scribble but interspersed with words she could actually write (*mummy, and, the*) and with a drawing on the cover. The stories she wrote from 5:6 onward were in cursive script with headings in capitals. She was by this time reading a good deal, mainly the little animal stories by Beatrix Potter and Alison Uttley.

Turning from the general pattern to the detail, Clare at the age of 3 played very often with a set of inch-high letters made of plastic in various colors. Among more random, playful uses, she learned to make her name in these letters and she was interested in what each letter was called. (One effect of this play was evident: When first she attempted to write words, an "E," for example, was an "E" for her whether it faced right or left or up or down.) One of her activities represented a link between letter recognition and writing behavior in general: At 3:5, in imitation of picture alphabets she knew, she was drawing a series of objects and writing the initial letter of each beside the drawing. Most of them she knew, but she came to one she did not: "rhubarb." When I told her, she said, *R—that's easy—just a girl's head and two up-and-downs!*

(5) The final stage in Vygotsky's "developmental history" is that by which the written language ceases to be second-order symbolism, mediated by speech, and becomes first-order symbolism. I can offer no evidence of this from the records of Clare, and indeed I seriously doubt whether that transition is ever entirely appropriate to the written language we have been concerned with, that of stories.

(6) I think the most important conclusion to be drawn from the case of Clare and other children who have taught themselves to write by writing stories is a point that is central to Vygotsky's argument, that of the effect of INTENTION on a child's performance. It would appear that the spoken language effectively meets young children's needs in general, and we must surmise that it is only as they come to value the written language as a vehicle for stories that they are likely to form an

intention to write. Much of Clare's behavior indicated that she had done so. Slobin and Welsh (1973) have effectively demonstrated that mastery of the spoken language cannot be adequately assessed without account of "the intention to say so-and-so"—a lesson that as teachers or researchers we have been slow to learn.

Writing and Reading

Clare continued to read and write stories for many years. Animal fantasies predominated until the age of 7, pony stories and adventure stories (often featuring an animal) followed until, from the ages of 12 to 14 she gave herself up almost entirely to reading women's magazine stories and writing herself at great length in that vein. Here, to represent successive stages, are some opening lines:

At 6:   *I am a little Teddy Bear. I've got a pony called Snow and I live in a little house with a thatched roof.*

At 8½: *Mrs Hedgehog had just had three babies. Two of them were like ordinary hedgehog babies, covered with soft prickles. But the third had none.*
It was a dead calm as the Sand Martin and crew glided out of the small harbour at Plymouth. Phillip and Jean were the eldest. They were twins of fourteen.

At 11:   *Fiona Mackenzie lay in bed in her small attic bedroom. She turned sleepily over, but the morning sun streaming in at her small window dazzled her, and she turned back.* (A story about horses in the Highlands.)

At 12:   *Derek looked into her face, and his green eyes burning fiercely with the white hot light of intense love gazed into the liquid of her melting, dark brown ones.*

At 14:   *The dance was in full swing, and Giselle was the acknowledged belle of it. More radiant, more sparkling than ever before, she floated blissfully in the arms of James Wainforth.*

Her comments on her reading and writing were sometimes illuminating. At 3:8 she described the Cinderella story as *A bit sad book about two ugly sisters and a girl they were ugly to.* At 8:7 she was asked what sort of things she liked reading. *Well,* she said, *there's* Treasure Island—*that's a bloody one for when I'm feeling boyish. And* Little Men, *that's a sort of half-way one.* "And don't you ever feel girlish?" she was asked. *Yes. When I'm tired and then I read* The Smallest Dormouse. At 10:2 she wrote a story about children finding a treasure: *It's like Enid Blyton's story mostly,* she said, *except longer words.* A few months later she was struggling to get through Mrs. Craik's *John Halifax, Gentleman,* but gave up with the comment, *It's a*

*bit Lorna Doonish, a lot of cissy boys in it. It's so sort of **genteel**—I
can't stand it!*

Spectator Role and the Beginnings of Writing

In the light of current school practices, it is as important as ever
today to stress Vygotsky's view that learning to read and learning to
write must be seen as inseparable aspects of one process, that of mas-
tering written language. We have come to recognize the way this process is grounded in speech but have not yet acknowledged the essential contribution of other forms of symbolic behavior, gesture,
make-believe play, pictorial representation. In my account of Clare's
development, I have added one other activity, that of manipulative
play with the substance of written language. Bruner (1975) has pointed
out that such play contributes to learning because it is a 'meta-process,'
one that focuses on the nature itself of the activity. (Children learn to
walk for the purpose of getting where they want to be; PLAY with
walking—early forms of dancing—involves a concern with the nature
of the walking process, an exploration of its manifold possibilities.)

It remains for me to point out that make-believe play (embracing
the social environment children construct with their playthings),
storytelling, listening to stories, pictorial representation and the talk
that complements it, story reading and story writing—these are all
activities in the role of spectator. As I have suggested, I believe it is
this characteristic that develops a need for the written language in
young children and the intention to master it. In such activities children are sorting themselves out, progressively distinguishing what is
from what seems, strengthening their hold on reality by a consideration
of alternatives. Clare, for example, at the age of 8:6, writes what at first
sight appears to be a variant of the kind of animal fable she was familiar with from earlier reading of Beatrix Potter:

Hedgehog

*Mrs Hedgehog had just had three babies. Two of them were like
ordinary hedgehog babies, covered with soft prickles.*

*But the third had none. He was like a hedgehog in any other
way. He ate like a hedgehog and he lived like a hedgehog and he
rolled up in a ball like a hedgehog, and he went to sleep in the
winter like a hedgehog. But he had no prickles like a hedgehog.*

*When he was a year old a fairy came to him and said, "Go to
China and get three hairs from the Emperor Ching Chang's
seventh guinea-pig. Throw the hairs in the fire, and then put it
out with six bucketfuls of water. Put some of the ash on your
head, and leave it for the night. In the morning you will be
covered with prickles." Then she faded away.*

[The story tells how he carried out these instructions, and concludes:]

> *He went to sleep beside the stream. In the morning he woke up feeling rather strange. He looked at his back. It was covered in prickles. He spent four days in China, then he went home in the boat. His family were very surprised to see him!*

For those who knew Clare, it was not difficult to recognize here an account of her own struggle to establish herself in the family in competition with a more confident and more relaxed younger sister. *His family were very surprised to see him!*

It has often been pointed out that in one sense a tiny infant is lord of his universe, and that growing from infancy into childhood involves discovering one's own unimportance. But the world created in the stories children write is a world they control and this may be a source of deep satisfaction. As one of the children recorded by Donald Graves remarked, she liked writing stories because "you are the mother of the story."

Whether to read or to write, a story makes fewer demands than a piece of transactional writing since one essential element of the latter process is missing in the former. The reader of an informative or persuasive piece must construct himself the writer's meaning and inwardly debate it (an essential part of the piecemeal contextualization process); the reader of a story accepts, so to speak, an invitation to enter a world and see what happens to him there. The writer of a transactional piece must attempt to anticipate and make provision for the reader's inner debate; the writer of a story constructs a situation to his own satisfaction, though thereafter he may be willing, even eager, to share it.

Expressive Writing

Edward Sapir observed that "ordinary speech is directly expressive [1961, p. 10]." Because expressive writing, though it differs in substantial ways from speech, is the form of written discourse closest to speech, the London Writing Research team suggested that it provided a "natural" starting point for beginning writers, assisting them at a time when they have rich language resources recruited through speech, but few if any internalized forms of the written language. Progress from this point consists, we believe, in shuttling between those spoken resources and an increasing store of forms internalized from reading and being read to. (It may prove that vocal reading, whether their own or somebody else's, is in the early stages a more effective route to that internalization.)

We might describe this early form as an all-purpose expressive. As the writer employs it to perform different tasks, fulfill different purposes, and increasingly succeeds in meeting the different demands, his all-purpose expressive will evolve: He will acquire by dissociation a variety of modes. Expressive writing is thus a matrix from which will develop transactional and poetic writing, as well as the more mature forms of the expressive.

What the Young Writer Needs to Know

My argument has been that Vygotsky's account offers an explanation of the phenomenon I have noted, that of Clare and the other children who mastered written language by producing storybooks at an early age. Let me now go on to ask, "What does a writer acquiring mastery in this way need to know?"

First and foremost he must know from experience the SATISFACTION that can come from a story—perhaps first a story told to him, but then certainly a story read to him. Sartre (1967, p. 31) has commented on the difference: Accustomed to having his mother tell him stories, he describes his experience when first she reads to him: *The tale itself was in its Sunday best: the woodcutter, the woodcutter's wife and their daughter, the fairy, all those little people, our fellow-creatures, had acquired majesty; their rags were magnificently described, words left their mark on objects, transforming actions into rituals and events into ceremonies.*

Then he must know something of the structure of a story, a learning process that Applebee (1978) has very helpfully described in developmental terms for stories told by children between the ages of 2 and 5 (but with implications for later stages). He sees two principles at work, one of **centering,** a concern for the unity of a story, and one of **chaining,** a concern for sequence; and in terms of these two principles he outlines a series of plot structures that parallel the stages of concept development described by Vygotsky (1962). It should be noted, at the same time, that recall of events in narrative form is something that all children achieve a year or more before they are ready to tackle the written language.

Some forms of story writing will only be possible if the writer is familiar with the conventional associations that govern our expectations in listening to stories—the role expected of a wolf, a lion, a fox, a witch, a prince, and so on (Applebee, 1978, chap. 3). Such built-in associations are, of course, a resource that a young writer may in his own stories exploit, improvise on, invert, or ignore.

Knowledge of the linguistic conventions of stories—the *Once upon a time* and *happily ever after* conventions—are often familiar to children before they can read or write, as are more general features of the language of written stories. (I saw a story dictated by a 3-year-old which contained the sentence, *The king went sadly home for he had nowhere else to go*—a use of *for* which is certainly not a spoken form.)

But production of these and all other written forms relies, of course, on a knowledge of the written code itself, the formation of letters, words, sentences. How this is picked up from alphabet books and cornflake packets, picture books, TV advertisements, and street signs remains something of a mystery, though two governing conditions seem likely: a context of manipulative play and picture-making, and the association of this learning with the purpose of producing written stories. I am sure we underestimate the extent of such learning when a powerful interest is in focus. In my recent experience of reading stories to a 3-year-old, I have been amazed at her ability to fill the words into gaps I leave when the story I am reading is one she cannot have heard very often. Michael Polanyi's account of the relation of subsidiary to focal awareness certainly helps us to see this learning process as feasible (Polanyi, 1958, chap. 4).

Finally, the writer must know from experience the SOUND of a written text read aloud. How else can he come to hear an inner voice dictating to him the story he wants to produce? An apprenticeship of listening to others will enable him later to be aware of the rhythms of the written language in the course of his own silent reading.

A Final Speculation

I believe the successful writer learns all these things implicitly; that is to say, in Polanyi's terms, by maintaining a focal awareness of the desired performance that acts as a determining tendency guiding and controlling his subsidiary awareness of the means he employs. I believe, further, that any attempt to introduce explicit learning would be likely to hinder rather than help at this early stage. When we are dealing with poetic writing, there is much that could not in any case be made explicit: We simply do not know by what organizing principles experience is projected into a work of art.

It is this problem that Susanne Langer has been investigating over many years. Her distinction between discursive and presentational symbolism—between a message encoded in a symbol system and a message embodied in a single unique complex symbol; her recognition of the key role of the arts as offering an ordering of experience alternative to the cognitive, logical ordering achieved by discursive symbolism—these are foundation stones in our theory of language functions.

From her exploration of the laws governing a work of art she makes one very interesting suggestion: that in all works of art there is a building-up and resolution of tensions and that the intricate pattern of these movements, this rhythm, somehow reflects the "shape of every living act [Langer, 1967, chap. 7]."

To speculate on her speculations: We give and find shape in the very act of perception, we give and find further shape as we talk, write or otherwise represent our experiences. I say "give and find" because clearly there is order and pattern in the natural world irrespective of our perceiving and representing. At the biological level man shares that order, but at the level of behavior he appears to lose it: The pattern of his actions is more random than that of the instinctual behavior of animals. In learning to control his environment he has gained a freedom of choice in action that he may use constructively and harmoniously or to produce disharmony, shapelessness, chaos. When, however, he shapes his experience into a verbal object, an art form, in order to communicate it and to realize it more fully himself, he is seeking to recapture a natural order that his daily actions have forfeited. Understanding so little of the complexities of these processes, we can do no more than entertain that idea as a fascinating speculation.

References

A. N. Applebee, *The Child's Concept of Story*, University of Chicago Press, 1978.

J. N. Britton, Literature, in J. N. Britton (ed.), *The Arts and Current Tendencies in Education*, Evans, 1963, pp. 34–61.

J. N. Britton, Response to literature. In J. R. Squire (Ed.), *Response to Literature*, National Council of Teachers of English, 1968, pp. 3–10.

J. N. Britton, T. Burgess, M. Martin, A. McLeod, and H. Rosen, *The Development of Writing Abilities, 11–18*, Macmillan, 1975.

J. S. Bruner, The Ontogenesis of Speech Acts. *Journal of Child Language*, 1975, 2, 1–19.

G. Gusdorf, *Speaking*, Northwestern University Press, 1965.

D. W. Harding, The Role of the Onlooker, *Scrutiny*, 1937, 6, 247–258.

D. W. Harding, Psychological Processes in the Reading of Fiction, *British Journal of Aesthetics*, 1962, 2, 133–147.

D. W. Harding, Response to Literature: The Report of the Study Group. In J. R. Squire (ed.), *Response to Literature*, National Council of Teachers of English, 1968. pp 11–27.

D. Hymes, The Ethnography of Speaking, in J. A. Fishman (ed.), *Readings in the Sociology of Language*, Mouton, 1968.

R. Jakobson, *Selected Writings* (Vol. 2), *Word and Language*, Mouton, 1971.

W. Labov, *The Social Stratification of English in New York City*, Center for Applied Linguistics, 1966.

S. K. Langer, *Feeling and Form*, Routledge and Kegan Paul, 1953.

S. K. Langer, *Mind: An Essay on Human Feeling*, Johns Hopkins Press, 1967.

J. Moffett, *Teaching the Universe of Discourse*, Houghton Mifflin, 1968.

M. Polanyi, *Personal Knowledge*, Routledge and Kegan Paul, 1958.

L. Rosenblatt, *The Reader, the Text, the Poem*, Southern Illinois University Press, 1978.

E. Sapir, *Culture, Language and Personality*, University of California Press, 1961.

J. P. Sartre, *Words*, Penguin Books, 1967.

T. Sebeok, *Style in Language*, M.I.T. Press, 1960.

D. I. Slobin, & C. A. Welsh, Elicited Imitation as a Research Tool in Developmental Psycholinguistics, in C. A. Ferguson & D. I. Slobin (eds.), *Studies of Child Language Development*, Holt, Rinehart and Winston, 1973.

L. S. Vygotsky, *Mind in Society*, Harvard University Press, 1978.

H. G. Widdowson, *Stylistics and the Teaching of Literature*, Longman, 1975.

II
Language and Intention

7

The Speaker

The child, the kitten, the cub, the fledgeling arrive to inhabit the same world but they take up residence in vastly different ways. The fledgeling may lie in a nest that its mother has worked to construct, and the cub learn to use a water track that its elders cut through the jungle: but the child is quite likely to be so surrounded by the work of men's hands that for a long time he rarely sets eyes on anything else—excepting of course those hands themselves and the faces that go with them. There is, however, a more remarkable difference even than this: for every item in the human child's environment there exists, side by side with it, a verbal counterpart, and much of his parents' energy is given to the manipulation not of the things but of the words.

The infant is born into a world of daily newspapers and letters of congratulation, news bulletins and Reith lectures, books on child rearing and traffic notices, 'Hey diddle diddles' and 'God save the Queens': and, above all, the buzz of conversation, for, from the very first, people talk at him and to him and about him. He takes little notice of it for a while, but there arrives a time when he too, after a good deal of babbling, becomes a speaker.

It has all started afresh. Language and all it comprises—its registers and dialects, its phonology, grammar, lexis and semantics—is put to use by another individual. It is the use he makes of it that I want to consider here, as briefly as I can.

Language in fact serves his purposes long before he can speak it. After four or five weeks of existence he can distinguish the speech of his mother from all other sounds and invests it with special significance: his response to it is to 'take heart', to stop whimpering. We can only surmise that the sound stands for her presence, even when she is out of sight, and therefore for the possibility of satisfaction in a world which may otherwise be confusing and threatening. That human speech should come to be associated with the activities of the parents, the life of the family, seems to me a fact of great importance. The family is to the infant his whole theatre of operations: and the funda-

First published in *Talking and Writing*, 1967. London: Methuen for the University of London Institute of Education.

mental 'satisfaction of progress' must lie in entering more and more fully into its activities. Before words have any meaning for him he seeks contact with members of the family by babbled 'conversations', by vocalization: and once he can give meaning to a few of the things he hears—'Give it to mummy', 'Fetch Teddy'—the eagerness of his response reflects the same pleasure in contact, the increased contact of actual co-operation through language. When, later, he tells himself to 'Give it to mummy' and 'Fetch Teddy', and obeys his own commands with equal eagerness he is still in a sense co-operating, having taken over with the language the authority-of-the-family with which he himself invested it.

It is during the first year of speaking that he makes the discovery that everything he sees has a name: thereafter, by dint of constant questioning, he learns a great many of these names. When he has increased his resources in this way he begins to chatter to himself as he plays, naming the objects as he handles them and saying what he is doing with them. He has, thus, two kinds of talk at his command: monologue and dialogue, talking to himself and conversational exchange. At first the two kinds are indistinguishable in form, but later they become differentiated; by the time he is about three and a half the tone of voice in which he speaks when he wants an answer is different from that of his monologue, his 'running commentary'. It is the difference in function, however, that concerns us here: the running commentary represents a first stage in a far-reaching sequence of mental developments.

Talking to himself about what he is doing helps him in two ways: first he interprets to himself the situation that confronts him, clarifying and defining it; secondly, he organizes his own activity within that situation. At this stage his monologue is in a strict sense 'a running commentary': he talks about what he *is* doing for the powerful reason that he is able to use only words about things actually present and actions actually being performed. It is a major step forward when, after about eighteen months of this here-and-now speech, he acquires the ability to use words *in place of* things, to refer to things not present and actions not being performed.

Freed of this restriction his language becomes a much more powerful instrument for the two purposes I have mentioned. Now his interpretation of the situation is enriched by reference to past situations. Indeed the *interpretative function* of language appears in its true light as the bringing to bear of the past upon the present. Similarly, in organizing his own activity within the situation, he begins to envisage what *might* be done, potentialities not tied to the means of achievement actually present: he can speak now of what he will do rather than what he is doing. Moreover the process of putting into words the possible courses of action reinforces his ability to resist random distractions—those shin-barking obstacles to achievement—and pursue the activity he has envisaged.

Language (or, as we shall see, forms of mental activity derived from language) continues to perform these two functions throughout life: by means of it we *interpret* experience and *regulate* our actions. Before we consider the general significance of these functions, however, we must trace a further specific change in the form of the child's monologue. While his powers of conversational exchange become more and more efficient as communication, able to deal in words with more complex experiences, and with an increasing range of past experience, his other mode of speech, monologue, develops in what might almost appear a contrary direction. It begins to be both *abbreviated* (a series of predicates, perhaps, with the subjects omitted) and *individuated*—using words for the meaning they have acquired from particular personal experience, regardless of their intelligibility to a listener. In both respects we may liken such language to the cryptic conversational utterances of two people who know each other intimately and find themselves in a highly meaningful, unambiguous, 'eloquent' situation; and then remember that when the child talks to himself he shares a situation with a listener who is very much *en rapport*.

By the time he is about seven years old this speaking to himself has more or less disappeared. It requires no great feat of the imagination to suppose that the changes we have noted have turned it into 'inner speech': that the omitted—or, rather, unspoken—subjects have been joined by unspoken predicates: that the continuing traffic in personal, individuated meanings has left him with verbal symbols that would be less and less useful in public interchange but more and more useful in organizing his own experiences. Speculating further, we can postulate the development from 'inner speech' to 'verbal thinking', when the forms employed would be still less like the grammatical forms of overt speech and the meanings still less like conventional word-meanings. What began then as one form of language behaviour (a joint activity—conversation), has become two, and the two are very different in character because they serve distinct purposes. I should add that what I have referred to above as 'speech to (one) self'—the first differentiated stage—is more often and more significantly called 'speech *for* oneself'—for reasons that will now be clear.

Speech and verbal thinking continue, however, to operate in close conjunction. In an unfamiliar area of experience a child will need to talk before he can think. And our loftiest speculations as adults are seldom achieved without a good deal of talking, and writing and reading, in addition to, and in very close relation with, our thinking.

We interpret experience, then, and regulate our actions in the course of both our talking and our thinking and it is language that, by its nature, enables us to do so. The most dramatic stage in the development of the regulative function is that we have already described: the child who puts into words what he is doing and what he is going to do increases his persistence and is better able to carry out his plan. That this should be so must in part be due to the power language gained for him when, in his infancy, it represented the security and order of the family. But, as adults, we can still catch an occasional sense that language retains its power to regulate: if we approach an event with misgiving we may well find ourselves preparing for it by putting into words—silently or even aloud—hypothetical courses of action: and caught in an unexpected difficulty we may sometimes be aware that a word comes into mind at the moment of deciding what to do. Examples of *other people* using language in an attempt to 'regulate' what we do are too frequent and obvious to need elaboration. That in the interchange of conversation we can influence each other's behaviour is clear, and the idea is familiar that we may also use a listener as a 'sounding board' assisting us to arrive at some decision, and so setting the course of our further action.

Language begins to operate as a means of interpreting experience from the very first exchange of words between an infant and his mother about what is going on: the shared situation is organized, given shape, by the words spoken in it. It need hardly be pointed out that the experience is at first more fully interpreted for the infant in the mother's words than in his own: but he continues the process for himself when he speaks his own running commentary on what he is doing. A new phase is entered when he begins to use words about things not present—now in telling his mother what he *has done* he shares through words experiences which she did not share in actuality. Here the onus for selecting, shaping, interpreting in words is on him, though of course her questions and her comments may supply the main 'members' on which he sets up his structure.

It must be stressed that until a child has acquired powers of verbal thinking, it is only by actual speaking that the interpretative process can function for him. Eventually his talking, reading, writing and thinking all contribute to it.

The interpretative function of language is essentially the use of words to 'give shape to experience'. But there is something unsatisfactory about this description: 'give shape' might suggest that I can use words to give any shape I please, whereas 'interpret' indicates that the experience itself will set limits. We need in fact a way of describing the process which allows for both these aspects—for the shape we *give* and for the shape we *find*. For this reason, risking its offence as jargon, I shall use the verb 'to structure'. As a noun, 'structure' may refer either to 'a construction' or to 'the relations between elements making up a whole', and we shall import both these senses into its use as a verb.

By means of language, then, we structure experience: experience itself—what is structured—is of course far more than language: it is the sum total of our responses to environment, whether in action, thought or feeling; and all that our senses report. It is difficult for us to realize how much we rely upon language simply to sort the material provided by the senses—difficult because the essential early stages of the sorting were accomplished in infancy. The child who says 'Mummy's chair, Daddy's chair, Baby's chair' has in the common sound 'chair' a tool for classifying—a pigeon-hole or a filing-pin. Without that filling-pin 'chair' as a category distinct from 'table' or 'bed' or 'washing machine' would never be established. Thus, a child learning names is at the same time sorting the objects of his world. As things fall into categories, and categories into a network of relationships, we are able to take into the area of our activities more and more of the environment: we respond to more and more of the world, in other words, by very reason of the fact that it presents itself increasingly as order and not chaos. The uniqueness of every moment of life must imprison us until, with the help of words, we begin to generalize.

The rough analogy of a word as a filing-pin upon which successive experiences are filed has already brought us, in attempting to explain our growing response to the present, to think in terms of an accumulation of past experiences. We must look more directly at this aspect. Clearly it is not the meaningless flux of sense impressions that we accumulate as experience succeeds experience, but organized, interpreted versions of those experiences. (Memory itself is organized, has taken on, so to speak, a narrative form.) The outcome, as the days and years go by, is a highly organized, continually modifying representation of the world as we have found it. And that is the world in which, each as individuals, we continue to live. It constitutes a frame of reference for every new experience, a body of expectations to be selectively aroused, every waking moment, either by some stimulus outside ourselves or by some continuing activity in our own minds. It is probably true to say that we could make no response to a situation to which we brought no expectations: without this interpretative process, experience would remain a largely meaningless flux of impressions.

It will be clear that though each of us must build his representation, his picture of the world, for himself—and each individual picture will be unique—we do not do so alone. The young child's talk with his parents is, as we have seen, crucial for the help in structuring experience that he receives from it: and how much we can later compensate for a failure at this point we do not yet know. To a very large degree, in any society, we build in common a common world picture. If the topic of any conversation can be said to have an existence at all, it exists as the relevant parts of the world picture of each of the participants—and the effect of the conversation will be to modify in some degree those parts of the picture both in ourselves and in our fellow-talkers.

It is this process of building in common that most clearly distinguishes man from other animals: their response is to the stimuli of the immediate environment, while man responds to a representation of the situation made in the light of past experience—a representation that is susceptible at all stages to the influence of other people. Thus animals learn from experience, but from their own experience: through language man learns from the experience of other men, present or absent, living or dead.

In the young child's picture of the world as it seems to him there is much that further experience will correct. A new experience may require the modification of whole areas of the structure, for gathering experience is no mere process of rolling a snowball over fresh snow. Many of the adjustments required may be achieved in the actual process of responding to the new situation, but there will be others which will be too deep-seated to be so readily achieved. If the experience is not to be rejected he needs in some way to go back over it and work upon it: and the rejection of experience means that the required adjustment is not made and the child is left with a false picture, erroneous expectations.

Fortunately, the child is already in the habit of going back over past experiences, re-enacting them, improvising upon them, for the sheer fun of it. Make-believe play is at its zenith at the stage of existence when deep-seated adjustments are most frequently demanded: how much of this play is to be explained as merely for the fun of it and how much as a means of coming to terms with past experience, it is impossible to say.

In re-enacting the experience in his own terms, as a game, freed from the obligation to respond socially that holds in real situations, the child adjusts his expectations to conform more nearly with what the actual world has manifested. Speech will normally play an important part in the game: what is said will often represent indeed the essential substance of the readjustment that has been made.

We can in fact parallel all that we have said about make-believe games in the realm of speech without re-enactment. The child in his talk will draw upon past experience, improvise from it, spinning long yarns of imaginary events around the briefest encounters, for example, with a bus conductor or a door-to-door salesman or a neighbour. All this is for the joy of it, but it is itself a process of extending (if on a somewhat 'provisional' basis) his world picture by incorporating his own view of other people's views of the world: it is at least a first step away from his exclusively individual angle of vision.

But the same kind of talk—talk with no practical purpose, talk as play—is available also when the need arises to come to terms with intractable experience. Small children's tales about witches constitute a recurring example of such talk: hearing so often in the witch's speech the tones of a scolding mother one cannot doubt that the utterance serves a purpose in adjusting the child's picture of the world to include the phenomenon of an angry mother.

Whenever we go back, in mind or in talk, over past experiences, to understand them better or to accept them more fully or simply to enjoy them again, we are as it were in the role of spectators of our own lives. When we gossip about other people or read biographies or novels or plays, we are in a similar way spectators of other men's lives, real or imaginary. Let me distinguish then two roles: as participants we *live* life, we interact with people and things, we take part in the world's affairs in some way or other: *as spectators,* we 'stopped the world' in order to 'get off'. The need to act and decide are marks of a participant's role: a spectator, freed from this need and looking to no practical outcome at all, is able to respond more fully to the *forms* of experience—the pattern of events, the network of personal relations, the configuration (if it may be so called) of the emotions that lie beneath both the events and the relationships; free to respond also to the *forms* of the *language* which, at its most successful, are an integral part of the total construction.

In most of our speaking and writing, language exercises a social, communicative function. When we write or speak or read or think in the role of participants, language has for us both a regulative and an interpretative function, and the two interact at all points: when we write or speak or read or think in the role of spectators, it is the interpretative function that is dominant.

I have considered some of the ways in which a child uses his own language to further his own development. I have done little more than elaborate the statement that he uses it to structure his experience. In conclusion, it seems to me that when the child comes to school his work in the subjects of the timetable, whether it be environmental studies, or science or history or geography, will encourage him to continue this structuring process in those areas in which impersonal, objective, socially approved bodies of common knowledge exist. But when these areas, which in the child are areas of shared curiosity, have been removed, what is left is all those experiences in which children differ most from each other—an area that may be roughly described as 'personal experience'. Moreover, it is in this area that all experience is integrated, becomes part of the individual's world picture. It seems to me that to look after this area is the primary task of the English teacher. I do not see him then as a teacher of literature: for this defines his function in extrinsic terms: rather I believe that the process of structuring personal experience demands the writing and the reading of what is essentially literature—language in the role of spectator. Again, it is certainly true that for the purposes of his own social and intellectual development a child needs to extend his linguistic powers, and the English teacher must regard this as a part of his responsibility. It seems to me, however, that acquiring skill *in* language must be secondary to achievement *through* language—and what is to be achieved through language in English lessons is the organizing and interpretation of the child's personal experiences and their extension in an organized way. This demands of the teacher as full an understanding as possible of what language is and the way it works.

8

Words and a World

As human beings we cannot escape the influence of language. It pervades all we do: the activities of every waking hour bear its stamp and it shapes more or less directly the material of our dreams. Perhaps it is principally for this reason that we find it as difficult to answer the question, 'What do we use our language for?' as we would to satisfy the child who says, 'What are people for?'.

We might catalogue situations and kinds of utterance and try to give a particular answer as to what each is for—small talk at the tea party, chat in the launderette, the sermon on Sunday, a monograph on lepidoptera, or Keats' 'Ode on a Grecian Urn'. But what would the answers have in common? What major features would shape an answer to the *general* question?

More promising perhaps to consider what effect language has upon a young child's behaviour when first he acquires the ability to use it. The small child who learns to speak begins to live in a new way. Hitherto, all that he has done has been a contribution to the family activities, its corporate existence; now he begins to contribute more of what he *is* than what he *does* could reveal. But, to feel the justice of the claim that he 'begins to live in a new way', we have to think not of the family's point of view but of the child's; and from his point of view, this contribution of himself through speaking bears the aspect of 'becoming' rather than of 'revealing'. In speaking he *discovers* more of what he is than he could discover in action. And since he has at first no inner dialogue with which to operate, all this discovery, this 'becoming', is spoken aloud for all to hear.

The change does not, of course, take place overnight. In the course of a year or eighteen months, two notable stages mark its progress. The first is the discovery that things have names, and that this is a fact about the world—in other words that *everything* may be assumed to have a name. Most children at this stage play what has been called 'the naming game', but is perhaps more usually a 'touching and naming game'. Here is the performance of an eighteen months old girl at

Published in *Children Using Language*, A. Jones and J. Mulford (eds.), © Oxford University Press, Oxford, 1971.

breakfast time: 'Bun. Butter. Jelly. Cakie. Jam. Cup of tea. Milkie.' To understand its significance we must imagine the game being played in the middle of a great sea of the un-named and hence (with some exceptions) the unfamiliar, the as yet undifferentiated. After the speaking of names has conferred a new status upon what was already familiar by use, the learning of new words adds fresh conquests—fresh objects are 'possessed' as they are differentiated. Then as further instances crop up and naming occasions are reduplicated, the word becomes a means of building up a category. ('Shoe. Another shoe. Two shoes.'—again at eighteen months.)

The second stage is reached when naming has progressed so far from touching that words begin to be used about things not present, and about events not actually taking place; and when words, in this way, come to be used *in place of things* they take on a much more powerful role. The naming game, in fact, represents a process of 'bringing into existence' the objects of the immediate environment, the here-and-now. But when the second stage is reached, the objects that *have been* named, but are no longer present, are brought in to assist in classifying what is present and relating it to the familiar. (On first meeting strawberries at two and a half: 'They are like cherries'—and, tasting them, 'They're just like sweeties'—and, finally, 'They are like ladybirds'.) What is being called into existence at this stage is an abiding world, a world that stays there when we move away or go to sleep—a world that provides prospect and retrospect as well as a here-and-now.

There is a paradox at the heart of all this. The words are old: they constitute a language that served the child's grandfathers and great-grandfathers before him. But every occasion for speaking them is a fresh one: in use, whether by child or grandfather they are on all but the most routine occasions not indeed newly minted, but newly meant. And the paradox is at its sharpest with the infant for whom there is no back-log of experience of what the words may in speaking be used to do.

Thus it is that in young children's efforts we recognize more clearly the nature of the process: how speech is generated not only to suit the situation—each new situation as it arises—but also to influence it in accordance with the speaker's needs and purposes. In other words he speaks to do more than meet the demands of the situation upon him—he speaks to *make something of it* for himself. What he makes of it, the direction of his curiosity, the tenor of his interpretation, the tentative constructions he places upon events—these in the course of his speaking reveal something of the sort of person he is becoming. He declares his individuality. And by a gradual process over a period of years he discovers his own individuality reflected in the responses other people make to his declarations.

To put the matter directly, all this amounts to saying that in speaking we represent the world to ourselves, and ourselves to other people. 'To represent' here means to 'make a representation', in the sense that we make a representation of a chair when we draw a chair, or a representation of the neighbourhood when we draw a map; in this sense also, that when we catch sight of a familiar face, what we have seen has matched something that we must have carried with us from previous seeing, a 'representation' of a face: and when our ears catch a familiar tune, the sound that has just been made must chime with an inner 'representation' of a sound we had heard on some previous occasion.

Language then is one way of representing experience, and before we can appreciate its particular role we must look at the importance of the process of representation itself. Learning in its broadest sense might be described as turning the unfamiliar into the familiar—not in a random way as my last examples might suggest (the chance heard tune, for instance) but in such a way as to relate one familiar item of experience with another. I knew a dog who grew very excited if he found a member of the household sticking stamps on to a letter: not only was the process familiar to him from past experience but it had been related, by experience, with another familiar event—being taken for a walk, and of course it was the anticipation of this that excited him.

Whatever might be said about dogs, it has been claimed that human beings internalize their experience of the world in the form of a *representation* of the world: and that whereas the lower animals respond directly to the stimulus of the actual environment, human beings react not directly but *via* this representation. The fruits of our past experience of the world are there in a coherent or organized form to assist our interpretation of what confronts us at a particular moment of time, the present. As I stick the stamps on a letter I too may anticipate the walk to the post-box, but I am likely to have in addition a far more complex and far-reaching set of anticipations taking into account such things as the appearance and personality and situation of the person I am writing to, and the probable outcomes of the news I have communicated. Moreover I can choose at any moment to think of that person, to recall his circumstances, to clarify my anticipations of his likely responses: it seems very unlikely that the dog can do anything at all like thinking quietly to himself 'It would be nice if someone were to write a letter and take me to the post'—he requires rather something in the present environment to set off the chain of expectation.

A representation lasts in time in a way that events themselves do not. One consequence of this we have seen—that we store experiences (to put it crudely): there are two other important consequences. First, we may work upon the representation: given the fact that our picture of what the world is like is subject to modification—as well as extension—by every new experience, we add now the notion that we may deliberately go back over experiences in order to make sense of them. That is to say, we work upon the representation to make it more orderly, more coherent. Secondly, a matter of the greatest importance, other people may work upon it too. The small boy who tells his mother what has been happening to him at school, goes back over the experiences, works upon the representation: but the representation is also very much affected by what she says in response. Thus, though each of us builds his own representation, what is built is in very large measure the picture of a world in common. We become experienced people in the light of other people's experiences as well as our own: the unfamiliar becomes familiar to us by virtue in part of our confidence in what other people have heard and seen and done.

We build in large measure a common world, a world in which we live together: yet each of us builds in his own way. My representation differs from yours not only because the world has treated us differently but also because *my way of representing* what happens to both of us will differ from yours. We are neither of us cameras. Admittedly, we construct a representation of the world we both inhabit: on your screen and mine, as on the sensitive plate in the camera, is reflected that world. But we are at the same time projecting on to the screen our own needs and desires. In this sense then, we build what is for each of us a representation of the world and at the same time is to each other a representation of a different individuality, another 'self'. More literally, it is by knowing in what terms I think of and respond to the objects and people and events of my environment that you know what sort of a person I am.

We interpret the present instant in order to turn what it offers us to our own advantage: that is to say we 'make something of' the situation (in one sense) in order to 'make something of' it in another sense. Past, present and future are interwoven here: we interpret the present by referring it to our representation of the world as we have experienced it, by bringing, in other words, the past to bear on it. Our purpose in doing so is to choose the appropriate response: in other words, to anticipate future events. Let me only add that as more and more of the world becomes familiar to us, the context into which we fit new experiences, by which we 'place' and interpret new experiences, becomes more complete and more effective as a basis for our predictions. Contrast the two-and-a-half-year-old confronting her first strawberries with the botanist identifying a rare plant.

Language is only one way of representing experience, but as such it plays a key role because it becomes the means of organizing all the other forms of representation. It is for this reason that it has already found its way into our discussion of the representation-making process. First, it is as we have seen a way of classifying. The naming and touching game shows words in the closest possible relation with the use of the senses. To take one example of the importance of this, what is potentially a vast number of different colour sensations must be grouped under the word 'red' and this group related to other potentially vast groups under the words 'blue', 'green' and so on, before a child's colour experiences can enter significantly into his expectations about the world. In all his activities, words become the filing pins upon which successive encounters with objects and events are filed. (We must add a reminder that the language-using-cum-exploratory activities interact to feed each other at all points: that a child is stimulated to activity by the enticements of the world to his senses: and therefore that an environment rich in such enticements plays an essential part in the growth of his powers.)

Secondly, by reason of its own complex internal organization language can be used to impose, as it were, a grid upon the multiplicity of sense impressions. Built into language are relations of likeness, of oppositeness, of sequence, of hierarchy, of consequence; and as a child learns to operate the language systems he applies these relations to reduce to order the multiplicity of things in the world. He does not merely imitate sounds and so arrive at speaking; he learns to operate a system. Thus at first 'flower' may be simply another name for 'daisy' and 'animal' another name for 'dog' but in due course he discovers he can use 'flower' to say things about buttercups and daisies and an immense number of other such objects. (And also that there is no satisfactory answer to the question 'What kind of a tail has a dog?' for the same sort of reason that he would not even ask 'What sort of a tail has an animal?') At a later stage he discovers that what seems *wide* on one occasion may seem *narrow* on another, and then he can begin to make sense of the fact that even the very, very narrow thing has width, just as the lowest things have *height,* and the lightest things *weight:* and that he can sensibly ask 'How heavy is your bag?' when it looks very light and 'How old is the kitten?' when it must be very young. In other words, he finds (but not in so many words) that oppositeness is a relationship that language systematically caters for.

Let us, in the third place, observe the fact that we habitually use language as a way of going back over experience, a way of *working upon* our representation of events. If we brood over something that has happened, our thinking has some of the characteristics of an inner dialogue and certainly it will take the form it does as a result of our past experiences of talking. (As Charles Morris explains it, we may not be using language symbols, but we shall certainly be using 'post-language symbols'.) But very frequently we in fact engage in talk as a means of going back over events: nothing is more familiar than the kind of gossip that goes on among participants after the 'big event'— the play, the party, the open day, the match, the wedding. There may well have been plenty of talk while they were still participating: but this is a different kind of talk because, no longer participants, they are in the role of spectators. Participants respond to ongoing events—they are 'responsible': spectators have no such responsibility, but are free to *savour* the past events in a quite different way. They will enjoy the behaviour of their party guests, for example, in a way that they could not while the guests were still behaving. They will savour and enjoy even the hardships and anxieties of the match—or 'the march'—in a way that they certainly did not enjoy them at the time.

The distinction between participants and spectators very roughly corresponds to a distinction linguists have made between two uses of speech. In the first, the participant form, speech and action are so closely complementary as to be often interchangeable. Interaction between two people—in a shop, for example—may be thought of as a chain of items any one of which may be speech, or action, or speech with action. The shopkeeper may say, 'Can I help you?' or he may merely stand opposite you in an expectant way: you may say, 'I'll take this, please' or pick up a bar of chocolate and give him the money. If you ask him, 'Have you a half-pound block?' he may say 'I'm sorry I haven't' or he may say 'Yes' and hand you one, or he may simply hand you one. Again, looking at another example in a slightly different way, if you have a bulky parcel to take through the door, you may manipulate the door somehow yourself, or you may use speech as a way of keeping the door open—by somebody else's agency.

You may agree that even in the simple examples given, speech may be seen to be used to organize our behaviour, to regulate both our individual and our co-operative activities. It would be more fully so, of course, when a group of people were engaged on a complicated joint enterprise. Such use of language by participants constitutes one way in which we construct a representation of experience and continue to adjust it—in our stride—as we come across the unexpected. Edward Sapir has suggested that it is from such uses 'in constant association with the colour and the requirements of actual contexts' that language acquires its 'almost unique position of intimacy' with human behaviour in general.

In the second of these two uses of speech, that corresponding to the role of spectator, language is used to refer to, report upon, and interpret action, rather than in substitution for it. Freed from the responsibility for action and interaction, we speak above all in order to shape experience, to interpret it—to work upon our representation of the world. I want to distinguish three ways in which we may do this—though in doing so I must observe that in any one conversation it is likely that all three ways will be used to some degree. If I go back as a spectator over my own past experiences in conversation with you, then you are also in the role of spectator. It may well be that my incentive for doing so at all is to share these experiences with you, to savour them, enjoy them with you: at the same time I am shaping and interpreting them and your comments will be helping me to do so. But the experiences I relate will sometimes be ones in which what happened was too unlike what I anticipated for me to adjust my world view, my body of expectations, while I was participating in them. In this case there is a positive *need* for me to go back and adjust, to 'come to terms' with the past events; and while in such situations you as a listener may sometimes be no more than a sounding board, you may of course sometimes be the major influence in bringing about the adjustment required. That is the first way of using conversation in the role of spectator: the events are those of my own experience and I shape them in order to share them. The second use could be illustrated from the same situation, seeing it from your point of view: let us, in all modesty, turn it round. Suppose as our conversation continues, you take up the role of spectator of your experiences and invite me to do the same. I am still engaged upon the shape of the world as I know it, but as I respond to you I shall be extending my picture to include in it some things that I have not experienced but you have. Of course, I cannot take over your experiences as though they were my own: inevitably it is still my own experience that I am working on: as I listen to your story I recombine elements of my own past experiences into new structures that correspond to the shape of your experiences. My representation is extended by this multiplication of its forms. My ability to anticipate events rests in this way partly upon the shape that experience has taken for other people.

Both these uses might have been regarded as ways of *improvising* upon my representation of the world: however the word applies more obviously to the third category of use. When in conversation we talk not about what has happened but what might happen, we open the way for a whole range of activities. I may speculate about what may happen to me with a close eye on actual possibilities—as might be the case if we were planning a joint undertaking. But in day dreaming the relation between what is imagined and what is likely to happen may be a very remote one: and of course we do carry on conversations which are a sociable form of day dreaming. The 'might-be' and the 'might-have-been' are pleasant topics of conversation and cover a whole range from sober, fairly realistic wish formulations to the extravagant fantasies of a Walter Mitty or a Billy Liar. Though the pleasure of improvising in this way upon our world representation may lie in the abandonment of any concern for the relation to reality and so for the predictive value, I would still see in such improvisations (in a world in which the strangest things sometimes happen) some connection with our urge to anticipate events or create the fullest context for whatever may occur. I see them, then, as a kind of testing out to the limits the possibilities of experience.

It should be added here that, if we accept as a rough definition of 'literature', 'the written language in the role of spectator', the literature we write may fall into any of the three categories we have considered and the literature we read may fall into the second or the third.

Thus, while it is true that we use language to shape experiences even as we participate in them, the shaping more typically takes place as we go back over experience in the role of spectators. Freed from practical responsibility, we are able to *savour* the feelings that accompanied events rather than act upon them, attend to the pattern of actions and circumstances, evaluate against a broader framework than we were able to apply in the course of the actual experience. Do we *give* this shape, or do we *find* it? The question must remain an open one: it seems probable that the structure of our world-picture reflects both order in the universe and our own particular way of *representing* the world—the shaping force of our own inner needs and desires.

To speak of language in the role of participant and in the role of spectator is to make a broad division in terms of the relation between the speaker and the situation. I want now to look more closely at language itself and suggest a three-fold division.

A great deal of talk is of the kind that Sapir called 'expressive'. It tends to tell us as much about the speaker as it does about the subjects of his talk. It is speech that follows the contours of the speaker's consciousness, a kind of verbalizing of the self. Often it will be intelligible only to someone who knows almost as much about the situation of the speaker as he does himself. Sapir suggests that as expressive speech sheds its more personal, unique, individual, subjective features and refers more explicitly to the actual world, it turns into 'referential' speech—the speech by which we participate in the world's affairs— informing people, explaining things, arguing, persuading, asking questions and so on. I want to add another 'wing' to Sapir's diagram; if expressive speech remains in the centre—a matrix, speech not subjected to the kind of pressure that makes it referential—then I should put referential (or transactional) speech on the one side, and 'poetic' or 'formal' speech on the other. This is also arrived at by subjecting expressive speech to particular demands, but they are demands of a different kind. They concern the *formal* characteristics of the utterance, and in particular its coherence, unity, wholeness. As speech, it is rare; the nearest examples will be occasional utterances in the course of successful dramatic improvisations: and this may serve to suggest the nature of the demands I have referred to—they are the kind of demands any artist makes upon himself in order to produce an object, a work of art.

Writing is of course rooted in speaking, though the two processes are very different. Because writing is *premeditated* utterance, because there is a time gap between its utterance and its reception, the shaping process I have been writing about may be fuller or deeper or sharper in its effect than it normally is in speech.

It seems probable that children's first attempts at writing will naturally rely heavily upon their speech experience, and will be of a kind we should classify as expressive: and that with more experience we shall find it differentiating in the two directions, both towards the referential and towards the poetic. Let me in conclusion suggest that the following extracts indicate better than I could explain the transitional categories that very much good writing in the Primary School will fall into. The first is by a ten-year-old boy: the practical task in hand has shaped his writing in the direction of the referential:

How I Filtered my Water Specimens

When we were down at Mr. Harris's farm I brought some water from the brook back with me. I took some from a shallow place by the oak tree, and some from a deep place by the walnut tree. I got the specimens by placing a jar in the brook and let the water run into it. Then I brought them back to school to filter. . . . The experiment that I did shows that where the water was deeper and was not running fast there was a lot more silt suspended as little particles in the water. You could see this by looking at the filter paper, where the water was shallow and fast there was less dirt suspended in it.

There are, as you see, expressive features interwoven with the referential: it *was* an oak tree, and it *was* a walnut tree—he knows because he was there—for him this was a part of what happened but they are features of his landscape rather than features of the experiment he sets out to describe.

The next example I can only leave with you. It is a catalogue by a seven-year-old girl—a kind of writing we are familiar with. But in this case I believe the rhythms she set up in the writing began to exercise some control over what she wrote: the writing, I suggest, moves towards the artistic, towards the language of poetry.

Class I had Monday off and Tuesday off and all the other classes had Monday and Tuesday off and we played hide-and-seek and my big sister hid her eyes and counted up to ten and me and my brother had to hide and I went behind the Dust-bin and I was thinking about the summer and the butter-cups and Daisies all those things and fresh grass and violets and roses and lavender and the twinkling sea and the star in the night and the black sky and the moon.

9

Language and Representation

From many diverse sources has come the idea, the hypothesis, that the importance of language to mankind lies not so much in the fact that it is the means by which we co-operate and communicate with each other as in the fact that it enables each of us, as individuals and in co-operation, to represent the world to ourselves as we encounter it: and so to construct—moment by moment and year after year—a cumulative representation of 'the world as I have known it'. In infancy the representation is made in talk; as for example this four-year-old who represents to herself, at the moment of encounter, the objects and events that engage her as she plays with her toy farm—to which had recently been added some model zoo animals:

> I'm going to have a zoo-field . . . now we've got more animals . . . three more, so I think we'll have a zoo-field (Whispering) Well, now, let's see . . . let's see how it *feels* . . . Get this pin now—there, you see. Haven't got a case . . . should be a zoo man as well . . . Look, must get this zoo man, then we'll be all right. Really a farm man, but he can be a zoo man . . . Depends what their job is, doesn't it, Dad? (She goes off and fetches him.) There now, you see . . . What do you want . . . Well, if you could look after these two elephants . . . I'll go and see about this . . . this panda. Well, all right. He squeezed out, and he got in. Shut the gate again . . . He said Hello . . . He said Hello. Dad, what I want to know is if the bear sitting up and the mother can fit in the house . . . Spect she can though . . .
>
> The bear . . . Dad, I'm going to call the fellow Brumas, the polar bear fellow. Look, the man and the lady are talking. The man's looking after the elephant and the lady's looking after the polar bear. They're talking over the wall. . . . You didn't see any polar bears, did you?
>
> When a person's standing it's taller than when it's sitting . . . when an animal's sitting it's taller than when it's standing. Spect

Introduction to *Speech and the Development of Mental Processes in the Child*, A. R. Luria and F. Yudovich, Penguin Books Ltd. 1971 Reprinted by permission of Penguin Books Ltd.

it's because they've four legs. It's because of the legs . . . your legs go up on the ground, don't they? But really an animal's front paws is really its hands, isn't it? When he sits up (i.e., the polar bear) he's as tall as the lady . . .

Daddy, are we in our house, Daddy? (Yes.) Well, why shouldn't the polar bears be in *their* house?

Her chatter constitutes a verbal representation of the things she sees and the things that happen—in this case mainly the events she causes to happen. Some of the more general formulations may be important elements in her cumulative representation of the world (as for example her conception of 'home' in the final comment quoted): all may be seen as facilitations at some level of subsequent encounters. On one occasion, over a year earlier, when she turned reluctantly from her engrossment with that same toy farm she said: "Oh why am I *real* so I can't live in my little farm?"—a representation that surely would persist and evolve through the years.

We continue of course to use talk as a means of representing the world: and that would serve to describe a great deal of the chat and the gossip that most of us devote our time to so generously. But we use writing also, and we use thought—going over in our minds events of the day, for example—and those two processes would not normally be possible to us unless we had built their foundations in speech.

I have arrived at this point, as many others have done, from a desire to understand the nature of language and how it works for us. What I have now to go on to—or back to—is a realisation that language is only one of a number of means by which we represent the world to ourselves; furthermore, that what makes us unique among the animals is not our ability to speak *per se*, but our habit of representing experience to ourselves by one means or another. We do so in terms of our own movements, in terms of our perceptions, and probably, more fundamentally still, in terms of our feelings and value judgments, though this remains a speculation and a mystery; and we do so in language.

We have no difficulty in recognizing the distinction between the process of looking at a face and the process of calling that face to mind, nor in realising that the two are in some way related. Our ability to call the face to mind is what allows me to talk about a *representation* of the world in terms of perception; the effects of my looking have not been utterly lost when I close my eyes or go away; what I have perceived I have 'represented to myself', and I may go back to the representation long after the face has disappeared from the range of my looking.

Being a man of parts, I can play 'God Save the Queen' on any ordinary piano on request (though three parts of me still wants to call it 'God Save the King'). If, however, you asked me to play the chords that accompany, say 'send her victorious', I should not be able to do so without actually playing, or rehearsing in mind and muscles, the phrases of the tune that lead up to it. I *have* the representation—the fact that I succeed in doing as you ask me would prove that; but it is a representation largely in terms of my movements (in relation to my perception of the piano-keys) and only minimally in terms of the appearance of the notation on the page. Hence I need to go through the repertoire of movements in order to re-capture it.

Piaget and Bruner have shown that young children represent the world to themselves first in terms of perception-cum-movement—and I put it that way to indicate that the two are inseparable; and later also in terms of visual imagery, or in perception freed from movement; and that the *simultaneity* of visual representation compared with the *serial* nature of perception-cum-movement results in a better organised system of representing, a more effective filing system for experience.

These two modes of representation are well-established before the third, the linguistic mode, comes into operation. When, at about two years of age, a child begins to speak, so achieving this third system, his talk is used as a means of assisting the modes of representation previously acquired; that is to say the modes of movement and of perception. In fact, his language is at first tied to the 'here and now', limited (with a few notable exceptions) to speech about what may be seen and handled in the immediate situation. It is speech-cum-action, or as Luria calls it, 'synpraxic speech' Its function as such is to facilitate activity in the here and now, activity in terms of movement and perception. Parts of the monologue of the four-year-old we quoted above will serve to illustrate this earlier stage. ("Well, if you could look after these two elephants . . . I'll go and see about this . . . this panda. Well, all right. He squeezed out, and he got in. Shut the gate again . . ." etc.) As we read it with imaginative insight, I believe we can sense the fact that her speech operates as a way of assisting her moves in the game.

But at one particular point in that monologue we find language operating differently. She talks of things she *wants*, things that are *not* there in front of her—first 'the cage', and then 'the zoo man': and having spoken of him, off she goes to get him.

This indicates what really amounts to a fourth kind of representation. Just as movement-cum-perception provided the basis from which the second stage was reached, that of perception freed from movement, so language tied to the here-and-now forms the basis from which there develops linguistic representation freed from these bonds, freed from its dependence upon movement and perception. At this fourth stage words come to be used not *with* objects but *in place of them.* As our example directly suggests, the ability to use words in this way further assists exploratory activity by breaking out of the immediate situation.

Things previously éxperienced may be imported into the situation, as the zoo man is: ideas derived from past experience may be brought to bear upon present problems. The result is a wide extension of a child's activities, the enrichment of the possibilities of the here and now by drawing upon the resources of the 'not-here' and the 'not-now'.

We are not concerned here simply with what the use of language may import into a situation: we are concerned also with *the way language does so*. Luria has demonstrated in a number of experiments that what is formulated in language carries a special power to influence a young child's behaviour; that from obeying the verbal instructions of an adult he goes on to instruct himself in words, both directly and indirectly; and that for him *to say what he plans to do* increases his ability to persist and complete an undertaking: that language, in short, performs a *regulative function*.

It has long seemed to me that the great importance of Luria's work in *Speech and the Development of Mental Processes in the Child* lies in its indication of the close relation between language ability and the scope and complexity of human behaviour in general. Of the two outcomes his experiment reports—the effect of encouraging normal speech performance in both the twins, and the further effect of speech training upon one of them—it is the former, the changes of behaviour in both boys after their speech had become 'normal', that is without doubt the major effect. By the same token, Luria's hypothesis that language acquires a regulative function, a power of co-ordinating, stabilising and facilitating other forms of behaviour—and the evidence and explanations with which he supports it—form one of the most important contributions he makes in this book to a general reader's understanding of the way language works. His Chapter VII is for this reason a key chapter, and his formulation has acquired, in my copy, a kind of illuminated border more often associated with 'texts' of another kind:

> With the appearance of speech disconnected from action . . . it was expected that there should also arise the *possibility of formulating a system of connections transcending the boundaries of the immediate situation* and *of subordinating action to these verbally formulated connections*.

That, taken at its very simplest level, is how the zoo-man got to the four-year-old's model zoo-field.

That same four-year-old had a sister two years younger than herself. One Saturday morning when they were respectively four and a half and two and a half, I tried, for about fifteen minutes, to keep a record of all that happened and everything they said. During the course of it, the older child, Clare, sat on the sofa with coloured pencils and a drawing block and, in spite of interruptions from Alison, the younger child, she completed two pictures; one of a girl riding a pony and one of a girl diving into a pool—both of them references back to things she had seen and done on her summer holiday three months earlier. She talked to herself from time to time about what she was doing ("Want to make your tail a bit shorter—that's what you're wanting.")—but sometimes inaudibly.

Meanwhile, Alison

1. pretended she was a goat and tried to butt Clare,
2. tried to climb on to the sofa,
3. came over to me and claimed my pen,
4. saw a ruler on the table, asked what it was, wanted it,
5. crawled under the table,
6. came out and asked me what I was doing,
7. climbed on to a chair by the window, looked out and made 'fizzing' noises,
8. climbed down, saw her shoe on the floor and began to take the lace out,
9. came over and asked me to put the shoe on her foot,
10. saw the other shoe, and did the same with that,
11. went over to Clare and pretended to be a goat again,
12. climbed on to the sofa and claimed the pencil Clare was using.

It will be clear, I think, that Alison's behaviour arises almost entirely in response to the various stimuli of the here and now, and is in this respect in direct contrast to Clare's sustained activity. A principal conclusion from Luria's experiment would be that language is the primary means by which the behaviour typical of the four-and-a-half-year-old is derived from that typical of the two-and-a-half-year-old—a gain which might crudely be called one of 'undistractability'. The story Luria tells of the twins in his experiment may in fact be seen as an accelerated journey between the stages represented respectively by Alison and Clare. For those of us who from observation and experience know more about children than we do about psychology, that starting point may prove a helpful approach to what Luria has to say.

As a child acquires the ability to use language to refer to things not present, it becomes possible for him to represent in words 'what might be' rather than simply 'what is'. As he does so his formulation may equally be a *fiction*—a make-believe—or a *plan*, and sometimes the two will be indistinguishable. A two-year-old child is able to make the first moves in this direction: but the ability either to sustain the make-believe or to carry out the planned activity is one that is developed as the facility in verbalising grows.

The habit of verbalising originates in and is fostered above all by speech with an adult: the appropriateness of the adult's early 'instructions' to the child's own concerns, and the eagerness and confidence with which he 'obeys' them constitute the criteria of favourable conditions. As Luria reminds us (in Vygotsky's words) "a function which is earlier divided between two people becomes later the means of organisation of the child's own behaviour."

10

Writing to Learn and Learning to Write

My lecture derives from some work that I've been doing for the past six years as director of the British Schools Council Research Project into Development of Writing Ability in Children (ages 11–18). We're still working on the data of that, so I shan't be referring to it very much more. But we began by collecting writings in all subjects from children eleven to eighteen from about sixty-five schools. We had about 2000 children in all and we drew a sample of 500 children's work in English and other subjects. And what I want to discuss is the thinking that has arisen in connection with sorting and interpreting those papers. I shall be quoting one or two of them to you.

The first of these was written by an eleven-year-old called Jacqueline, for her science teacher. She writes on how to make oxygen and this is what Jacqueline says:

> It is quite easy to make oxygen if you have the right equipment necessary. You will need probably a test tube (a large one), a stand with some acid in it. You will also need a Bunston burner, of course you must not forget a (glass) tank too. A thin test tube should fix neatly in its place. When you have done that, fill the glass tank and put the curved end upwards. Put the (glass) tank on the table and fill with water. Very soon you will find that you have made oxygen and glad of it.

It's the "glad of it" that interests us here. I wonder where that came from. On the whole she is trying to tell you what she did, so if you are really keen to make oxygen, well, you know how she went about it and you can go about it. That is what she is trying to do, but that bit at the end seems to come from somewhere else, doesn't it? I can just imagine her mum saying, "Yes, I dropped in and had a chat and a cup of tea, and glad of it." It comes straight out of speech. It is a sort of spoken fragment. I wonder what her science teacher thought of

Published in *The Humanity of English: NCTE Distinguished Lectures 1972.*
Reprinted by permission.

it. Do you think *he* would think he was glad of it, or that this was something she might well have left unsaid? I think from what I know of the situation that he was glad to know that Jacqueline was glad she'd made oxygen and wasn't simply going through the hoops for him. On the other hand, while I would welcome that expressive feature, that feature taken from speech, in that writing at that stage, I hope you would agree with me that in the long run, ultimately, if she's out to inform us and wants us to have the information necessary for making oxygen, that at least is inappropriate—is not required.

What about this? This is another piece from the research by a fifteen-year-old boy from a school just off the old Kent road, which is a dockland area of London—a tough school, a school in a rough area.

> School, ugh. Dad is up having a wash, Mum has gone to work, sister has got up, and me, I don't get up till I'm told to. If I had my way, I wouldn't get up. Still I get up, have a wash and go to school. On the way you see some funny people about these days. Take that old man who lives round the corner. He says that he cannot go out to get his pension [that's the old age pension, and he has to go to the labor office to get it] but when someone gets it for him, he is round the pub like a shot. Crafty old man. At any rate, to get back to walking to school. School, what a terrible word, whoever invented it should have been shot. I know parents say schooldays are the best days of your life but that was in those days. School was good because you started work when you were twelve so school was good. For the time you were there.

Obviously a good deal of that comes out of speech also—in fact, the whole area is fairly near to speech, isn't it? He says "cannot" instead of "can't." He got that from books, not from speech. But most of it comes pretty directly from speech. And it has other features which make it like speech. He rather assumes that we're in his context. He invites us to accept an assumption that we know the sort of thing he's talking about, so he says, "You see some funny people about these days."

"Take that old man who lives down the corner." Well, what old man? We've nothing leading up to him. He's come straight out of the boy's context and he's offering it to us to accept and assume the context, which is again like speech and which is again why I want to call it "expressive." The whole piece is expressive. This is not a case of expressive features in a piece which is out to do something else. This chap isn't trying to inform us, to tell us things he believes we want to know; he's simply sharing a slice of his experience with us, letting us into it, which is an expressive function. It's a way of being with him. It is also loosely structured. He moves to the old man, for example, and then back to school again. This loose structure is again typical of the expressive. The expressive is a term I take from the linguist, Edward Sapir. He is usually called the father of American linguistics, but I think he deserves to be called the father of modern linguistics. Sapir says that in all language, two strands are interwoven inextricably, one an expressive pattern and one a referential pattern. Referential means you're talking about what's in the world and you are using your reference to what's in the world for useful purposes. You are informing people, instructing people, persuading people, and so on.

But the expressive bit of it. How does language get that? Sapir gives us one answer. He says that it is expressive because "language is learned early and piecemeal, in constant association with the color and the requirements of actual contexts."[1] In other words, we pick it up as we go. "Early and piecemeal," and it never loses its ability to revive the actuality of these contexts with all their colors and all their requirements.

So I want to define expressive language as language close to the self; language that is not called upon to go very far away from the speaker. The prototype for linguists is the exclamation. You know, the noise you make when you drop the hammer on your toe. And if you are by yourself it's purely expressive. In other words, merely vents your feelings. If somebody else is there, then it is also a communication. It won't have any meaning unless a person can see the plight you're in and knows you, because we have different habits of exclamation; what might be a very mild exclamation for you might be a rather severe one for me. You need to know the person and the situation in order to get the full meaning of that communication. Well that's also true, in general, of the expressive. You need to know the speaker and the context.

Expressive language is giving signals about the speaker as well as signals about his topic. And so it is delivered in the assumption that the hearer is interested in the speaker as well as in the topic. In fact if I had to tie myself to one thing about the expressive I'd say that that was the most characteristic. It relies on an interest in the speaker as well as in the topic. It's relaxed and loosely structured because it follows the contours of the speaker's preoccupations. I sometimes take my wife for a drive, and I drive and she talks. And that talk is highly expressive. It's about anything that comes into her head. Things she sees from the car, things she remembers suddenly, things that she's forgotten in the kitchen and so on. It's highly expressive talk, loosely structured, only really communication to me because I am also in the context, because I know her and what has been happening around her. If I want to argue with her—if she says something that I disagree with—or if she says something I am curious about and want some information about, then her language is likely to move away from the expressive, further away from the person speaking and a bit nearer to the actualities of the world. Nearer to what Sapir calls the referential.

I'm saying all this about expressive because I do believe it's very important. I believe it has a very important function. Its function in one sense is to *be with*. To be with people. To explore the relationship. To extend the togetherness of situations. It's the language of all ordinary face-to-face speech. So it's our means of coming together with other people out of our essential separateness. But it's also the language in which we first-draft most of our important ideas. In other words, most of the important things that there are in the world were probably first discussed in expressive speech with somebody who was in the context. And if you put those two things together I think you'll see why I claim for it, in the third place, and it's the form of language by which most strongly we influence each other.

I was in New Orleans when Martin Luther King was shot, and of course the talk was everywhere. Talk on street corners and church porches, in bars, indoors. I really do believe that the quality of that talk, what it was able to achieve in influencing people's opinions, was a material factor in forming public opinion and hence the political outcome of the event. It's far more influential than sermons in church or printed political manifestos.

Expressive writing is primarily written-down speech, and that is, I think, why it is important as writing. Being written-down speech, it does something which I want to describe in two ways. First, it maintains the contact of the writing with the resources the writer has, resources which come from speech. We recruit and keep fit our linguistic resources, above all, through speech. So when we are using expressive language, we are writing in such a way as to maintain the closest contact with those resources. And then saying that same thing a second way, expressive writing is also important because in it, we make sure the writer stays in the writing and doesn't disappear. We'll come back to that.

Nevertheless, writing, even expressive writing, is very different from speech and this is pretty obvious. In speech you have a face-to-face situation. You have immediate feedback. When you are writing, you are left on your own. You have to work in a vacuum with no feedback. You have to imagine your audience and hold him fully in mind if you are to take his needs into account. What's written here and now is to be read there and then; some other time and some other place. I think we need to conjure up an audience for this rather lonely task, and this is one reason why I hold unorthodox views on the role of the teacher with regard to the child's writing. I think the teacher needs to extend to a child a stable audience. I think when a child is learning to write in the first stages, this business of meeting the needs of a reader is one of the real difficulties of coping with writing. The kind of encouragement the teacher can give—in other words, the extent to which the teacher is a good listener, a good reader—can make that easy for a child, and the stability of having the same reader from occasion to occasion is also, I think, very important to those stages.

And then there's the effect of the time lag. You write it here and now, and it's read elsewhere at some other time. How do you use that time lag? How do you use the time lag between the transmission and the reception? In speech, we usually trust the process of "pushing the boat out." Are we wrong in not trusting it also in writing? How far in writing ought we to have faith in the process you might call "shaping at the point of utterance?" Or how far do you think this premeditation is something we should be much more deliberate about? We all know how expressive speech works; we all know about its importance for children. How in telling about what's been happening to them, for instance, in sharing their experiences, children are also shaping those experiences and therefore making them more accessible for their own learning. We don't learn from higgledy-piggledy events as they strike our senses; we learn from events as we interpret them, and one of the main ways of interpreting them is by talking about them—by giving them shape in language. And the incentive to do that is to share them with somebody else. Can this work with writing? Can the constant audience of the teacher and the even sharper shaping process that goes on when you write about experience—can this—continue to serve for the child as the talk with his parents has served him in infancy?

Let me refer again to "and glad of it." We judged that to be ultimately—I judged that on your behalf—to be ultimately irrelevant. That is, writing as written-down speech won't go the whole way. Something else has to happen side by side with it. I had this something else illustrated to me not too long ago when I was visiting a colleague of mine at home. I was shown a story which my colleague's wife had typed out at the dictation of their four-year-old boy. And the four-year-old boy's story included this sentence: "The king went sadly home for he had nowhere else to go." Well I was very interested in that from a four-year-old because you see "for he had nowhere else to go" is not a speech form. He hadn't heard his parents say that. He hadn't used it in speech. It had come directly to him from the printed page. He hadn't read it but it had been read to him. In other words, he has done what the linguists would call internalized a form of the written language, and he's using it in an appropriate place. He's telling a story. He's using the storyteller's language as he had got it from the printed page by somebody's reading.

And that is the other process that has to go on alongside the written-down speech. As a child extends his reading, so he internalizes more and more the patterns of the written language. I don't mean that globally—and I mean *many forms* of the written language appropriate to many different kinds of tasks. I think this process, once we understand it, needs to be gradual. I think we can easily short-circuit it if we're too deliberate about it. I don't believe in setting the written model for their writing. I believe in reading for reading's sake and the kind of internalization that comes from reading for reading's sake will then articulate, interlink with the spoken resources. The linguistic resources which have in general been recruited at the spoken level. In other words I'm asking for a kind of metabolism. You know, language in any case is outside in the world, not in the child. He has to internalize it in order to speak. There is another internalizing job when it comes to the written form. In both these cases, just as we internalize substances of the world and create our own bodies out of them by a process biologists call metabolism, so we need a metabolic process in internalizing language. In other words it is highly selective and it depends upon internal structures already in existence. It's a personal job, a personal selection and internalizing in terms of individual needs and interests. So I don't think we can hasten it. I think the way in which we treat reading in relation to writing sometimes is in danger of being too deliberate.

Reporting how she made oxygen was for Jacqueline a concern with the outside world. I'm suggesting that this sort of writing makes its best start in the expressive. Here's another little example. This is a ten-year-old country boy who lives in Suffolk.

> On Sunday I made some coal gas. I got a large peanut tin and punched a hole in the top. I filled it one-third full with small bits of coal. Nothing happened when I first put it on the fire, but after a while brown stuff came out. It was gas. I immediately tried to light it, but it did not light. I tried to light it every five minutes. After fifteen minutes it lit. It lasted for eight minutes. My second try lasted one hour three minutes. Each time it did not turn to coke. The back of the tin was red hot.

Well, it's fairly near to speech but he's moving toward the language in which you would expect him to perform the kind of transaction he's after—giving us information. Pretty concrete. How about its shape? Well it simply takes the shape of his activities.

Here's a much later one and a very different one. Another stage in the journey. This is a sixteen-year-old black girl from a school in Connecticut.

> When I first moved into my neighborhood twelve years ago it was a predominantly Jewish community. From the minute I moved in till just a few years ago I was an oddity looking for acceptance. I had no one in my neighborhood I could call a true friend. The air of prejudice hung so heavy in the air it choked the life out of the neighborhood. Slowly I watched the For Sale signs pop up, and

gradually I watched most of the Jewish families move out. Until I was about eleven I never knew quite why. But when I was older I realized it was because of my family and the few other black families in the area. And that's why today there is a little hurt left in me from knowing that people can be so thick-headed and narrow-minded they would let false ideas force them to move out of their homes. Today I am fighting to keep myself from inflicting my hurt on someone else and trying not to let prejudice become a part of my life.

Attempting to do a job in the world but a much more advanced job at a much more abstract level. Much more exploratory. Much more a matter of theorizing in order to solve her own problems.

Let me add very briefly, I believe the writing and the reading are complementary processes and we need both. We need to test out in writing what we can do with the written forms, what meaning we can derive from the written forms, what meaning we can communicate in the written forms. The written language forms a gateway to most further learning. And perhaps this becomes of particular importance for children from linguistically deprived homes, from dialect homes; because here will be the first and perhaps the greatest opportunity of coming to terms with this language which will prove so valuable later on.

But all that is only half the story. It's the more familiar half. I want to move on now to what I think is the less familiar half. And to do that I want to go back to a sort of beginning, a theoretical basis. I've already made brief reference to it. The most fundamental and universal kind of learning for human beings is learning from experience, which means bringing our past to bear upon our present. To do this we need to interpret, to shape, to represent experience. One way of representing, interpreting, and shaping experience is by talking about it. And we all do a great deal of it. Joseph Church, an American psychologist, has this to say about the process: "The morning after the big dance, the telephone system is taxed while the matrons and adolescents exchange impressions until the event has been given verbal shape and so can enter into the corpus of their experience."[2] I'm sorry I can't help smiling about that because he starts off like a human being and finishes like a psychologist, doesn't he? That last idea is the important one I'm after. There is such a thing as "a corpus of experience" and talking does shape experience in such a way as to add to it—no doubt adding to what has in fact also been created largely by talk. There are, of course, many ways of representing the world to ourselves, and language is one of them.

Sapir suggested, many years ago, that we operate in the actual world not directly, but by means of—through the mediation of—a "world picture," a representation of the world. Ernst Cassirer, a German philosopher mostly writing in America, in his book, *An Essay on Man*, reports that, according to a German biologist, man is slower to react to an immediate change in the immediate environment than any other creature is and he puts forward a hypothesis to explain it. He suggests that all creatures have a system of nerves carrying messages from the outside world into themselves and a system of nerves for carrying from themselves to the outside world their responses to those messages. And these two systems are linked together—the incoming stimulus and the outgoing response. But in man, for the first time, a third system is shunted across those two, and that's the symbolic system. A system of representation. So that man receives the signals from the outside world, builds them into his world picture—his representation from past experience of what the world is like—and responds, not directly to the incoming signals, but in the light of his total representation: he responds, in other words, to the incoming signals *as interpreted by the representation*. If that sounds a very involved process, I can think of a very simple example. If I say to you, as I might well, "I thought I heard somebody coming upstairs," I've expressed my response to an immediate change in the environment in terms heavily clothed in past experience. I think you'd find it very difficult to do it in a way that wasn't. We habitually take the signals in and interpret them in the light of our past experience—of stairways, and people, and the world in general.

A representation lasts in time in a way events don't. So you can work on it. You can go back over experiences and work on them. Not only you but other people also. When the small boy comes home and tells his mum what's been happening in school, an important part of what he builds into his representation of his day in school is what his mother says as well as what he is saying. So we can affect each other's representations. You might say what I have been doing is to work upon (or try to work upon) your world picture in certain areas to do with schools and children and language.

Representing experience is a cumulative process. Looking back, our representation is a storehouse of past experience, selective of course, not total. But looking forward, that same storehouse is a body of expectations as to what may happen; a sheaf of expectations from which we can draw as appropriate in accordance with the stimulus that meets us. It's a cumulative process, but it's not like a snowball, rolling around gathering more snow on the outside. Because every new experience is liable to demand a change in the picture of the world as a whole. Mostly we can adjust in our stride. If an event is too unlike our expectations we have to respond as best we can, because events don't wait for us; but we are left, after it's over, with an undigested event, an undigested experience.

The expectations from which we draw, and which we put to the test in actual experience, are our hypotheses. And we modify our expectations in the light of what happens, just as the scientist puts his hypotheses to the test and modifies them in the light of what happens in the laboratory. So we are actively predicting experience at every moment in the light of this storehouse of past experience.

Let me draw a little picture of your world representation—the world as you have found it—a nice simple one—and then add an event, something happening to you at the moment.

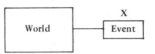

What's happening to you, you can only interpret in the light of your total representation: in other words the small square is subject to change in the light of what is in the large square. On the other hand, your total world representation is open to modification in the light of any new experience—that is in the light of this (or any other) event. So the large square also is subject to change. Now while the event is happening, you are called upon to *participate* in it. For this reason your attention (represented by "x" in my diagrams) will be focused upon changes to the smaller square: I have suggested that we can normally adjust to new experiences in the course of their happening. But if what happens is too unlike our expectations, then we are left, after the event is over, with an unmodified world representation and an undigested experience—still with a large square and a small square. But suppose the event is *not now happening*. Let me indicate the difference. Here, the small square stands for an event which *has happened* and is being reconstructed in talk. And because it is not now happening, and we do not have to participate in it, we are free to concentrate upon changes in the total world representation, the large square.

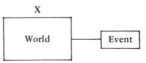

The difference of focus is very important: what we now have is a process of surveying the *total* in search of order and harmony and unity.

Actually, the whole scheme as I have depicted it is too simple, and I have very briefly to make it more complicated in the light of what sociologists would tell us. Now what the sociologists would point out, of course, is that I've spoken as though this were an *individual* matter, with only very cursory references to mothers and other people. Sociologists will point out that the building of the world is to a great extent done cooperatively. The worlds we build are very like each other in many respects. So they would want to say we build by scanning, interpreting, acting *in* and acting *upon* situations. So that from joint action in encounters with other people we build a shared social world. I want to see that in two steps: take it first at a momentary level. In any encounter each member of the group interprets the situation in his way and acts in the light of that interpretation. To act, which includes speaking, of course, is to present oneself. So in this encounter, each member of this group is presenting himself. To act is also to *modify* the situation. But *interaction* means that these interpretations and self-presentations embodied in action are offered like pieces in a jigsaw, and it's the fitting together of the jigsaw that in fact confirms and modifies the individual interpretations and shapes the outcome of the encounter.

And now, very briefly look at that as a cumulative process. Day by day and year by year, we classify, further interpret, and store these interpretations and these self-presentations and so construct a social world and an individual personality within it. Thus, when sociologists look at us, the teachers in schools, what they see (and I'm quoting here a young British sociologist called Geoffrey Esland)—what they see is that "the relationship between teachers and pupils is essentially a reality-sharing, world-building enterprise."[3]

I want now to go back to the diagram and add a little to it. The two sides of this page represent two different relationships between *language* and *events*. On the left side, as we said, the events are actually happening, and the language constitutes a part of what is going on, a way of participating in events. Whenever we talk or write or read for some functional purpose—to get things done, to make things happen—we are using "language in the role of participant."

On the right hand side, you will remember, the event is no longer happening: you are going back over it in talk. Therefore, for what I hope will be obvious reasons, I want to call that "language in the role of spectator."

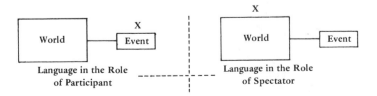

And in theory, at any rate, the distinction is clear. In the role of spectator we use language to reconstruct events, to talk about what is not now going on. However, it is not quite so easy as that. Suppose I invite you to be spectator of my past experience. I had a lovely weekend in New Orleans recently. Suppose I want to talk about it, in order to enjoy it again. I take up the role of spectator of those events for their own sake, for the pleasure of it. I might prevail upon you to listen and then you would take up the role of spectator of my past experience.

On the other hand, I might begin to tell you about my past experiences and after you had listened patiently in the role of spectator, you might suddenly find you were in the wrong role, because what I was doing was working up to asking you to lend me a fiver—working up to raising a loan. A hard luck story. Well that's not the spectator role because that's participation. I am pursuing my practical purposes here, talking to make things happen—and so, participating in events. So even though I'm reconstructing past events, because they are the means to something I am now pursuing, they are not in the role of spectator.

We could contrast that with hospital talk. I don't know whether you've visited a hospital or been in a hospital, but you know on visiting day in hospitals the talk is all about operations, symptoms and illnesses and pains and aches. And all this is spectator role talk. Going back over things in order to come to terms with them—to deal with as yet undigested events. On the other hand, in the doctor's consulting room, you may also reconstruct past experience and talk about your symptoms and your aches and your pains. That's quite different. You are contributing there to a diagnosis. Participant role. And if you got into the kind of vein you would use in the hospital, the doctor would soon recognize it and pull you out.

Another example; think of a party, and the party is over, and you and your fellow hosts are discussing the behavior of your guests in order to discover who it could have been that left a ring on the wash basin. Well that's very helpful of you. It's very useful. You are doing part of the world's work. So you are in the participant role. On the other hand you'll probably find that the conversation soon drifts into another vein, and you find yourselves discussing the behavior of your guests in order to *enjoy* their behavior in a way you couldn't when they were still behaving. And that's pure spectator role.

We can take up the role of spectator of our own past experiences and since you can of mine and I can of yours, we can become spectator of other people's experiences, real or unreal. Spectator of imagined experiences. Spectator of our own possible futures in our daydreams. So I'm including under this role of spectator a whole range of possibilities. In spectator role, we are free from the need to interact. Our attention is upon events that are not happening, interactions with people that are not now present. (We are, of course, in a situation and interacting with our listener. But we are minimizing our interaction. We may offer him a drink as he listens to the story, but this is likely to be felt as an interruption to what we really are doing—which is to concern ourselves with events not now happening, for the sake of doing so.) Free then from the need to interact, we use that freedom, I suggest, first of all to pay attention to *forms* in a way that we don't when we participate. And the forms of language, particularly.

If we are in a spectator role, then the way you tell your story is part of my enjoyment in it, and the forms of language and the way you form language will be an essential part of what you are doing. And particularly this is true of the form or pattern of feelings. You know, if a mother during the day has a small son to look after who gets into all kinds of trouble, the feelings aroused in her are likely to be above all sparked off in action. But when her husband comes home in the evening, as long as he knows the boy is safely tucked up in bed, he loves to hear about the hairbreadth escapes. They both now are in spectator role. They can both enter into and appreciate the feelings of fear and anxiety and horror and excitement and pride, and so on in a way you can't when you're participating. One is somehow able to savor feeling *as feeling* in a spectator role in a way one isn't free to savor it in a participant role.

And finally, something not unconnected with that. We also use the participant role to evaluate. We bring onto the agenda of our talk with neighbors and other people a great deal of human experience by taking up the spectator role. I suggest that we take up the spectator role out of need—when we need to go back and come to terms with undigested experience. But we also take it up for fun and pleasure— because we never cease to long for more lives than the one we've got. We've only got one life as participants. As spectators, countless lives are open to us. They are extensions of our own. And what is afoot when we are extending our experience into each other's as we gossip is above all an exploration of values. As I recount a story of events, I'm offering evaluations and I am looking to you listening to me to come back with your evaluations. I want to establish this as an important feature, because I believe we are dealing with a basic social satisfaction.[4]

I've suggested that in the spectator role we show a concern for the total world picture, a concern for the total context into which every experience has to be fitted. I've suggested that creating a world is to some extent a social process. Now the physical part of our world is very easy to corroborate. Corroboration that you have the same idea of this room as I do isn't going to be difficult. Where our world pictures are likely to be held vulnerable is not in the physical features, it's in the value system. It's in what we feel and believe about the world that we hold our world picture most privately and tentatively. So we're always offering evaluations to other people to see how they evaluate and in so doing are gaining the basic social satisfaction of having our value system, as it were, checked and calibrated against those of other people.

I now want to complete the diagram by adding a reference to the principal functions, or uses, of language, as we categorized them for the purposes of our research on writing.

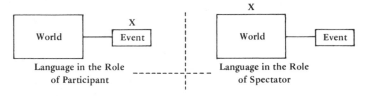

TRANSACTIONAL _ _ _ _ _ _ EXPRESSIVE _ _ _ _ _ _ _ _ _ _ _ POETIC

The middle term is one we've already talked about a good deal—the expressive function. Loosely structured, equally at home in the spectator role or the participant role—language close to the self. We saw Jacqueline attempting to meet the demands of a participant role, attempting to get something *done*. The kind of writing that fully meets such demands we labeled—for very obvious reasons—"transactional." It is important to see the line in the diagram as a continuous scale, a spectrum. We've already noticed that as the expressive moves towards the transactional, it has to make more explicit reference to the outside world. The personal features that are not relevant are omitted, and more of the context is filled in for somebody who is not in it already, not face to face sharing the same situations and events.

So those are the kinds of changes that go on as "expressive" moves out to "transactional." I could say a lot more about the transactional, but I'm going to leave that, because the important things I want to discuss come on the other half of the diagram.

From the expressive to the poetic. In other words, language in the spectator role. Once again, as a piece of expressive writing changes to meet in full the demands of the spectator role, it changes from expressive writing to what I want to label "poetic." I don't mean rhymes. I don't mean meter. I don't mean poetry in the usual sense; poetry is certainly at the core of it, but is not the whole of it. By poetic I mean language as art—poetic in the original Greek sense, something made, a verbal object. So as we move from the expressive to the poetic, once more meeting the demands of a wider audience, once more language gets further away from self, but in a quite different way because for a quite different purpose. The personal features are given wider meaning as they enter into a very intricate complex organization. Because the further you move along this scale towards the poetic, the greater is the attention paid to forms, to the organization of form. The forms of language, but also the forms of events, the plot of the novel, the pattern of feelings—forms in general. So what you are doing is to create an artifact, a verbal object. And it's this refinement of organization that gives personal features a kind of resonance by which they have meaning for an unknown audience. Transactional language is language that gets things done, language as a means. Poetic language is a construct, not a means but an end in itself. So language in the role of spectator is a spectrum that stretches, as far as the written language is concerned, from an intimate letter, a way of "being with" someone, writing in the expressive, to literature: novels, poetry, drama.

I'm saying in part what has often enough been said before. It was said very elegantly by W. H. Auden about poetry.

> For poetry makes nothing happen: it survives
> In the valley of its saying where executives
> Would never want to tamper.[5]

Poetry makes nothing happen. It's not transactional. One last point about that. I think perhaps I can make this clearer by contrasting the way we contextualize a piece of language, or make it our own. You know we have our own ongoing purposes. If a piece of language is to mean anything to us at all we have somehow to incorporate it in those ongoing purposes. In other words we have to contextualize it.

With transactional language, what goes on is *piecemeal* contextualization. If you read a piece of transactional language—an article on a subject such as how to teach composition, or this piece of mine—then you take what you want from it and leave the rest. You pick a bit here, you leave all this because you don't accept it or you knew it already. You pick here, you pick there, you make new relations between those bits, and you make your own relations between those and what you already know and think. That is piecemeal contextualization. What a writer of poetic language has to do at all cost is to avoid that piecemeal contextualization. What he's after is contextualization *as a whole*. In other words he wants to resist contextualization until the poetic object has been built up by his reader. He wants a hard skin around it.

Of course we do respond to literature in this piecemeal fashion. I've heard children reading Yeats say, "Oh, I didn't know Yeats was a spiritualist." Or even reading other poems say, "Oh, I didn't know there were camels in Tibet." We do contextualize literature piecemeal. There is no reason why we shouldn't. But we do it knowing that we are not playing the game for which the poem is written. In order to do that we need to resist this piecemeal contextualization. It doesn't matter whether there are really camels in Tibet—there are camels in Tibet in the poem and that's all that matters.

And yet, of course, we do in the end have to contextualize a piece of poetic writing. A novel can incorporate a message. What we must do is resist the piecemeal interpretation of that message because the message is embodied in the construct. When we have reconstructed the verbal construct, then we can make that our own—and I would call that global contextualization.

I want to stress the importance of that spectrum from the expressive to the poetic. I think I can illustrate this with two pieces which represent, in a sense, poles. They're both expressive still, but they're both moving towards the poetic in very different ways. One was sent to us from Canada from the Jessie Katchem Primary School in Toronto. It was written by a boy who lived with his mother because the father had abandoned the two of them several months before. This is what he wrote:

> Once upon a time there was a little boy and he didn't have a mother or father. One day he was walking in the forest. He saw a rabbit. It led him to a house.
>
> There was a book inside the house. He looked at the book and saw a pretty animal. It was called a "horse." He turned the page and saw a picture of a rabbit . . . a rabbit just like he had seen in the forest. He turned the page again and saw a cat. He thought of his mother and father, and when he was small and they had books for him and animals for him to play with. He thought about this and he started to cry.
>
> While he was crying a lady said "What's the matter boy." He slowly looked around and saw his mother.
>
> He said, "Is it really you?"
>
> "Yes, my son. I'm your mother."
>
> "Mother, mother . . . are you alive?"
>
> "No child. This is the house that I was killed in."
>
> "Oh mother why are you here?"
>
> "Because I came back to look for you."
>
> "Why mother? Why did you come back to look for me."
>
> "Because I miss you."
>
> "Where is father?"
>
> "He is in the coffin that he was buried in. But don't talk about that now. How are you son? You're bigger . . . I'm glad to see you."
>
> "It's been a long time mother."
>
> While the boy and the mother were talking his father came into the room and said "Hi son. How are you?"

"Fine," said the boy, "fine."

Suddenly the mother and father came to life.

The boy was crying, and the mother and father were crying too. God suddenly gave them a miracle . . . to come to life. The boy looked at the mother and father and said, "Oh Mother, oh Father."

Well, spectator role taken from *need*—in order to repair as far as you can the fragmenting of your picture of the world, to come to terms with events. But as I said, the spectator role is not only used from need. We habitually take it up for much more commonplace and enjoyable reasons. Here's a very different example written by another boy. An eleven-year-old boy called Malcolm in a school very near where I am working in London:

"Sir, can I have two pieces of paper?"

"Yes you can, Malcolm. What do you want it for?"

"To do a picture of a tiger, sir."

"All right then, Malcolm."

It took me two weeks to do that picture, but when he was finished he was Lord of the Jungle, he was magnificent. Lord of lords, Master of Masters.

The way I felt I just could not describe, but it was just the way Miss Harford felt. [Miss Harford was his English teacher.] Well, no one in this world could describe him, only someone out of this world could describe him. He was magnificent.

Poetry is a form of celebration. That is a celebration well within the expressive, but moving in the direction of poetry.

Everyone wants children to learn language to get things done, you know—even politicians and economists. If we as English teachers do not foster the kind of language which represents a concern for the total world-picture, the total context into which every new experience that comes to a child—a man—has to be fitted, then I don't know who will.

I am going to finish very briefly by picking up one or two points. I've suggested that as there is a metabolism of the body, so there must be a metabolism of the mind in learning. A child must draw from the environment (which includes books and teachers) but draw selectively in accordance with the structure of his own personality. In other words, learning has an organic shape. Like a plant or a coral. As teachers we very often think of the shape of learning as though it were frost on the boughs we provide or barnacles on the bottom of our boats.

A child's learning has its own organic structure. Hence, the value of writing in the expressive, which is the language close to and most revealing of that individuality. Hence, also, the importance of individual work and work in small groups, and of the sea of talk on which all our school work should be floated.

Given these conditions I want to suggest that children learn to write above all by writing. This is an operational view of writing in school. The world about the child waits to be written about, so we haven't the need to go hunting around for exercises or dummy runs. We have to set up a working relationship between his language and his experience, and there is plenty there to write about. An operational view implies that we have our priorities. Of course we care about spelling and punctuation, but not more than we care about what the language is doing for the child.

Reading and writing and talking go hand in hand. And development comes from the gradual internalization of the written forms so our standards, the standards we apply to their writing, must be such as to take care that we don't cut the writer out of the writing; or to put that another way, cut the writer off from his resources at the spoken level. Development comes in two main directions—towards the transactional and towards the poetic. And in either case, if we are successful, children will continue to write *as themselves* as they reach those two poles. Their explorations of the outer world demand the transactional; their explorations of the inner world demand the poetic, and the roots of it all remain in the expressive.

We don't often write anything that is merely communication. There's nearly always an element of "finding out," of exploration. So it's a very common process for us to be able to read into our own writing something which we weren't fully aware of before we started to write. Writing can in fact be learning in the sense of discovery. But if we are to allow this to happen, we must give more credit than we often do to the process of shaping at the point of utterance and not inhibit the kind of discovery that can take place by insisting that children know exactly what they are going to say before they come to say it.

I want again to mention the importance of writing in the spectator role. Chaos is most painful in the area of values and beliefs. Therefore the harmonizing, the order-seeking effects of writing and reading on the poetic end of the spectrum are highly educational, important processes.

And then finally the teacher as listener. We must be careful not to sacrifice to our roles as error spotters and improvers and correctors that of the teacher as listener and reader. I could sum it all up very simply. What is important is that children in school should write about what matters to them to someone who matters to them.

References

1. Edward Sapir, *Culture, Language, and Personality,* University of California Press, 1949, p. 10.
2. Joseph Church, *Language and the Discovery of Reality,* Random House, Inc., 1961, p. 113.
3. Geoffrey Esland, "Teaching and Learning as the Organisation of Knowledge," in *Knowledge and Control,* ed. M. F. D. Young, Collier-Macmillan, 1971, p. 72.
4. For an explanation of this and other important ideas I have drawn upon here, see D. W. Harding, "The Role of the Onlooker," in *Scrutiny* VI, No. 3, 1937, pp. 247–58.
5. W. H. Auden, *Collected Shorter Poems, 1930–44,* Faber and Faber, 1950, p. 65.

11

Talking

What Do We Mean by 'Meaning'?

A study of talk has particular interest because it constantly forces us back to a consideration of what we mean by 'meaning'. We may approach the problem circumspectly by recognizing that meaning has to do with some one thing standing in for another. At a most obvious level, a child might ask, "What does 'rapacious' mean?" and be happy with the answer, " 'Rapacious' means 'greedy' "; where the text then says 'rapacious', the child says to himself 'greedy'—for as long as the equation remains in mind. Of course, we have to recognize that substitution covers far more cases than substitution in meaning: I may use a nail-file to unscrew my lighter, and if it does the job I have substituted a nail-file for a screwdriver. We shall need to say that meaning is associated with a substitute used for the purposes of *understanding* and not for any other kind of performance.

If 'rapacious' may stand in for 'greedy', it is equally true that 'greedy' is a word that substitutes in our understanding for some element that is common to a whole category of recollections about *events,* about pieces of human (or other) behaviour that we have observed; in like manner, 'apples' substitutes in our understanding for a whole category of remembered (or imagined) objects of many shapes, sizes and colours. Further, the process works in essentially similar ways when words are not involved at all; a wind-sock pointing north may have meaning for me; that is to say, in my understanding it may substitute for the unpleasant experience, recollected or imagined, of trying to land a plane across wind. Or, to take a different example, a fragment of Venetian glass on my carpet may substitute for the horrifying sight of a treasured vase reduced to fragments. This example is different, of course, because the wind-sock was constructed *in order to* communicate a meaning, whereas the piece of glass was not *intended* to mean anything.

It is very unlikely that the child who was happy to accept 'greedy'

Published in *English in Secondary Schools Today and Tomorrow,* Watson and Eagleson (eds.), 1977. Reprinted with permission of the English Teachers Association of New South Wales and the editors.

as a substitute for 'rapacious' would have been equally happy if in answer to his question, "What does 'greedy' mean?" he had been told that 'greedy' means 'rapacious'. No, it is the familiar word that we need to have standing in for the unfamiliar one. More generally, with the meaning of signs or objects or events in mind, we might expect *the near* to stand in for *the far*, the obvious for the not-so-easily-perceived, and the thing that matters less to us standing in for the thing that matters more. (It would be absurd to suppose that an aircraft in difficulties with a cross wind could ever be useful as a means of discovering which way a wind-sock was pointing!)

Meanings We See and Hear

Intended and unintended meanings assail us, without the help of words, at every step. We take and use them, often entirely unaware that we have done so. Psychologists call it 'processing the data of our senses'. Novelists construct their narratives largely by bringing these processes to a conscious level for their readers. Here is C. P. Snow describing how Lewis Eliot, a principal character in this novel, made his way to his home in London after a few days' absence:

> I felt an edge of anxiety, a tightness of the nerves, as I always did going home after an absence, even an absence as short as this. . . . As soon as I reached Cheyne Walk, my eyes were straining before I was in sight of the house. When I did see it, the picture might to a stranger have looked serene and enviable. The drawing-room lights were already on, first of the houses along that reach; the curtains had not been drawn. . . .
>
> As I walked up the path, I did not know how she would be.
>
> The hall was brilliantly lit, pernicketily tidy, the hall of a childless couple. No voice greeted me. I went quickly into the drawing-room. Here also the lights attacked me, as in the dazzle I saw my wife. Saw her quiet, composed, pre-occupied. For she was sitting at a small table, away from the fireplace, looking down at a chess-board. . . . So far as I could see, she was not playing a game, but working out a problem.
>
> 'Hello, you're in, are you?' she said. 'You'd better help me with this.'
>
> I was flooded with relief, relief so complete as to be happiness, just as I always was when I found her free from strain. Whatever I had expected, it was not this. I drew up a chair opposite her, and, as she bent her head and glanced at the board, I looked through the tall pieces at her forehead, the lines of which were tightened, not as so often with her own inner care, but with simple calculation.
>
> 'I don't see it,' she said, and smiled at me with great light-filled grey eyes.

(After a paragraph describing how her appearance has changed since first he knew her, he goes on:)

> Seeing her through the chess pieces, I noticed none of these changes, for I was only concerned with her state from day-to-day. I knew the slightest change in her expression, but I could not see what would be obvious to others. Trying to keep her steady, over the hours, the days, the years, I had lost my judgement about whether she was getting better or worse. All I knew was that to-night she was gay, anxiety-free, and that for this night, which was as far as I could see ahead, there was nothing to worry about.[1]

The meanings we see and hear, the information we glean through our senses, are of particular importance to anyone who wants to study talk, because talking is the mode of language which is most inextricably embedded in these other ways of deriving meaning. 'I don't see it', for example, spoken in the above situation would have been quite unintelligible to anyone who could not 'read' the situation itself—the chessboard, the woman sitting preoccupied, her look indicating that she was puzzling over something. Notice above all, however, that the reader learns a good deal about the 'set-up' (the characters and their relationship), not by having it *explained* to him, but rather by being shown objects and events that convey a meaning to him.

We might speculate that this way of handling meaning may have deep roots in us because there was a time, in our earliest years, when no other mode of handling it was available.

Two-way Traffic in Meanings

I realise that in speaking of 'handling meaning' I have blurred a distinction that has to be made clear. We must distinguish between arriving at a meaning for oneself and communicating meaning to somebody else. The distinction once made, however, we may find a complicated set of relationships between the two processes. The first thing to be clear about is the fact that we cannot take over somebody else's meanings ready-made. One of the popular errors in educational thinking is to polarise the difference between 'being told' something and finding it out for oneself. In fact, 'to be told', successfully, we have to go through a process very like finding out for ourselves. In order to accept the new information offered to us we have to *have somewhere to put it:* and having somewhere to put it means having a network of past knowledge and experience into which the new information will fit and make connexions in such a way as to make sense of it for us. Where we have difficulty in doing this, the normal procedure is to draw out connexions by *talking* about the new information; and talk with an expert who does not understand our ignorance may be less helpful than talking with others who share our experiences and share our ignorance. (There is no argument here for witholding information from people who can use it: in daily life we live in a regime of asking and telling, and so it should be in school.)

There may be rare occasions when we find ourselves employed in conveying a meaning from one person to another without any understanding of that meaning on our part. A child, for example, might be sent to the baker's to ask for 'a seedy bloomer' without knowing that that is a loaf, or what kind of a loaf it is. To take the opposite case, we may sometimes be aware of arriving at an understanding which we nevertheless cannot communicate to anybody else. How far, in fact, can we ever be sure that what we have, for somebody else's benefit, formulated (put into words or expressed in gesture or mime or by other means) is the precise equivalent of the meaning we have arrived at? Where an understanding is at all general, we should perhaps regard 'communicating', 'expressing' or 'formulating' it as somewhat akin to *applying it* to a particular situation: this may help us to account for a feeling we have that our most fruitful ideas are those which we re-formulate most often. Something that lies behind each re-formulating process is more powerful and more precious than any formula arrived at, and to cling to the formula rather than undergo again the labour of reformulating may be to rob the idea of its power.

Very often, of course, we arrive at a meaning (with or without the help of 'being told') and there we rest, without attempting then to communicate it to anyone else. More often, I believe, the two processes are interlocked: we come to an understanding in the course of communicating it. That is to say, we set out by offering an understanding and that understanding takes shape as we work on it to share it. And finally we may arrive co-operatively at a joint understanding as we talk or in some other way interact with someone else. One of the most important things to be said about talking in this chapter is that it is the normal way in which we endeavour to make sense of our own experiences, so that we store in memory not the raw data of events but the meaning we have come to attribute to them. Speech is of all language modes the best suited to this task because it has grown its roots, in infancy, deep into our first hand experiences. Or, as Sapir has put it, speech has 'an almost unique position of intimacy among all known symbolisms' because it is 'learned early and piecemeal, in constant association with the colour and requirements of actual contexts.'[2]

Our Earliest Meanings

Until recent years, linguists who studied the way infants learn to speak were primarily interested in analysing the grammatical structures of their early utterances and noting the successive stages by which they arrived at the grammar of the language as we know it.

Much that is of interest and importance was learned from this work, for it is the grammatical structure of languages that makes them the most highly specialised system of human communication. Sometimes these linguists justified this focus by claiming that the ability to use language is innate and being so could not be observed until it became operational and manifested itself in the act of speaking.

Recent years have seen a change of emphasis. It has been recognized that observers who arrive on the scene only when a child is able to talk have missed a great deal of interesting earlier behaviour— behaviour in which he exchanges understandings with his parents and begins to discover meaning in the world around him. Today, psycholinguists in many parts of the world are providing evidence of the way an infant's earliest uses of speech evolve from, and depend upon, ways of handling meaning that do not employ language.

Thus, Bruner's observations of the behaviour of young babies with their mothers form part of a fascinating new chapter in language study. He suggests that shared looking and listening and shared activity, mother and baby, are key processes in the infant's first attempts to make sense of the 'meaningless flux' that engulfs him. Between mother and child patterns of action are set up: to the child, these emerge, as it were, from the flux and become recognizable as they are repeated. As the mother follows the child's direction of gaze, and the infant's comes to follow the mother's, objects are picked out for attention and routines of action embodying the objects become established. Expressive gestures and sounds and (from the mother) speech accompany the actions and accentuate their patterns. Some of the patterns are, as Bruner says, 'in earnest'—that is to say they are concerned with 'mothering', with feeding habits, for example—but most of them are play. It is a characteristic role of the mother in these joint sequences to mark the completion, the climax—a hug at the end of peek-a-boo, perhaps, or a 'Good boy!' when the child successfully negotiates a mouthful of food.

The role of speech or speech-like noises in these sequences is strictly supplementary to the meaning already attached to the joint activity. Bruner suggests that conventional speech sounds, as spoken by the mother, are arrived at by the baby in gradual steps. He describes, for example, a mother and child who have established a routine of giving and receiving. When she gives the object—ball or rattle or whatever—to the child, the mother says, 'There you are', and she says 'Thank you' when the child gives it to her. After a while, the baby begins to add his noises to the exchange, but they are his own sounds and not recognizable words. Then at 9 months and 2 weeks, Bruner records, the baby says 'Kew' when the mother takes the object he has offered; a month later, he says 'Kew' whenever she offers him something; and two months after that he says 'Look' when handing to her and 'Kew' when receiving from her.[3] Bruner points out that this piece of learning prefigures a later process in which an infant learns to use 'I' and 'you' appropriately: I once heard a 22 month-old girl ask for some cake at the table by saying, 'You have some of dat over dere'—a stage that will be familiar to many parents.

As an infant grows older, the patterns of his playful activity will rely less upon the initiative of the mother. He will devise his own routines, and he may co-operate with other people he meets, even strangers. Here is an example from my own experience when I visited some friends last Christmas. Rowan, aged 22 months, was a grandchild of the house, staying there over Christmas with her parents. She was allowed to wait up to see the guests arrive, and though she didn't say a great deal she moved about without any shyness, quite capable of occupying herself. At one point she began to collect up any drink-mats that happened at that moment to have no drinks standing on them; she had four when she approached me. I held out my hand in invitation and she quite happily gave me all four. I handed them back one at a time and said 'There you are' or something of the sort with each. She gave them back to me in the same way, one at a time, without a word, and I said 'Thank you'. This time, however, I had no sooner received the last of them than she reached firmly out and took all four at once— and proceeded to hand them back to me one at a time. After several performances of this pattern, she began to initiate each repetition with the word 'Now!', spoken with emphasis in a tone that reminded me of a conjuror signalling the beginning of his next trick. This was repeated many times, with minor variations—I don't know how long she would have kept it up if her bedtime had not intervened: she readily ex- changed this ploy for the more familiar one of piggy-backing off on her father's shoulders. Patterns, ploys, routines—it is certainly in these ways that behaviour escapes from randomness and unpredictability and takes on what we can only call 'meaning'. Furthermore, the one word Rowan used brought to a focus in an entirely appropriate way the nature of this particular routine: it was a bonus, heightening the mean- ing that was already present in the behaviour itself.

Bruner makes the important point that the routines devised by mother and child introduce and ring the changes upon basic elements of person-to-person and person-to-object interactions. Thus, there is an *action,* a doer or *agent,* sometimes the *object* of an action, the *recip- ient,* an *instrument* with which the action is performed; there is *loca- tion, change of location* and *possession*—a list that strongly reminds us of the lists compiled by linguists when they catalogue the grammatical *cases* that may be found in a language.[4] Gordon Wells in Bristol uses similar categories and his systematic study of the speech (and speech contexts) of one-and-a-half and three-year-olds is based on a similar hypothesis.[5] And Roger Brown, in his book *A First Language: The Early Stages* surveys a number of language acquisition studies center-

ing on Harvard which in general support this view.[6] What is evident
from these and other studies is that precursors of many of the features
of adult grammar are to be found in children's earliest utterances and
in their pre-speech behaviour. It is not enough to explain that in the
course of his evolution man has come to perceive and act in ways
derived from the structure of the language he uses: we have also to put
forward the alternative hypothesis that the structure of language has
developed to reflect the nature of man's cognitive processes, the ways
in which he attends to and interprets experience. Or, in Bruner's
words, 'language is a specialized and conventionalized extension of
human co-operative action.'[7] The three researchers we have referred
to, among others, relate sensori-motor behaviour, as Piaget has described it, to the meanings that pre-verbal or early verbal behaviour
expresses or encodes. It is becoming evident that meanings established before language is achieved provide an entry for the child into
verbal meanings, and thereby into language structure. Language
moves within his grasp when he can begin to match meanings of words
and verbal utterances with what he has already learnt about the world.

Home as a Language-workshop

Much has been said about the importance of the language a child
experiences at home in infancy as a basis for his later social and mental
development. From the studies we have just described we can justifi-
ably claim that the good effect begins long before the child begins to
use language—that the co-operative activities, in play or 'in earnest',
provide an essential basis for all that follows. Other studies suggest
that the give-and-take, the rough-and-tumble of language as it is un-
selfconsciously used for work and play in the home constitutes a better
learning situation than would anything more deliberate. The home, in
other words, provides a language workshop, an environment of
language-in-use—often interrupted, often fragmentary—and it now
seems likely that such experiences are more productive than any focus
upon language, any attempt to give language instruction in the home
would be.[8]

Indicators of progress in the home are multiple: the average
length of utterance becomes consistently longer, the structures more
complex and more varied; more of the meanings in co-operative activity become verbalised; as we have noted, autonomous activity, the
development of the child's own ploys, increases with maturity, and in
course of time he begins to assist his solitary activity by adding a verbal
commentary, talking to himself about what he is doing; and, to conclude with a non-linguistic development, whereas a child derives
meaning in the early stages by establishing pattern (cooperatively) in
his own activities, he becomes more and more capable of perceiving
patterns in other people's behaviour, taking meaning from sequences

that he has not himself actively devised. The importance of the destination here, his ability as a mature adult to process the data of his senses, to interpret what he sees and hears, is something we have stressed in an earlier section.

The earliest form of speech to be established is conversational exchange: the child joins in the family conversation that has enveloped him from his earliest days. Though some of this conversation will consist of an expression of wants and needs, most of it will be by way of *comment:* in Susanne Langer's words, 'Young children learn to speak . . . by constantly using words to bring things *into their minds*, not *into their hands.'*[9] It is a characteristic achievement of the human race that we store representations of the world as we encounter it and respond to immediate experience in the light of past experience, that is, in the light of our stored representation, our 'world picture'. The various ways of handling meaning that we have already considered are, in fact, modes of representation, and among those modes language comes to play a key role as an organising instrument. As we talk about experiences, we further shape and interpret them (and this, again, is normally a co-operative undertaking) and it is in this form that we store them. What is, looking backward, a storehouse of an individual's experience is, looking forward, a body of expectations as to what may yet happen to him. From that body of expectations he draws, in accordance with the immediate environment to which he is attending, knowledge of the world which will enable him to make sense of the present and, when necessary, keep a prudent eye on the future.

Young children, however fluently they may talk, are in one sense poor conversationalists, since they are comparatively unable to put themselves into somebody else's shoes and see the world from their point of view. In course of time and experience, they become better able to take account of a listener's needs and expectations at the same time as they are acquiring a greater ability to use the words we use and to mean by them what we mean, and gaining control of a greater variety of language structures.

Most children, after conversing for something under a year, discover another function for language, one I have briefly referred to above. They talk to themselves about what they are doing. Vygotsky and Luria,[10] Russian psychologists, have claimed that this running commentary has a very important purpose: it is in fact the young child's way of thinking out answers to the problems that face him in solitary activity. When first produced, the running commentary takes the forms and intonation patterns of the child's conversational speech, but as time goes on the forms adapt to this different function. The commentary ('speech for oneself', Vygotsky called it) becomes abbreviated or fragmentary and may show an idiosyncratic use of words, the use of 'private meanings'. Its evolution, that is to say, is essentially in the opposite direction to that of conversational speech. Since the commentary is not spoken to be understood by another person but to serve the speaker's own purposes, this relaxing of the rules and conventions of language may in fact be an advantage. It was Vygotsky's contention that this function became progressively 'internalised', and when, by the age of six or seven the running commentary no longer occurs, it is because outward speech has turned into 'inner speech' or verbal thought. On this hypothesis, speech in infancy is a foundation upon which later thinking is built.

We have looked briefly at the importance of play in the co-operative activities of mothers and babies, and we must note now some of the ways in which young children will play with language. It is in the nature of play as an activity that it tends to focus attention upon the activity itself rather than upon anything to be gained by doing it. For example, most children reach the final stage of being able to walk under stimulus of a desire to get from where they are to somewhere else: walking is the means, the instrument. But once they have mastered the art of walking they begin to 'play' with that activity: focusing upon the activity, they elaborate the movements in a variety of ways: that is to say, they *dance*—a pleasurable occupation not concerned with getting from here to there. Commenting upon mothers' and babies' co-operative activities, Bruner notes that 'the rituals of play become the objects of attention, rather than being instrumental to something else' and underlines the value of this: 'Play has the effect of drawing the child's attention to communication itself, and to the structure of the acts in which communication is taking place.'[11] Play of this kind with language may occur spontaneously as part of a conversation or breaking into a running commentary, or in isolation. The story is told of a psychologist's son who danced up to his father (who was with a group of colleagues) to the chant of 'Maximum capacity! Maximum Capacity!' Some children go in for a more extended and deliberate form of playful activity which bears the nature of 'a performance'. It is consistent and characteristic enough to be reckoned a third kind of talk in the home, alongside conversation and the running commentary. The speech is often delivered in a kind of rhythmic sing-song, and may be accompanied by a dance-like walking up and down. I call it 'the spiel'. Here is a brief extract from the spiel of a three-year-old. She has just finished her dinner, as her interpolation indicates: it shows also that she recognizes what she is doing as an 'it', a performance:

> There was a little girl called May
> and she had some dollies—
> and the weeds were growing in the ground—
> and they made a little nest out of sticks

for another little birdie up in the trees
and they climbed up the tree—
and the weeds were growing in the ground
(*I can do it much better if there's some food in my tum!*). . . .

Later examples of such performances are likely to be more straight-forwardly narrative in form. I have a tape of a five-year-old boy who spins a long breathless yarn about motor-bicycles and racing cars, talking at great speed to the very last words, 'And that is the end of my story what I told.'

Finally I must refer to a fourth kind of talk, the dramatic talk of make-believe play. In its earliest stages it is likely to be a monologue, played out in a variety of voices, and with the help of one or more dolls, teddy-bears, toy animals or whatever. When the child is at an age to co-operate with other children, the activity becomes a joint one, and the dolls and teddy-bears are likely to fade out of the picture. In talk of this kind the context, the situation is *invoked:* it is therefore a more accessible form of speech than story-telling, where the situation has to be put into words.

Each of these forms of talk embodies its own kind of learning, capable of development into distinctive adult activities; in each, in various ways and to varying degrees, verbalised meanings are supported by intended and unintended meanings derived through the senses from the situation shared by speaker and listeners. The first two forms are, on balance, concerned with the organisation of the *objective* aspects of our experience, the 'thingness of things'; the third and fourth—those related to play—are concerned with the organisation of the *subjective* aspects of our experience, the 'me-ness of things'. Both aspects have their sophisticated linguistic forms of expression in adult society; it is important that we concern ourselves with both in school.

The use of language in the pre-school years yields an enormous dividend to the child, a dividend in terms of the evolution from more or less helpless infancy to the self-possessed status of a five-year-old. Here in the home, then, there is a direct means-end tie-up between speech and what it achieves for the speaker. Can we preserve that direct relationship throughout the years of schooling?

References

1. C. P. Snow, *Homecomings*, Macmillan, 1956, pp 3–5.
2. Edward Sapir, *Culture, Language and Personality*, University of California Press, 1961, p. 10.
3. Jerome Bruner, "The Ontogenesis of Speech Acts" in *Journal of Child Language*, Vol. 2, No. 1, 1975, pp 20–21.

4. Charles J. Fillmore, "The Case for Case" in Emmon Bach and Robert T. Harms, eds., *Universals in Linguistic Theory*, Holt, Rinehart and Winston, 1968, pp 1–87.
5. Gordon Wells, Project Director, Language Development in Pre-School Children. Second Annual Report, University of Bristol School of Education, 1974.
6. Roger Brown, *A First Language: The Early Stages*, Allen and Unwin, 1973, pp 168–201.
7. Jerome Bruner, *Op. Cit.*, p. 3.
8. Courtney B. Cazden, *Child Language and Education*, Holt, Rinehart and Winston, 1972, p. 128. Cazden quotes from an earlier work (Brown, Cazden and Bellugi, "The child's grammar from I to III" in J. P. Hill, ed., *1967 Minnesota symposium on child psychology*, University of Minnesota Press, 1969): "We suspect that the changes sentences undergo as they shuttle between persons in conversation are . . . the data that most clearly expose the underlying structure of language."
9. Susanne K. Langer, *Philosophy in a New Key*, 3rd edition, Harvard University Press, 1960, p. 121.
10. L. S. Vygotsky, *Thought and Language*, trans. Eugenia Haufmann and Gertrude Vaker, M.I.T. Press, 1962. A. R. Luria and F. I. Yudovich, *Speech and the Development of Mental Processes in the Child*, Penguin Books, 1971.
11. Jerome Bruner, *Op. Cit.*, p. 14.

12

Notes on a Working Hypothesis about Writing

The speech of children in their infancy has a 'here-and-now' quality about it. They make comments, ask questions and make demands relating to the events going on around them and the people and objects involved in those events. Thereafter, a major dimension of their linguistic growth lies in their increasing ability to use language at further and further remove from the immediate context, the 'here and now' in which they speak. This does not mean, of course, that they abandon one form of language in favour of another as they might abandon one pair of shoes when they needed a bigger one. As adults we continue to rely on 'context-bound' speech as the currency of our everyday exchanges with the people we meet. "Development" lies in a bifurcation, an ability to do two things with language where previously we could do one.

Adding mastery of the written language to mastery of the spoken reflects one aspect of this development from context-bound to context-free utterance. A written communication—transmitted here and now for reception elsewhere, later—must of necessity be put into terms that can survive that transplantation. But again, this does not mean that all speech is context-bound and all writing context-free; simply that there will be an overall tendency in that direction.

Being context-bound (relying heavily for its interpretation upon the situation in which it is uttered) is one of the characteristics of 'expressive language' as a number of linguists have defined it. But it is only one part of that definition. In our Schools Council Writing Research Project we distinguished three major functions for writing and labelled them 'Transactional', 'Expressive' and 'Poetic'. We described the expressive as utterance that relies on an interest in the speaker (or writer) as well as in what he has to say about the world. We called it an utterance that 'is not projected very far from the speaker'—a communi-

Published in "The National Writing Project Network Newsletter," 1 (3), May, 1979.

cation between intimates rather than a public speech or a letter to a stranger. As such, it will tend to carry information about the speaker as well as conveying his message about the world; revealing, for example, the speaker's *attitude* towards his message, towards his listener and towards his present state of mind, himself. Expressive forms of speech capitalize on the fact that both speaker and listener are *present:* expressive writing simulates that co-presence, the writer invoking the presence of the reader as he writes, the reader invoking the presence of the writer as he reads.

Our experience of chatting with people we know well in a relaxed and loosely structured way is thus a major resource we draw upon when we write expressively. And whether we write or speak, expressive language is associated with a relationship of mutual confidence, trust, and is therefore a form of discourse that encourages us to *take risks*, to try out ideas we are not sure of, in a way we would not dare to do in, say making a public speech. In other words, expressive language (as a kind of bonus) is a form that favours exploration, discovery, learning.

Transactional language is the medium of a verbal transaction, a means of getting something done through language—whether it be asking or giving information, instructing or persuading. Poetic language, in its fully developed form, is the language of literature—stories, poems, plays. We saw it as language not for *doing* something but for *making* something, a verbal object; and it seemed to us that the child who writes a fictional or autobiographical narrative, giving shape to real or imagined experiences, should be seen as performing at his untutored level essentially the same task as the novelist or poet achieves at a higher level, in a more finely organised way.

It was the main purpose of our publication, *The Development of Writing Abilities, 11–18*, to describe those categories (among others). But in addition to describing them we set up a developmental hypothesis, the hypothesis that expressive writing should be regarded as a matrix from which the other two categories would develop. That is to say, expressive writing might be seen as a beginner's all-purpose instrument; and 'learning to write' would involve the progressive evolution both of the other two forms, transactional and poetic, and of the mature forms of expressive writing that we continue to use in personal letters and the like. It should be noted that this hypothesis is not a part of the conceptual framework we evolved, the description of the function categories, but a broad hypothesis about the kinds of distribution of function categories that might occur. We speculated that distribution patterns might reveal 'routes of development' in writing ability and that one route was likely to be a more successful one than others. The reasoning behind this speculation is simple enough, though a full spelling out of the stages begins to look complicated:

1. A great many children who cannot yet write are able to converse fluently in favourable conditions.
2. Those conditions include a relaxed situation, and someone they know and trust who will be receptive to what they say.
3. The speech in which they will be fluent in such situations will be expressive speech as we have defined it.
4. Expressive writing (as we have defined it) is the form of writing that most nearly resembles expressive speech.
5. At the stage when they first try their hands at writing, most children have rich language resources, in terms of syntax and vocabulary, but they are with few exceptions spoken language resources. If they are to become writers, they have to adapt these resources to the new demands of writing: the more the written forms resemble spoken forms at their command, the easier the transition is likely to be.
6. 'Dissociation' in the special sense of 'successive differentiation' is familiar enough as a mode of learning. Young writers who begin by employing an all-purpose expressive writing might by a process of dissociation arrive at differentiated forms of discourse as they meet and solve the range of problems presented by different kinds of writing tasks. (The slogan, 'Learn to write by writing' must imply some such procedure.)
7. Stress must here be laid upon what the writer is reading, or having read to him; in other words on written 'models'. Progress is likely to depend upon the degree to which he is internalising the forms of a variety of written discourse, and his ability, in the process of writing, to 'shuttle' between these new resources and his consolidated spoken resources.

That brings us to first base, but an analysis in terms of *learning* in general (not learning to write) is an essential part of our hypothesis. Thus:

8. A learner meeting a new concept needs to see its relevance to what he already knows (what he knows from experience as well as what he has learnt from formulations previously met). Since learners vary as to their prior experience and knowledge, they cannot be appropriately *helped* (by teacher or other learners) to make these links unless they have some opportunity to verbalise their experience etc.
9. For these reasons, talk has a heuristic role to play, and expressive talk (being relaxed talk, relatively free from fear of making errors) is likely to be more strongly heuristic than, for example, the more formal exchange of teacher question and student answer with a whole class as audience. But (a) writing, as premeditated utterance, may have the effect of sharpening the process of seeking

relevance, as well as harvesting for the writer connections first explored in speech, his own and other people's. And (b) writing puts the onus for effort on each member of the class. Hence the hypothesis that expressive writing has an important role to play in the initial stage of grappling with new concepts.

10. If the dissociation process (as we described it above) works according to hypothesis, the learner will be acquiring mastery of informative writing at the same time as he succeeds in more effectively organising his understanding of the concepts he is writing about. This dual achievement should enable him increasingly to go through the exploratory stages of grappling with new ideas *without* committing those stages to writing. And at the same time the teacher may recognize that there is less and less need for him to assist in those exploratory stages or monitor them, hence less and less call for expressive writing. This would be reflected in a distribution of function categories that showed (or intended to show, for there would be difficulties of interpretation) a transference of activity in writing from expressive forms to informative ones as learners become more mature.

That might be said to bring us to second base, though it is a minimal statement and many interesting ramifications could be added. To take one example:

11. Our characterisation of learning in (8) above is a pretty traditional and conservative one—that of the learner who is introduced to new concepts. We have talked to science teachers who believe that one of their first tasks is to assist learners to distil facts from their own first-hand experience—as a necessary foundation for a learning career in which they must take many facts on trust from the reported experiences of other people. They therefore see a special virtue in expressive writing in that it will tend to record in one and the same account both the experiences and the facts being drawn from them. By this means the teacher is allowed to perceive and assist the *act of learning,* that of sorting experience from fact in order to select and organise the facts. It is not only at the earliest stages that 'learning science' may involve an open-minded contemplation of some 'bit of the world' (a plant, a soil sample, a crystal or whatever) so that the learner may decide for himself what facts need to be formulated in order to solve a specific problem; and return for more focussed looking at the object in the light of the facts so formulated. Expressive talk and writing are suitable modes for verbalising the initial process, the open-ended contemplation, and informative writing a suitable mode for formulating the appropriate facts.[1] It will be obvious, I

think, that the teacher's skill in selecting a sequence of problems to be solved will be directed to ensuring that the particular facts required for the solution of each build up to a coherent study of a scientific principle or concept, and beyond that to a coherent study of a particular branch of science. There is more to be said about science teaching in relation to the broad hypothesis we are considering, but it must await its turn.

In (6) to (11) above we have looked at the learning we associate with the expressive/transactional spectrum of the function categories. The development from expressive to poetic is associated, in our view, with a learning process, but one of a different kind (perhaps one that is not often thought of as 'learning'). This is our next concern:

12. Most children who have had the opportunity will like to listen to stories, read or told, and will frequently tell stories of their own making. There is in fact some evidence that written stories constitute the only justification some children can accept for the existence of a written form of language.

13. Most children who have the encouragement of an interested listener will narrate some of their own experiences.

14. Narrative versions of our own experience are *compositions* and as such subject to 'embellishment'; fictional stories often display, however indirectly, aspects of the writer's own experience. Thus 'autobiographical/fictional narrative' might be seen as a continuum.

15. When we talk about our own experiences, I believe we usually do so in a way that suggests we want our listener to share the feelings we ourselves have about those experiences—to sympathise with us when we feel we were hardly done by, to admire when we are proud of our achievements, etc. This is consistent with the explanation D. W. Harding has given of gossip about events and of fictional narratives, both of which he includes under the term 'imaginary spectatorship'.[2] He suggests that they constitute 'detached evaluative responses' to experience or to the possibilities of experience; and he associates our engagement in such activity with the maintenance of our value systems. In offering evaluations we are looking for corroboration, since to have our value systems 'sanctioned' by fellow members of our society constitutes a 'basic social satisfaction'.

16. These purposes seem to us to differ in important ways from the purposes of informing, persuading, theorising, etc. that are the typical activities of transactional discourse. We see them as requiring a different kind of discourse, one organised on quite different principles. The existence at the most developed end of this

spectrum of a work of literature supplies a clue as to the nature of this alternative organisation; cutting many corners, we have described it as the 'construction of a verbal object'. The change from expressive narrative (gossip about events) to poetic narratives (verbal objects) is therefore seen as one of increasing organisation-for-unity. 'Organisation' may include the ordered disposition of sounds, words, word-meanings, sentences, events, feelings, thoughts, images.

17. The move from speech to writing in this spectrum (paralleling that described in (9) above) will allow the shaping towards unity to be carried out in a premeditated way that is impossible in ordinary speech situations. (It is interesting to notice that speech may achieve poetic form when it occurs in a situation that is highly charged emotionally.)

18. While the fully developed written outcomes of work in history, geography, social studies, science will always be transactional forms of discourse, there are initial stages when writing in the expressive/poetic spectrum may be valuable from time to time. 'Imagine you are a boy or girl in Roman Britain and describe your experiences' has been a familiar assignment in history lessons, and if some geographical region or some social milieu be substituted for 'Roman Britain', a similar task will have appeared in a good many geography and social studies lessons. The value of such tasks, as we interpret the matter, lies in encouraging students to empathize with the human elements in the topic under study, and while inaccurate or inadequate knowledge of the facts may disable the effort, the primary effort does not lie in getting the facts right but in what can be constructed within the factual framework. It is possible that even in science lessons this move towards the poetic could fulfil a purpose: commenting on the study of biology, Michael Polanyi has said, "our understanding of living beings involves at all levels a measure of indwelling; our interest in life is always convivial."[3]

19. A further item needs to be added to our analysis, and it brings us to fourth base—and home. It has been pointed out that the ease with which in expressive language we move from the transactional side of the borderline to the poetic, and back again, gives to that form of discourse a flexibility which serves its particular purposes of exploring and developing interpersonal relationships.[4] Expressive writing for such purposes is not a form of discourse transitional to any other form; its development throughout the years of schooling will be to mature forms of expressive writing.

Since the publication of our report, a number of surveys have been carried out in terms of our function categories, some in England, some in Australia, some in Canada and some in U.S.A. What they indicate is that expressive writing is very little encouraged in most schools, far too little for there to be any evidence regarding our hypothesis that expressive writing is the best starting point for writing in any of the function categories. We hold to our conviction that the quality of learning could be improved if fuller use were made of the heuristic potential of expressive writing. The alternative hypothesis to which teachers must be working might be phrased as follows: "If you limp around long enough in somebody else's language you may eventually learn to walk in it."

References

1. I owe acknowledgements here to an unpublished paper (1972) by Peter Medway of the Schools Council Development Project on Writing across the Curriculum.
2. D. W. Harding, "The Role of the Onlooker", reprinted in *Language in Education,* Open University Source Book, Routledge and Kegan Paul, 1972.
3. Michael Polanyi, *Knowing and Being,* Routledge and Kegan Paul, 1969.
4. John Dixon, *Growth Through English,* Third Edition, Oxford University Press, 1975.

13

A Reader's Expectations

When I think of the variety of things we do in the course of a day
and the vastly greater variety of things that are going on all about us I
find myself bedazzled. Some of the things we do we choose to do, in
others we seem to have no choice: and to say that is, I suppose, to
comment on two ways in which the things we do are related to the
things that go on around us. We are accustomed to thinking of an act, or
an event, as taking place in a context, the context being a kind of halo
that surrounds the event. But then we have to see that life is like a pit
full of snakes—anything may be seen as part of the context to something else, and none of it stays still for a moment. Yet in the multiple
interactions that make up this flux we constantly manage somehow (if I
may switch my metaphor) to bring our argosies home to port; individually, yes, but more importantly, as a partnership or a team or a family.
How does it work?

Perhaps the word 'enterprise' is a useful one to bring in—a course
of action directed towards some desirable end. During a single day we
might contribute to or carry to completion a number of enterprises,
some long term, some short term. If I say we *ride* an enterprise as
though it were some bucking bronco, that's one way of putting
it—but makes it sound too violent, as though everything were always
only just under control. If I say we constantly, every waking moment,
process the data of our senses and pursue some appropriate enterprise
in the light of our findings—that sounds far too deliberate and meth-
odical, perhaps even mechanistic.

The fact that an enterprise on my part is directed towards some
end that seems desirable to me is an important part of the idea: the
motive for our data-processing is normally, directly or indirectly, *a
glimpse of some possibility ahead.* We are, as it were, drawn on by the
future: only in apathy or despair are we driven on by the past. Though
processing the data of experience is a skill or an art we must each of us
learn, I believe a poor performance at it is more often due to a lack of
incentive than to a lack of skill. Putting it crudely, we 'make some-

Published in "The English Magazine," No. 1, 1979.

thing of experience' above all in order to 'make something out of it'—
either for ourselves or for someone we regard for the moment as 'one of
us'.

Reading the Game

Take as an example this moment in a football match when the
centre-half, say of the home team, passes the ball out to the left wing.
Every player on the field is interpreting that action as an item in a
series of events in the course of being performed. It *means* something
to him (and enables him to respond) insofar as he is able to see it as part
of a series and not an isolated act. To do this he 'reads' the immediate
context, the situation—the position of all the relevant players on either
side, their direction of movement, anything he knows of their capabil-
ities and weaknesses and temperaments. The sequence of moves on
the field that led up to this particular action is another aspect of context. More broadly still, the context includes such things as any deliberate strategies discussed and practised in training; strategies of the
opposing side as they are known from experience or reputation; what
the score stands at, and, behind that, the status and reputation of each
team; what the player knows about and expects of *himself*. Each
player must read the signs, process the data, in order to know what to
expect and so be in a position to take action himself. And 'knowing
what to expect' is rarely as simple as that may sound: it ordinarily
involves entertaining many possibilities and assessing their comparative likelihood.

The example puts a premium on processing the data of our
senses—what we directly perceive around us—and it is right that the
emphasis should lie there. However, had we chosen to look in, not on
the match itself, but on a training session on the field, we should
probably have found that all that took place was supported by a running commentary of *speech*. The data a player had then to process
would have included the things he was *told* as well as the things he
saw. And the two, the speech and the action, would have been locked
into one. The speech alone—heard later on a tape-recorder,
perhaps—would have been virtually meaningless; and likewise the
value to the players of what they did and were done to (the point in fact
of the whole activity) would have been lost if there had been no speaking. There would, of course, be training sessions of another kind (as for
example briefing before the match) when all the data being offered and
processed took the form of speech.

De-briefing

Thus, to go back to the match, when the players interpreted a
move in the game by placing it in its full context, a considerable part of
that context consisted in the outcomes of processing other people's

talk—information, in other words, which they had acquired by being told. Further, it is important to note here in passing a point we shall return to—and that is the notion that a man's own speaking is one of the principal ways in which he processes data of all kinds. What in the jargon is called a 'de-briefing session'—the post mortem after a match—serves as a good example of how we may talk our way to a better understanding of past experiences.

We referred, in speaking of the training session, to the way speech may be interlocked with action. A great deal of our speech is of this kind: linguists seem to prefer furniture-removers to footballers as illustration of it ('Up a bit, Alf! Steady! To your left. Mind the lamp. O.K., towards me.'). Infants who have been busy processors of the data of their senses for a couple of years or so readily handle this second source of information once they have mastered the code; from then on it is one of the directions of their development that they learn to interpret, and to originate, speech at greater and greater remove from action. Our example has crudely illustrated what we may now call three phases in the processing of data. During the football match the data offered took the form of action without speech; during the training session on the field it was action-cum-speech; and at the briefing session it was speech divorced from action.

A last word to finish off the football match: if the centre-half aimed accurately and if the outside-left formed appropriate expectations and made an appropriate response, then we may suppose that a winning goal was scored. And if the referee then blew for the finish, one more argosy was brought home to port. And the whole incident has brought us to a proper beginning: we are committed to a consideration of *reading*. And whoever heard of a practising footballer who spent no time reading about the game, whether it was the book of rules or the match reports?

Which is to indicate that our fourth stage of data processing is the reading of the written language. It follows logically from stage three (interpreting speech divorced from action), because the written language by its nature takes the disjunction of language from action a step further. A spoken utterance belongs to a moment and goes by with events. (If we record it and replay the recording we resurrect a moment of the past.) A written utterance has no such simple relation to time. Perhaps the only constant in a multiplicity of time relations is that a piece of writing is normally 'transmitted' at one time for 'reception' at a later one. (And there are exceptions to that generalisation, as when we use writing to 'talk to' a deaf person.)

The break with the stream of time has important consequences for the data processing task. Interpreting data, we have suggested, involves seeing an item not in isolation but in context. A speaker and a listener normally share the immediate context—the situation in which the words are uttered—as well as a great deal more in the way of shared knowledge and shared experience. If the talk is by long-distance telephone, the domestic, national and world situations of speaker and listener (insofar as they are relevant and known to both) represent a shared context that is the background to all that is said. But if I post a letter to you this evening and then die in the night, any assumptions you might make about a shared context will be sharply dislocated.

Generating Expectations

As a simple summary of what we have said so far, we might plot a child's progress diagrammatically in this way:

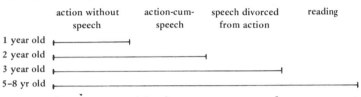

I remember being told of an experiment that was carried out years ago, I believe in Daniel Jones's phonetics laboratory at University College, London. A recording of a conversation between two people was played to a group of students, but it was so distorted a recording that they could not understand a word of what was said. They were then told that the conversation had taken place in a tailor's shop between a customer and a fitter. Armed with this knowledge, this very general expectation, they were able, on a second hearing, to make out quite a lot of the conversation. Very broad or general aspects of the context in which an utterance is made may be a powerful influence on our ability to interpret it; and this for the simple reason that they rule out so much. They limit the range of possibilities, narrow the area of experience we have to scan in order to pick up the sense of what is said. The process of listening or reading, then, is best understood as one of generating expectations as to what a speaker or writer *might* mean, and selecting from those expectations to match what we hear or what we see on the page.

There was a mode of communication used in the Second World War by which a base station could keep in touch with isolated outposts able to carry only light signalling equipment. The base station transmitted a powerful 'carrier wave' and the outpost sent out a weak signal which was enough to 'modulate' the carrier wave; the base station received back its own carrier wave thus modulated, and read the message. This is the model we want for reading: no transmission, no message; no expectations, no meaning.

However, the reading is part of a larger picture, as we have already suggested. We constantly generate expectations relating to our many enterprises; one of these enterprises may take us to a book to find out something we need to know. Or, at other times, the book may be a chance encounter or somebody else's prescription. In any case, what we find on the page will meet, take up and modify some of our expectations. Our other intentions, meanwhile, will wait in the wings.

Let us say we take up a book because it has been recommended to us, or because the author is familiar, or because the title suggests that it will tell us what we need to know; and the appearance of the book itself indicates that it is not too long, the type is not too small, the words are not too difficult for us. All these are a part of the expectations active in us as we approach the reading: and what we read will proceed to change the pattern of our expectations. It is likely that the first few sentences we read will make the sharpest modifications of all. The book may quickly prove, for example, not to be the kind we took it for. Where, on the contrary, we find it immediately rewarding and worth going on with, this is likely to be because the words have thrown *new light* upon notions that formed part of the expectations we brought to the reading. The focus of our attention is not upon the words as we read them, but upon a pattern of meaning. We do not, as we read, add word meaning to word meaning—like watching coaches come out of a tunnel; rather it is like watching a photographic negative in a developing-dish, a shadowy outline that becomes etched in with more of the detail as we proceed. The finished picture represents a transformation, brought about by the text-as-we-have-interpreted-it—a transformation of our initial expectations.

It is this emergent pattern, this set of expectations undergoing modification, that enables us to construe word meanings right as we read. If we come to an unfamiliar word we 'jump the gap' by supplying a meaning from our expectations, and read on. If the meaning we supplied for a key word was an altogether mistaken one, there will develop an increasing mis-match between what we expect and what we find. The words on the page will no longer be etching in the details of an emerging pattern, but confusion or puzzlement will spread like a stain on the negative. What we normally do then is to go back in the text to a point where all was going well, and try again. When we arrive at and identify the point of our misconstruing, we may simply make another guess and try that one out, or we may seek help—from an expert, say, or from a dictionary.

This view of the process may help to explain why we sometimes find it worthwhile to read a book for a second time. Most of us know books (usually on subjects we are in the process of trying to master) which have yielded vastly more on a second reading. What we have gleaned from the first reading, especially in highly general ways, has provided us with a more appropriate set of expectations, a better framework for the detail.

I. A. Richards put us into this way of thinking years ago. In a little book called *How to Read a Page*[1] he examines the difficulties an adult might encounter in trying to read a complicated text, and the final advice he comes up with is, 'Read it as though it made sense'. I remember thinking when I first read this that it was little comfort for a teacher struggling to help a child over his initial reading difficulties. But much more recently I have come across an account by a research worker of the way a five-year-old had taught himself to read. Jane Torrey visited John, child of a black working-class family, in his home and watched him while he read to her:

> "John's phonic knowledge and his word attack skills were strictly subordinate to the task of reading what is said. I interpreted his intonation patterns in reading to signify that he understood that strings of printed symbols represented language as it is spoken, not a series of sounds or words. When he did not understand what he was reading, he slurred over it, skipped words, converted it into something that was normal for him to say or just rejected the task of reading it. He never did anything remotely like sounding letter by letter a sequence that wasn't a word he knew or calling word by word a sentence whose meaning escaped him. *He read as though he always expected it to say something understandable.*"[2] (My italics)

As I now see it, the point Richards was making, and the strategy John was operating, are support for the idea that in reading we do not focus upon the words beneath our noses: we look *through* the words in order to focus upon the meaning that emerges from them. And there are encouraging signs that teachers of reading today are more and more basing their methods on the strategies of successful readers rather than on the pitfalls encountered by the poor reader.

In another of his books (*The Philosophy of Rhetoric*[3]), Richards makes an interesting point about the nature of word meanings. He suggests that the meaning of a word in a sustained utterance is of a different order from the meaning of an utterance. A word is not to be regarded as a self-contained unit of meaning which, taken with other word meanings, builds the meaning of an utterance. Rather, a word has potential contributory meaning and what it finally does contribute to a particular text will be the resultant of an interaction in the reader's mind. Richards saw two interacting elements, the *literary context* of a word (the other words with which it keeps company in a particular text) and its *determinative context* (the reader's accumulated experience of the word in previous contexts, his sense of the various meanings it has contributed to utterances in which he has met it before). The determinative context thus presents a reader with a range of possible contributory meanings; he makes a choice from this range *in the light of the literary context*—the sentence, paragraph, chapter that in the present instance contains it. For the reader this is an act of interpretation, and Richards points out that he may do it badly by paying too much attention to either of the elements and not enough to the other.

When, in his poem *East Coker*, T. S. Eliot wrote of 'a raid on the inarticulate' as a way of describing what a poet does when he writes a poem, he was using the word 'inarticulate' in a new and unfamiliar way and no dictionary in existence at the time would have listed what he meant by it. For a dictionary can do no more than list what a word *has been used to mean* in the past, and then only, as a rule, the focal or commonest uses. What Eliot means here by 'the inarticulate', put prosaically, must be something like 'all that has never yet been put into words'. Our determinative contexts for 'inarticulate' would probably focus upon a general sense of 'unable to speak', 'dumb'. The literary context then sets a problem by putting 'the' before 'inarticulate' and prods us into some such analogy as that with 'poor' meaning 'having too little money' alongside *'the* poor' meaning the mass—the collective category—of those who have too little money. But what sense can we make of 'a raid on the mass of those who cannot speak'? We are rescued, in all probability, by another determinative context, a recollection of some such phrase as 'inarticulate sorrow' in the sense of silent, unexpressed sorrow. So we arrive at the resultant, 'a raid on the body of all that has never yet been put into words'.

Richards' determinative contexts, then, are one particular example of the way expectations drawn from past experience are generated and matched with what we read; and, as we have seen, in the absence of any determinative contexts, any knowledge from past experience of what meanings a word may contribute, we leap the gap, supply a probable meaning, and try it out as we read on. We must add that where the gap is appropriately filled by these means we are in fact setting up our first determinative context for the unfamiliar word, and that this is *the normal means* by which we extend our mastery of word meanings. (Don't be put off by the *literary* nature of my example; similar processes are at work when I try to understand what the teenager meant by calling something 'wild', or when the immigrant meets a word that is thoroughly familiar in our culture, but not in his.)

These ideas lie at the heart of a comparatively recent breakthrough in the methods of teaching initial reading, a movement associated with the names of Kenneth Goodman in U.S.A. and Frank Smith in Canada. Goodman calls one of his articles, "Reading: A Psycholinguistic Guessing Game'.[4] The guessing is, of course, the supplying of meaning from the reader's expectations in accordance with the emerging meaning of the passage and as confirmed by the marks he sees on the page. He makes the point that this promising strategy is discouraged by teachers who regard reading as a very precise process involving detailed identification of every mark on the page. Reading should rather be seen as the gaining and using of meaning, and the most effective way of achieving this is to develop meaningful expectations and use minimal visual cues to confirm or disconfirm those expectations: in other words, good-enough guessing is the right approach. (There is a story current around Melbourne of a teacher in a one-teacher country school who knitted her way through her day's work. When a pupil looked up from his reading to say, 'Please Miss, what does so-and-so mean?', she would reply, 'Say Moses and read on'. In fact, of course, this would only work when the child successfully construed the missing word and so set up an appropriate 'determinative context': where he failed, the teacher would need to drop her knitting and help him.)

The main point I have been making here is that reading should be seen as an aspect of our general strategy for processing information. We continue to require, of course, all four aspects of the process (as set out in the diagram on page 133), and we shall have simple as well as complex problems offered in each—a fact which my serial ordering must not be allowed to obscure. (We may for example have no difficulty in processing the data offered by the word 'Danger' on a signboard, but considerable difficulty in perceiving directly what it is in the situation that threatens us.) Since reading represents the least accessible form of data, it is important to remember that it relies upon information gathered by prior data-processing of any or every type; hence that reading difficulties may be solved by regressing to earlier modes—by conversation about the text, for example, or by direct sense experiences of the events or objects referred to in the written text, where this is possible. Making sense of a text is part and parcel of the larger task of making sense of the world in general. We make a grave mistake if we treat a child's difficulties in reading in sole regard to the reading task.

The whole enterprise of 'making sense of the world in general' is kept in movement by expectations, by glimpses of possibilities ahead. Any teacher who can discover what is, or with his help could become, a glimpse of something ahead in a child's life worth making for—intellectual, social, moral, constructive, artistic or simply playful, but ahead and worth aiming at—is for that child a good teacher and a good teacher of reading.

References

1. I. A. Richards, *How to Read a Page*, Routledge, 1943.
2. Jane W. Torrey, "Learning to Read Without a Teacher" in Frank

Smith, *Psycholinguistics and Reading*, Holt, Rinehart and Winston, 1973, pp. 147–157.
3. I. A. Richards, *The Philosophy of Rhetoric*, Routledge, 1936.
4. Kenneth S. Goodman, "Reading: A Psycholinguistic Guessing Game" in *Journal of the Reading Specialist*, May, 1967.

14

Shaping at the Point of Utterance

The two words, 'spontaneity' and 'invention' as we ordinarily use them must surely have something in common: an element of surprise, not only for those who encounter and respond to the act or expression, but also for those who originate it. I want to suggest here that rhetoricians, in their current concern for successive drafts and revision processes in composing, may be underestimating the importance of 'shaping at the point of utterance', or the value of spontaneous inventiveness. It is my claim, in fact, that a better understanding of how a writer shapes at the point of utterance might make a major contribution to our understanding of invention in rhetoric.

In all normal speech we do, almost of necessity, shape as we utter. Syntactically, we launch into a sentence and hope somehow to reach closure. We had a Director at the Institute of Education where I once worked who was a very powerful speaker, but also a great 'um'-er and 'ah'-er. As you listened to him it would go something like this: "It seems to me, Mr. Chairman—ah—in spite of the difficulties Professor X has raised—ah—that what we most need—ah—in the present circumstances—ah—and—ah—at this moment in time—ah—in some way to bring to a conclusion this intolerably long sentence." Listening, we could tell precisely at what point he foresaw his total structure, the point at which he 'took it on the run'.

What is not so easily demonstrated is that the shaping as we speak applies not only to syntactic but also to semantic choices. When we start to speak, we push the boat out and trust it will come to shore somewhere—not *anywhere*, which would be tantamount to losing our way, but somewhere that constitutes a stage on a purposeful journey. To embark on a conversational utterance is to take on a certain responsibility, to stake a claim that calls for justification: and perhaps it is the social pressure on the speaker to justify his claim that gives talk an edge over silent brooding as a problem-solving procedure. Heinrich

Reprinted from *Reinventing the Rhetorical Tradition*, edited by Aviva Freedman and Ian Pringle (Conway, AR: L & S Books, for the Canadian Council of Teachers of English, 1980), copyright by the Canadian Council of Teachers of English and reprinted by permission.

Von Kleist, the early 19th Century German writer, puts this point boldly in an essay he called, "On the gradual fabrication of thought while speaking": "Whenever you seek to know something and cannot find it out by meditation, I would advise you to talk it over with the first person you meet. He need not be especially brilliant, and I do not suggest that you *question* him, no: *tell* him about it. . . . Often, while at my desk working, I search for the best approach to some involved problem. I usually stare into my lamp, the point of optimum brightness, while striving with utmost concentration to enlighten myself. . . . And the remarkable thing is that if I talk about it with my sister, who is working in the same room, I suddenly realize things which hours of brooding had perhaps been unable to yield. . . . Because I do start with some sort of dark notion remotely related to what I am looking for, my mind, if it has set out boldly enough, and being pressed to complete what it has begun, shapes that muddled area into a form of new-minted clarity, even while my talking progresses." As teachers, we are likely to have similar evidence from much nearer home: how often have we had a student come to us with his problem, and in the course of verbalising what that problem is reach a solution with no help from us.

Then what about writing? First it must be said that students of invention in writing cannot afford to rule out of court evidence regarding invention in speech: there must be some carry-over from expression in the one medium to expression in the other. Shaping at the point of utterance is familiar enough in the way young children will spin their yarns to entertain an adult who is willing to provide an audience. (A ten-minute tape-recorded performance by a five year old boy winds up: "So he had ten thousand pounds, so everyone loved him in the world. He buy—he buyed a very fast racing car, he buyed a magic wand, he buyed everything he loved, and that's the end of my story what I told you." A five-year-old sense of closure!) There is ample evidence that spontaneous invention of this kind survives, and may even appear to profit from, the process of dictating, where parent or teacher writes down what a child composes orally. That it is seriously inhibited by the slowing down of production when the child produces his own written script is undeniable. But it is my argument that successful writers adapt that inventiveness and continue to rely on it rather than switching to some different mode of operating. Once a writer's words appear on the page, I believe they act primarily as a stimulus to *continuing*—to further writing, that is—and not primarily as a stimulus to *re*-writing. Our experiments in writing without being able to see what we had written suggested that the movements of the pen capture the movement of our thinking, and it is a serious obstacle to further composition not to be able to re-read, to get 'into the tramlines' again.[1] An eight year old Newcastle schoolboy wrote about his own writing processes: "It just comes into your head, it's not like thinking, it's just there. When you get stuck you just read it through and the next bit is there, it just comes to you." I think many teachers might regard the outcome of such a process as mere 'fluency', mere verbal facility, and not the sort of writing they want to encourage. It is my argument that highly effective writing may be produced in just that spontaneous manner, and that the best treatment for empty verbalism will rarely be a course of successive draft making.

"It just comes into your head, it's not like thinking": it seems that Barrett Mandel would agree with the eight-year-old, for he calls his recent article on writing, "Losing one's Mind: Learning to Read, Write and Edit".[2] I quote his views here because they are in part an attempt to make room for the process of shaping at the point of utterance. He sets out the three steps that occur in his own writing process: "(1) I have an idea about something I want to write; (2) I write whatever I write; (3) I notice what I have written, judge it, and edit it, either a lot or a little." And his claim is that the relationship between (1) and (2) is not one of cause and effect; "rather, step one *precedes* writing and establishes a frame of mind in which writing is likely to occur." "It is the act of writing that produces the discoveries," he claims, and, by way of explanation, "words flow from a pen, not from a mind; they appear on the page through the massive co-ordination of a tremendous number of motor processes. . . . More accurately, I *become* my pen; my entire organism becomes an extension of this writing implement. Consciousness is focused at the point of the pen."

So far, so good, but since Mandel goes on to approve of his colleague, Janet Emig's, description of writing as 'a form of cognition' it seems to me a little perverse to propose (by his title, "Losing one's Mind") a mindless form of cognition. 'Freeing one's mind' would be more appropriate, the freedom being that of ranging across the full spectrum of mental activity from the autistic pole to the reality-adjusted pole, as Peter McKellar has described it.[3] Or, as we might speculatively describe it today, right brain and left brain in intimate collaboration.

I want to associate spontaneous shaping, whether in speech or writing, with the moment by moment interpretative process by which we make sense of what is happening around us; to see each as an instance of the pattern-forming propensity of man's mental processes. Thus, when we come to write, what is delivered to the pen is in part already shaped, stamped with the image of our own ways of perceiving. But the intention to *share,* inherent in spontaneous utterance, sets up a demand for further shaping.

Can we go deeper than this, penetrate beyond the process of

drawing upon our own store of interpreted experience? Perl and Egendorf believe we must if we are to provide a full account of writing behaviour. In an article they call "The Process of Creative Discovery"[4] they speak of a new line of philosophical enquiry, the 'philosophy of experiencing', and quote from the writings of Eugene Gendlin.[5] "Many thinkers since Kant," they suggest, "have claimed that all valid thought and expression are rooted in the wider realm of pre-representational experience". 'Experiencing', or pre-representational experience, "consists of continuously unfolding orders rather than finished products"; in Gendlin's words, it is "the felt apperceptive mass to which we can inwardly point." It is fluid, global, charged with implicit meanings—which we alter when by expressing them we make them explicit.

D. W. Harding, psychologist and literary critic, explores a similar distinction in his book *Experience into Words*[6]: "The emergence of words or images as part of our total state of being is an obscure process, and their relation to the non-verbal is difficult to specify. . . . The words we choose (or accept as the best we can find at the moment) may obliterate or slightly obscure or distort fine features of the non-verbal background of thinking. . . . A great deal of speaking and writing involves the effort to be a little more faithful to the nonverbal background of language than an over-ready acceptance of ready-made terms and phrases will permit." Perl and Egendorf comment on that effort as they observe it in their students: "When closely observed, students appear to write by shuttling back and forth from their sense of what they wanted to say to the words on the page, and back to address what is available to them inwardly." This is in essence the process they call 'retrospective structuring', and its near inevitability might be suggested by comparing writing with carving: the sculptor with chisel in hand must both cut and observe the effect of his cut before going on. But retrospective structuring needs to be accompanied by what the authors call 'projective structuring', shaping the material in such a way that the writer's meaning carries over to the intended reader. It is in this aspect of writing that 'discovery', or shaping at the point of utterance, tends to break down: a mistaken sense of a reader's expectations may obstruct or weaken the 'sense of what they wanted to say'—or in Harding's terms 'obliterate fine features of the non-verbal background of thinking'. Observing unskilled writers, Perl and Egendorf comment: "What seems particularly unskilled about the way these students write is that *they apply prematurely a set of rigid critical rules for editing* to their written products." 'Prematurely' might be taken to mean at first draft rather than at second or third, but I think this does less than justice to the authors' meaning. Minor editing—for spelling, for example—is better left, we can agree, to a re-reading stage. What is at issue here is a more important point: that too restricted a sense of a reader's expectations may result in 'projective structuring' coming to dominate the shaping at the point of utterance, to the exclusion or severe restriction of the 'retrospective structuring', the search for a meaning that in its expression satisfies the writer.

Such a conclusion would gain general support from a neat little study by Mike Rose, a study he calls, "Rigid Rules, Inflexible Plans and the Stifling of Writing".[7] A case study of five fluent writers and five with 'writer's block' leads him to conclude that "the non-blockers operate with fluid, easily modified, even easily discarded rules and plans, that are often expressed with a vagueness that could almost be interpreted as ignorance. There lies the irony. The students that offer the least precise rules and plans have the least trouble composing."

What I have suggested, then, is that shaping at the point of utterance involves, first, drawing upon interpreted experience, the results of our moment by moment shaping of the data of the senses and the continued further assimilation of that material in search of coherence and pattern (the fruits of our contemplative moments); and, secondly, seems to involve by some means getting behind this to a more direct apperception of the felt quality of 'experiencing' in some instance or instances; by which means the act of writing becomes itself a contemplative act revealing further coherence and fresh pattern. Its power to do so may depend in part upon the writer's counterpart of the social pressure that listeners exert on a speaker, though in this case, clearly, the writer himself is, in the course of the writing, the channel through which that pressure is applied.

I must now add the much more obvious point that in the initial stages of learning to write a child must draw upon linguistic resources gathered principally through speaking and listening, and apply those resources to the new task of writing. Some children, however, will also be familiar with some forms of the written language derived from stories that have been read to them. A four-year-old, for example, dictated a fairy story of his own composition in which he said, "The king went sadly home, for he had nowhere else to go", a use of 'for' that can hardly have been learnt from listening to speech. Thus, the early writer shuttles between internalised forms of the written language and his general resources recruited through speech: that he should maintain access to the latter is important if he is to embark on the use of writing to fulfil a range of different purposes. His progress as a writer depends thereafter, to a considerable degree, on his increasing familiarity with forms of the written language, the enlargement of his stock of 'internalised' written forms through reading and *being read to*. (The process of recreating the rhythms of the written language from his own reading must derive from that apprenticeship to an adult's reading.) To put it simply, if rather crudely, I see the developed writing process as one of hearing an inner voice dictating forms of the written language appropriate to the task in hand.

If it is to work this way, we must suppose that there exists some kind of *pre-setting mechanism* which, once set up, continues to affect production throughout a given task. The difficulties many writers feel in 'finding a way in' or in 'finding one's own voice' in a particular piece of writing, as well as the familiar routine of running through what has been written in order to move on, seem to me to supply a little evidence in favour of such a 'pre-setting mechanism'. Beyond that I can offer only hints and nudges. There is, for example, the phenomenon of metric composition. Read aloud a passage in galloping iambics and most listeners are enabled to compose spontaneously in that rhythm; young children's facility in picking up pig-Latin or dog-Latin is probably another example of the same sort of process. And by way of explanation, there is Kenneth Lashley's[8] longstanding notion of a 'determining tendency' in human behaviour: "The cortex must be regarded as a great network of reverbatory circuits constantly active. A new stimulus reaching such a system does not excite an isolated reflex path, but must produce widespread changes in the pattern of excitation throughout a whole system of already interacting neurons". Such a determining tendency, he argues, is related to an individual's *intention*. In this and other respects the notion parallels Michael Polanyi's[9] description of focal and subsidiary awareness. Applying that to the writing process, a writer is subsidiarily aware of the words and structures he is employing and focally aware of an emergent meaning, the meaning he intends to formulate and convey. And it is the focal awareness that guides and directs the use made of the means, of which he is subsidiarily aware. In similar fashion, a reader's attention is not focused upon the printed marks: he attends *from* them to the emerging meaning. To focus on the words would be to inhibit the handling of meaning by writer or reader. "By concentrating on his fingers," says Polanyi, " a pianist can paralyse himself; the motions of his fingers no longer bear then on the music performed, they have lost their meaning."

Painting in oils, where one pigment may be used to obliterate another, is a very different process from painting in water-colours, where the initial process must capture immediately as much as possible of the painter's vision. Do modes of discourse differ in production as sharply as that? And does our present concern with pre-planning, successive drafting and revision suggest that in taking oil-painting as our model for writing we may be underestimating the value of 'shaping at the point of utterance' and hence cutting off what might prove the most effective approach to an understanding of rhetorical invention?

Acknowledgements

I am grateful to Geoffrey Summerfield of New York University and Frank Smith of the University of Victoria who introduced me to the articles by Heinrich Von Kleist and Kenneth Lashley respectively.

References

1. James Britton, Tony Burgess, Nancy Martin, Alex McLeod and Harold Rosen, *The Development of Writing Abilities, 11–18*, Schools Council Research Studies, Macmillan Education, 1975, p. 35.
2. Barrett J. Mandel, "Losing One's Mind: Learning to Write and Edit," *College Composition and Communication*, December, 1978, pp. 363–5.
3. Peter McKellar, *Imagination and Thinking*, Cohen and West, 1957, p. 5.
4. Sondra Perl & Arthur Egendorf, "The Process of Creative Discovery: Theory, Research, and Implications for Teaching" in Donald McQuade, ed., *Linguistics, Stylistics and the Teaching of Composition*, Studies in Contemporary Language No. 2, Department of English, University of Akron, 1979, pp. 121–27.
5. Eugene Gendlin, *Experiencing and the Creation of Meaning*, Free Press, 1962.
6. D. W. Harding, *Experience into Words*, Chatto and Windus, 1963, pp. 170–2.
7. Mike Rose, "Rigid Rules, Inflexible Plans, and the Stifling of Writing: A Cognitivist Analysis of Writer's Block", unpublished paper, 1978, Department of English, University of California, Los Angeles.
8. Kenneth Lashley, "The Problem of Serial Order in Behavior," in Sol Saporta, ed., *Psycholinguistics: A Book of Readings*, Holt, Rinehart and Winston, 1961, p. 194.
9. Michael Polanyi, *Knowing and Being*, Routledge and Kegan Paul, 1969, p. 146.

III
Perspectives on the Profession

15

A Note on Teaching, Research and 'Development'

Perhaps We Don't Want to Know

To risk a sweeping generalisation, it seems to me that the attitude to research of teachers in England differs from that of teachers in America: and that each attitude has its inherent strengths and weaknesses. American teachers, as a result no doubt of their training, are more sophisticated readers of research reports, attach more importance to new findings, and are liable, I suspect, to make a too direct application of such findings to their practice as teachers. Teachers in England are less sophisticated in the language of educational research, expect much less in the way of assistance from this quarter, and are often suspicious of any advice that does not originate from classroom experience, or at the least confirm them along the lines of the convictions they have derived from their own experience. What is admirable about such self-confidence I need not underline: its weakness lies in the fact that as teachers we may be charged with attempting to hoist ourselves up by our own boot-straps. What linguists, psychologists, sociologists and philosophers can explain or suggest about the nature of human behaviour *ought* in some way to be available to us as an aid to our intuitive practice of the art of teaching.

Knowing and Doing

Our experience is a constant succession of confrontations: and what is meant by a 'confrontation' could hardly be more vividly illustrated than by thinking of a teacher facing his class. In order to act responsibly in any situation we must interpret what confronts us, and this involves *representing it to ourselves*. We are able to make such a representation because we are not new-born into each confrontation but can draw upon past experience: that is to say upon our store of representations of previous encounters with the world. This we may do

Previously unpublished paper prepared for the Schools Council English Committee, December, 1969.

badly or well: to do it well means, obviously, to represent as fully and faithfully as possible what is there. A principal reason for doing it badly is that we fall back on something ready-made: a formulation of a past situation is brought in to serve, with little or no adaptation, as a representation of the present. (This may result in our acting *irresponsibly*, as the psychologist George Kelly has pointed out: we shirk response to what is actually there by applying some ill-fitting ready-made formulation such as a school rule or a stereotyped status-image.)

What we *do* in any situation, then, is done in the light of the representation we make: and that representation is made in the light of what we perceive and what we *know*. Parts of this knowledge will be unsystematic and loosely formulated, as for example recognising that it is John Smith we are talking to and recalling a few random facts about John Smith's home circumstances: other parts of it will be highly systematic—as for example knowing the details of a psychologist's coherent analysis of the stages of mental development: or, to take a very different but not necessarily irrelevant case, knowing the structure of a Shakespeare sonnet in relation to the metrical principles that govern English verse forms. Our systematic knowledge, the fruits of our past thinking, the fruits of our past looking (and listening etc.), and—more mysteriously still—the fruits of our past intuitions, imaginings feelings—all these are frames of reference in the light of which we represent to ourselves the constantly changing situations that confront us.

Putting it crudely, it is the continual reformulation of what we know in the light of what we perceive that matters: and the hardening of what we know into a formula that we apply ready-made instead of reformulating—that is the danger. Thus, our most powerful ideas are relatively general, relatively unformulated starting points from which we constantly reformulate.

Research and Teaching

Research findings are things we can *know* which could have a bearing on what we *do* when we teach. And 'development' should be the name we give to the process of bringing this kind of knowing into relationship with this kind of doing. But how does it work?

The conclusions reached by a research team working in controlled situations cannot be directly apprehended and applied by teachers working in conditions where every variable is actively varying. For the teacher to reformulate from the general starting point to meet particular circumstances is in this instance a dangerous impossibility. The research team may step out of their quarters into the schools in order to produce materials that embody certain of their findings—a kit for the job, so to speak. For the teachers who work with the members of the team in the classroom this may be a very valuable kind of development work: it may enable them, that is to say, to modify their own insights in the light of the fresh thinking and so have at their disposal new knowledge that will enable them to represent more faithfully and more fully what confronts them in the classroom. But if the kit produced is then regarded as a means of persuading teachers to apply the research findings without undergoing the modification of insights—a means in other words of teaching better than they know— then clearly the stage that is essentially what we mean by 'development' has been omitted.

For development is a two-way process: the practitioner does not merely *apply;* he must reformulate from the general starting points supplied by the research and arrive at new ends—new not only to him, but new in the sense that they are not a part of the research findings, being a discovery of a different order. The value of the research lies in supplying the starting point for many such discoveries; the value of each discovery is limited to the successful solution of this particular problem at this particular time; but the power of the teacher to make that journey and make it again—there above all lies the value of the whole enterprise.

If there is to be a kit then, something we can call 'development' must go with it. Obviously there are not enough research workers to go round the schools working in turn with the teachers—even those who would welcome the opportunity. What then can we imply?

Teachers' Centres

I think there are implications here for those who plan educational research. A development aspect built into a research project from an early stage could act as a check upon the relevance of the enquiry and the operational value of the starting points it might provide: the nature of the enquiry in its details might be 'corrected' by such a monitoring process.

Clearly there are important implications for in-service training and initial training of teachers. But the implications I wish finally to pursue here are those for teachers' centres. The 'do it yourself' spirit that still makes the notion of teachers' centres an attractive one could, it seems to me, generate the kind of situation which provides the most fruitful point of application for the expert—the research worker and the theoretician—that makes possible in fact, the development process as we have described it.

It will take time. The 'do it yourself' impetus dies out if, after a while, nothing much seems to have happened. In other words, the pooling of experience makes the right beginning but needs to lead into a more clearly defined enquiry—a comitted attempt on the part of a group to make corporate discoveries. A measure of success in this is likely to lead the group to set itself more ambitious tasks, and at the point where the difficulties of achieving them seem insurmountable— this is the situation in which an experienced worker in a similar area may in fact find his most profitable audience. Again, the process is two way: the expert's knowledge can speak to the group in answer to questions they have already asked themselves: and the reformulating of his findings in the terms of their insights comes as an extension from that centre.

The most active field of research relevant to education today is probably that of language. The need for development work among English teachers is therefore particularly urgent. The need is urgent but the process cannot be hurried.

16

Take It from—Where?

We are not in an open situation with regard to the topic of this conference. Certain demands are being made upon us; there are pressures upon us to approach our job in a particular way—that of framing and working to behavioural objectives! (As I made my notes on this last night I found that I had written "behavioural *objections*"—a Freudian slip?) In these circumstances, it seems to me, we need to ask three questions: (1) Is the demand well-founded? (2) Is it practicable? and, if we fail to give a clear affirmative answer to either of those, (3) What alternatives do we propose? To reject the demands and offer no alternatives will certainly lay us open to the charge of being mere defenders of the status quo, content with the way things are in schools. I have seen no signs of any such self-satisfaction.

I shall start (quite illogically) with the middle question—Is it practicable?—because what I am able to say about it can be said very briefly. In the last analysis, only you can decide, in the light of your particular situation, what is practicable in your classroom. I can say some general things, yet even there my knowledge of the kinds of situations you operate in is very sketchy—though not quite so sketchy as it would have been three weeks ago. During the past three weeks I have visited a number of schools and colleges and sat in on a number of teaching sessions, and I must say I have enjoyed being flown around the continent by NCTE!

Let me refer you to Lanny Morreau's thirteen characteristics:

The student should be:

1. provided with the freedom to choose from alternatives.
2. provided with numerous alternatives from which to choose.
3. able to make inputs into educational planning and sequencing.
4. assured a minimal skill/knowledge level from which to make decisions.
5. provided with a precise description as to what is expected from him and how he will be evaluated.

Published in *Goal Making for English Teaching*, Henry B. Maloney (ed.), National Council of Teachers of English, 1973. Reprinted by permission.

6. provided with constant feedback regarding his progress.
7. able to progress at his own rate.
8. able to determine when he has been successful.
9. able to determine what he will gain from a specific course of study before he enters it.
10. provided with a learning environment that is free of punishment.
11. provided with a learning environment in which he can consistently receive positive consequences (reinforcement) for successful task completion.
12. provided with an environment where the focus of teacher behavior is on his individual needs.
13. able to increasingly assume responsibility for his own development.
    (from: Henry B. Maloney, ed., *Goal Making for English Teaching.* N.C.T.E., 1973, pp. 72–76).

I accept and endorse most of these. In fact, from reading these and from talking to Lanny Morreau, I would judge that he covets for his children what I have coveted for the children I have taught over many years—though I think he *would formulate that very differently* from the way I would formulate it. But that is a matter we shall come to later.

Number 5 does not go far enough for me: "The student should be provided with a precise description as to what is to be expected from him and how he will be evaluated." I want to make one minor amendment and stipulate ". . . a precise description of what *the teacher* expects from him" and then add a major loophole: "the student should be free to also seek evaluation from any other source of his own choice, this being a part of what is open to him and acceptable to the teacher."

Number 9 goes too far for me. I can only go so far as to say that the student should be able to estimate and assess *some aspects* of the outcomes—other aspects will be at least to some degree unexpected. If we have not set the course up in such a way that there are unexpected possibilities, I think we have set our sights too low.

Given the way things are today, I would strongly support number 13, "The student should be able to increasingly assume responsibility for his own development." But I would much prefer to challenge the way things are and rewrite that, "The student should at no point be asked to relinquish responsibility for his own learning." Before they come to us, children have that responsibility and our great mistake is to take it away from them.

But as you will see, I am in substantial agreement with these "Thirteen Characteristics of a Humanistic Environment." What I do not see is how to turn these broad statements into valuable, nontrivial behavioural objectives. I should like to learn; and I suspect that a great deal more study and experiment will be needed before this can be done effectively. In saying that, I am merely repeating what Lanny Morreau himself has said—that is, indeed what he is urging us to do.

The trivializing effect is a major difficulty. It does seem to me, for example, that reports we have had from obviously excellent—talented and committed—teachers in this conference have shown something of the trivializing effect. In other words, what they have set down on paper as their intentions seem far less worthwhile that what emerges as they talk about their work, their relations with the students, the quality of their face-to-face concern.

My second difficulty is the obvious one of devising, once you have written your objectives, valid measures of achievement. Quite new problems, I am sure, are due to arise here with the added difficulty that those best qualified to tackle them are likely to be those less well qualified from experience to conceive in their full complexity the desired achievements. Strenuous and sustained cooperation will be needed, and a great deal of tolerance on both sides.

Thirdly, there is the problem of record-keeping in the classroom—record-keeping of individual progress along individually chosen routes and with this the recognition that both student-evaluation and teacher-evaluation should lead to constant rewriting of the objectives (a point made by Lanny Morreau which I heartily endorse). All this seems to me to amount to something a teacher might carry out *instead of* but hardly *in addition to* his teaching role. (And I am thinking of the teacher in his revised, not his traditional, role—his tutorial responsibility, the availability of the resources within him, and the resources he has provided to meet the needs of individual students working on individual programmes.)

Here, if I may be allowed a digression, let me declare my support for individual programmes and at the same time put in a plea for the retention of two important processes—that of *learning from each other* and *learning with each other*. The first requires small group activities alongside individual ones, the second allows for the occasional shared experience involving teacher and student group as a whole: an experience of community. The teacher reading to the whole class would be a commonplace example which maintains the sense of a social group within which all the individual work can safely and happily go on.

In pursuing these questions of practicability, then, I should want to start with Lanny Morreau. He is well aware of the complexities of the behaviour he is trying to programme. He is well aware of the threat to teachers involved if behavioural objectives are seen as a teacher-evaluating device and is clearly opposed to such a use. Perhaps, if we can establish the unsuitability of this part of what is afoot, we may take the sting out of the whole enterprise. We may also welcome his emphasis on individual choice, individual rate, and individual route; and, if I may be allowed to add this, his contribution to an argument that has not yet seriously been engaged—the argument against an educational set-up in which one has to qualify as an eleven-year-old (for example) before being allowed to become a twelve-year-old. That, after all, is what the year-grade system amounts to. Morreau put forward as one of the advantages of individualised teaching that it offered a student the opportunity to repeat individual assignments and so avoid the wasteful and discouraging process of being asked to repeat a year.

Now back to my first and fundamental question: Is the demand for behavioural objectives well-founded? Are there facts about children's learning that are not taken into account? Does the demand imply a philosophy, a belief about the nature of man, the nature of learning, and the nature of experience? And if it does, is it a philosophy we accept or reject?

My first answer to this is that the demand does, to my mind, consistently imply an educational philosophy, a view of learning. It rests, in fact, on a behaviourist theory of learning with all its complexity and its implications. All I can attempt to do in this paper is to touch upon some of the issues that differentiate such a theory from its principal rival in the educational field, the humanistic theory. Let me begin by offering you a quotation from George Kelly, the American "personality psychologist." In the essay I quote he was concerned with a theme very close to our own, though its title, "Humanistic Methodology in Psychological Research," may not make that immediately apparent.

> Some of my literary colleagues leave me with the impression that 'the nature of man' puts more out of my reach than within my grasp. I expect better of them.
>   This is crucial: humanistic psychology needs a technology through which to express its humane intentions. Humanity needs to be implemented, not merely characterized and eulogized.[1]

As teachers of English, I believe we may very often have deserved such criticism ourselves. Eulogy is not enough. The humanities should reveal the possibilities of human life in such a way that there are steps by which children may make progress. Our objectives have too often been expressed in vague and Utopian terms. It is good that we should be asked to test the practicability of our intentions.

In that same essay, however, George Kelly points out that Skinner is the currently popular whipping boy for these humanists; and he asks why this should be so, since Skinner teaches men how to "actualize their intentions." "It is not," he adds, "that man is what Skinner makes of him, but rather that what Skinner can do man can do—and more. Skinner's subjects are not the model of man; Skinner is."[2] Now this, if we are to judge by the practice of behavioural objectives, is precisely to stand Skinner on his head, or so it seems to me. "Which responses to which stimuli are to be reinforced?"—I am as unlikely at the moment to hear an educator putting that question to a child as I am to hear Skinner asking the pigeon.

To the behaviourist, as to earlier schools of psychology, learning is a special kind of behaviour, roughly identified as "behaviour-changing behaviour"—a kind of behaviour that results in the establishment of new behaviour patterns. Here, I think, James Hoetker's contribution to the NCTE publication, *On Writing Behavioral Objectives for English*, is very helpful.[3] He distinguishes between "can do," "may do," and "will do" behaviours; and if we apply this to the rough definition of learning I have given, we find a curious complication. In "behaviour-changing behaviour" only the first behaviour can be rendered as "can do," "may do," or "will do"; the second behaviour is simply "did" behaviour—a once-and-for-all affair. I point this out to raise the question as to how valid and useful it is to consider learning in terms of the setting up of habitual behaviour patterns. Is this, in fact, a view of learning that is far too restricted?

George Kelly takes the scientist as his model for man in general (and hence, of course, his interpretation of Skinner). As a scientist frames his hypotheses, puts them to the test in experiment, and modifies them in the light of the outcome, so every man conducts his everyday behaviour. From past experience he derives expectations about the world he lives in; in any situation cues activate particular, relevant expectations, and these are his hypotheses (which he proceeds to put to the test of actuality, revising them in the light of what happens). Putting this more generally, in Kelly's own words, from an essay he called "Behaviour Is an Experiment":

> Behaviour presents itself as man's principal instrument of enquiry. Without it his questions are academic and he gets nowhere. When it is prescribed for him he runs around in dogmatic circles. But when he uses it boldly to ask questions, a flood of unexpected answers rises to tax his utmost capacity to understand.[4]

We should notice, in passing, the enormous implications of this statement for teacher behaviour and student behaviour in the classroom.

It follows that for Kelly, learning is not a special kind of human behaviour, but *behaviour at its most typically human.* And this view of learning is one that builds upon the broad basis of a great deal of philosophical thinking over the past fifty years or so. Summing up very crudely the view that emerges, we would claim that man—unlike the other animals—*represents the world to himself,* cumulatively as he experiences it, and reacts to every stimulus from the actual world—not directly and *ad hoc,* but by means of and in the light of that representation. Our "world representation" is both a storehouse of past experience and a body of expectations concerning the future. And, as Kelly would have it, it is the future that concerns us; behaviour is an experiment, every experience is an opportunity to improve our predictive apparatus.

With this sort of theorizing in mind, Skinner has commented: "The school of experience is no school at all, not because no one learns in it, but because no one teaches."[5] At an obvious level, this is of course true and undeniable. But does it not imply a very foolish disjunction between learning and teaching—as though one might judge a good school by its good teaching without ever attempting to discover how much was being *learnt?* It is this disjunction, or the possibility of it, that concerns us at the moment. The "school of experience" would seem to the behaviourists a place where learning is random, unfocused, and unstructured—no model therefore for the teacher-school. But there are others—George Kelly among them—who would want learning within school to be as much like everyday learning (in the school of experience) as possible. For one thing, a great deal of learning has been achieved before a child arrives at school; surely we must build on that. We may accelerate it, facilitate it, intensify it; but we should not, if Kelly is right, want to change its nature. Learning in the school of experience is the pursuit of curiosity; that means growth from an individual center on an individual, unified pattern. The growth of a plant is an organic process and is reflected in the organic shape the plant takes. If we could take this for an image of an individual child's learning from infancy and right through school we might be in a better position to plan our own teaching. We are more likely, I believe, to think of it in terms of frost forming on the boughs we offer him.

The view that in-school learning should be as like as possible to out-of-school learning is at its most vulnerable when we come to consider the basic skills. Here, at least, the behaviourist theory seems to have strong evidence on its side. Here, at the level of James Hoetker's "can do" behaviours, the writing of behavioural objectives seems most defensible. Let me at this point, therefore, take a second opinion. Michael Polanyi, scientist and philosopher, has some interesting things to say about skills in this recent book, *Knowing and Being*. He shows, for example, that *seeing* is a skill; it is not something that simply happens because the eye is what it is, but it is something we have to *learn to do*. And yet we acquire the skill without any teaching, without any consciousness of practice, without any awareness of a learning process; and many other more obvious skills, for example, riding a bicycle, we acquire in what is essentially a similar manner. The manner, if Polanyi is right, is acquired by concentrating upon the *desired performance* while maintaining a subsidiary awareness of the means, the details of technique. He gives a simple illustration. If we are trying to reach some inaccessible object with the help of a long stick, the focus of our attention is at the *far end* of the stick, and not at the near end, where the muscles of hand and arm are applying their pressures. What goes on there is the object of "subsidiary awareness." Moreover these subsidiary elements will often be "unspecifiable"; thus; in Polanyi's words, "we learn to ride a bicycle without being able to tell in the end how we do it." And again: "But does the successful teaching of skills . . . not prove that one *can* tell our knowledge of them? No, what the pupil must discover by an effort of his own is something we could not tell him. And he knows it then in his turn but cannot tell it."[6]

Polanyi's study of focal and subsidiary awareness is too complicated for us to go into in detail. I find considerable support in it for something that many teachers have arrived at by intuition. One of the best ways of acquiring a skill is to "have a go," to concentrate on the "desired performance," almost to imagine the action completed. And to focus upon techniques, to be over-explicit about them over-long, may very well be inhibiting. As Polanyi says: "By concentrating attention on his fingers, a pianist can paralyse himself; the motions of his fingers no longer bear then on the music performed, they have lost their meaning."[7]

All this is very like what Noam Chomsky has been saying to us for a long time about the way children acquire language; how they take on rule-governed behaviour "without a knowledge of the rules." Imitation and reinforcement are terms that he shows to be inadequate to describe how they learn to speak. Rather, he suggests, they scan the utterances of others in order to derive operating principles from them. By applying those principles, they produce utterances of their own, which are both new-minted and rule-governed, from a subsidiary awareness of the "unspecifiable" operating principles and a focus upon the desire to make themselves understood. This amounts to a very un-behaviouristic view of language learning. Chomsky, in fact, spells out his criticisms of Skinnerian theory in great detail in his review of Skinner's *Verbal Behavior.*

I have suggested that there are facts concerning the learning process that behaviourism does not explain. It is all very tentative and exploratory, and I have no wish to be dogmatic—even if I could. I recommend to you George Kelly's view of learning and Michael Polanyi's study of the relation between focal and subsidiary awareness. You will need, to use Peter Elbow's terms, to try on them "the believing game" and see how far it can take you. I certainly see no reason to feel smug about our situation. A great deal of strenuous thinking is needed; we need the help of people like Morreau to harden the nose of these tentative ideas and work out their practical applications.

I think we might, after such deliberations, find ourselves agreeing that there are skill-learning aspects of work in English that could be programmed in a Skinnerian manner, taught to a schedule of behavioural objectives, and backed by measures of the progress of individual children while claiming at the same time that student "response," "appreciation," and "interpretation," student attitudes, assimilative strategies, and beliefs, were also the concern of the English teacher and that in these cognitive-cum-affective areas of the curriculum no such programming was possible or desirable.

On the other hand, I prefer to believe that we shall be able to demonstrate what I have suggested above, i.e., these skills of language are best acquired when made incidental to the achievement of a desired performance, and the methods of teaching them will fall into line with those by which we discharge our more complex and imponderable responsibilities. I prefer to believe this for reasons that I must try to explain more fully.

It seems perfectly clear to me that in educational practice behaviourist psychology is not applied using Skinner as the model of man. The student to be taught comes into the picture as Skinner's *subject*. In other words, someone has to decide for them what sort of men and women these boys and girls ought to become.

I started teaching in 1930—that's a long time ago. Yet I can very well remember feeling, in those early years, that it was only the fact that education was no more than 20 percent efficient that made the job bearable. Who would dare to shoulder the responsibility if it achieved 100 percent efficiency? The point really comes home to me when I think of secondary schooling.

In the primary school it is different; every small child wants to grow up, and for him, every grown up may stand for what he wants to become. I am describing in a crude way what the sociologists call (without any pun intended) primary socialisation—the process of qualifying for mature membership in the society into which one is born. But in the secondary schools what is afoot is called secondary socialisation. This means *individuation*—going one's own way, fulfilling one's own particular blueprint, and, corporately, constructing from the interactions of these developing individuals a changed society. How can we—living in a society that corporately we have constructed (and individually we have grown to fit)—predict what society is to be like for our students in ten, twenty, fifty years' time? By some means, we must plan on the basis of what we *put into* the educational process and not on the basis of predetermined *outcomes*. (One of the resolutions of the York 1971 International Conference on English asked for "the redefining of our subject in the light of the language needs of all children and their probable needs in a kind of society we cannot predict—a kind of society that may emerge in part as a result of the successful teaching of our subject as re-defined.")

At the practical day-to-day level, this means that our lessons must leave ample room for the unexpected—for the occurrence from time to time of what surprises us, in spite of our wisdom and experience. Let me offer you an example of unexpected learning in a group of twelve to thirteen year olds. Their teacher was a friend of mine, a young woman of some four or five years' teaching experience. She had these boys and girls working in small self-chosen groups discussing their own writings—before and after the actual writing. On this occasion they were reading and talking about poems they had written about their families. The teacher is not present, the tape recorder is; and this is a situation they are familiar with. From discussing one of their poems they have wandered off into a general chat about grandparents. There are four boys in the group (Clive, Robert, Grant, and Daniel) and two girls (Anita and Sian):

C. My grandfather, he's always watching telly, cowboys and Indians.
D. Oh, my . . .
R. Does he . . .
D. He's still going strong then?
C. Yeh.
R. Are you *sure* he doesn't do anything else?
C. Not really.
R. My grandfather used to play golf.
D. Mine never watched telly, never watches it at all.
A. I watch about one-and-a-half hours a night.
S. I watch that much.
A. Yes. I suppose it's quite a lot.
D. I watch "Morecombe and Wise."
C. Yeh, that's a laugh.
D. Most programmes are useless.
R. Terrible.
C. My nanas [grandmothers] are both going strong.
S. Mine died. One of mine died in '63 or '64, I can't remember.

But soon they turn back to the poems. Robert reads the poem Daniel has written:

R. [*Reading*]

My Grandfather

He stood deep in thought
   While the milk on the stove
Boiled over
   His eyes with no sentiment
Flickered
   Stared on and on and gone

An old chair creaked as he sank down
  And his mind ticked on.
In endless fields of thought
  Of great rivers so long
Or wrought-iron bridges
  To cover the rolling mind
Of my grandfather.

S. That's good.
A. Very good.
S. Can I see it? I'll have to read it again.
C. Yeh, let's see. [*Murmurs*]
   [*Pause*]
S. It's very good. It's very true to life, true to his grandfather.
A. Do you know his grandfather, then?
S. No, but he's told me, he talks about him a lot.
G. I don't understand the last part, the bit, that line about "wrought-iron bridges."
R. I think it's there because it sounds good. I read it and thought, "That's good." But then I thought, "Well, what have wrought-iron bridges to do with it?"
D. Well, I suppose—I suppose I did kind of—well, write it—or it kind of came. But I think it is right.
S. Why?
D. Well, the main thing about him is he is like a bridge. I remember, well, he's always coped with things, climbed over obstacles, made kind of—well—bridges, you see, across, between things—between us too. Do you see?
G. I suppose so.
S. I think I see. Grandparents are often easier to get on with than parents. They patch up quarrels, don't they?
D. Yes, it seems to be—well—easier with them, they don't make such a big problem out of things.
A. My parents say my grandparents spoil me.
C. It's because they haven't got, well, the responsibilities parents have got.
D. In some ways they're like children again.
A. Yes! [*Laughter*]
D. "Wrought-iron" was because he does everything well and because in his days bridges were made of—well—were made of wrought-iron not cement.
R. Yes.
   [*Confusion of voices*]
G. He's thinking of the past, isn't he. Things, like, that have gone before. He doesn't notice what's happening now. Old

people are like that. My Gran, she remembers everything when she was a girl, but not what happened yesterday.

S. Yes.

A. That's right.

R. Yes.

S. I wonder if it's true?

G. I think . . .

R. If what's true?

S. Well, sort of what they remember, like it was always better then, in their days—even the weather.
    [Laughter]

A. Or else, "I didn't have all these things when I was a girl," and "I wasn't allowed to do that," and "Think yourself lucky."
    [Laughter]

R. Well, they can't just make it all up, though. It can't be—well—very nice to be old.

S. No, and not able to do things any more.

D. We all change things that happen.

A. What do you mean?

D. Well, if I do something wrong, or get—well, you know—embarrassed. Well, I think about it and do it again and again in my mind. I sort of act it out.

G. Yes, I know.

D. I make it—well—better, till it stops worrying me.
    [General murmurs][8]

In discussing that tape, teachers have sometimes criticised the waste of time on trivialities—those chatty comments at the beginning. But it seems to me that the trivialities play an essential role; they *constitute* a relaxed atmosphere and encourage unstrained relationships. From such a soil the discoveries grow, and I rate the discovery here very highly. Daniel, whose poem introduced this particular sequence of talk, comes out with it when he says, "We all change things that happen." They begin to explore the mysterious gap that lies between the totality of any experience and any representation we may make of it—a gap in which memories grow and change and die, in which fantasies take their formative effect upon us, and in which fictions place the dream alongside actuality.

No teacher in his senses could have programmed such a discovery, nor even (as you might well conclude from my attempts) have so formulated it that it could take its place in a sequential learning schedule. Why? Because it is too profoundly complex an idea; although we can recognize its value, we cannot explain or account for its occurrence. Such a learning process is in fact closely akin to the process

Donald Hall referred to when he described himself as "watching his right hand write the line he needed." If we try to write behavioural objectives for such acts of learning, I am afraid that what is precious about them will be lost in a kind of cognitive clutter.

I realize that I have been describing a philosophical watershed and am very ready to admit that I can see the landscape from my side of it very much better than I can see it from the other.

I must move on to my third question: What alternatives do we propose? Whatever misgivings we have, we cannot simply say no to behavioural objectives and leave it to be supposed that we are happy with the way things are.

It seems to me—and this is a no man's land—I shall tread very warily. A good deal more thought, effort, and time will be needed before the application of behavioural objectives in our field—even experimentally—will be seriously possible. I hope time will be given to it. Meanwhile, I suggest that we try alongside such an experiment, and as closely related to it as possible, an alternative experimental programme—one that embodies this other philosophy. All I can hope to do here is to suggest in outline what it might be like:

1. Its central notion would be that of learning from experience, i.e., a "school of experience" within the institutional school—one which deliberately sets out to make learning in school as much like out-of-school learning as possible.
2. It will be, in the broad sense, a language-based programme. In other words, it will focus upon the *uses* of language by the students, not to the exclusion of language *study* but relegating it to second priority (which means that where possibilities shrink it would be excluded at the teacher's discretion). It would emphasise above all the use of language for present satisfaction—the turning of a student's language upon his own world, or the gearing of his language to his experience.
3. It would be a programme in which operations or enterprises would be centrally in focus and not skills or techniques, which would be peripheral. By specifying operations I want to rule out "dummy runs" or practice exercises. By an enterprise I mean either some piece of first-hand experience dealt with in language (talk, dramatic improvisation, or reading) or experience which comes to us from others through language—secondary experience (in listening or reading). And in either case, talk is a primary way of dealing with the experience, whether first- or second-hand.
4. Among all the uses of language, the programme would concentrate upon what I define as "language in the role of spectator." Here I have to be ruthless and refer to a principle I have no time

to explain. This, to put it in shorthand, means a range of language use which is not directed at getting things *done* in the world (informing, persuading, instructing, explaining and so on) but at the recollection or reconstruction or fabrication of events for our pleasure and contemplation. It includes at one end of the scale the kind of chat we have with neighbours over the garden fence and at the other end novels, short stories, poems, plays—literature in its accepted sense. An utterance in the role of spectator is an end itself and not a means to some end outside itself. As we move from the chat end of the scale towards the literature end, this feature finds expression in a greater attention to *forms;* the utterance as end-in-itself becomes the verbal object, the construct that constitutes a work of art. Language to get things done, language as a means to other ends, has its own importance; but it will of necessity be mainly taught and learned where *it must be used—* that is to say, in almost every other lesson in the curriculum. If as English teachers we do not concern ourselves with language in the role of spectator, it is quite clear that nobody else will. (And please don't think that I am describing a literature-centred course; it is my purpose to see literature in the same context as the student's own uses of speech and writing.)[9]

5. The programme will recognize the importance of "expressive" language—informal, loosely structured language that relies on the listener's (or reader's) knowledge of the context and interest in the speaker (writer). It will recognize its importance as a starting-point, a matrix from which all other uses will be developed, and as an important continuing mode in itself.

6. The work would be carried out mainly as individuals or in small groups, but there would be provisions also for communal learning experiences. Individual modes of working and areas of interest will be recognized and encouraged.

7. The teacher will have two principal roles: as a provider of resources, over a wide range to allow for student choice; and as *a listener*—a stable, accepting, encouraging, and helpful audience for what the students say and write.

The two experimental programmes, representing the rival educational philosophies, should be run side by side and submitted to the same means of evaluation. Thus there would be evaluative measures contributed by each camp: objective tests of language skills; measures of the range of language uses—kinds of talk, kinds of writing, range of reading; multiply marked subjective assessments of the quality of the language products, and assessments of other imponderables such as student involvement, student commitment, student self-image. To devise these measures would in itself be a considerable challenge, although I suspect the work of George Kelly would give us a promising start.

I do not underestimate the difficulty of drawing upon recent scholarship in linguistics, psychology, and sociology in order to produce valid and viable measures; I realize the degree of tolerance demanded of both sides, if agreement is to be reached. But such an overall study has been an urgent necessity long enough. If the present impasse over behavioural objectives and humanistic goals in American education forces it upon us, the eventuality will be a happy one.

Let me finish, gratuitously, on another note. In recent years I have been more and more haunted by an idea—an image. It lies in wait for me when I watch a student in a secondary school doing his best with a class that will have nothing of him; or sometimes, when I watch a boy (or a girl) in the classroom—irked by everything, sullen and resistant when he is in the limelight of the teacher's attention, and then, as soon as that limelight is turned elsewhere, wrigglingly alive and responsive again. What haunts me is the feeling at these times that there is somewhere a kind of fine tuning device that only needs a slight touch—if only we could find it—to bring the blurred, chaotic picture into focus, to turn the incoherent sounds suddenly into intimate human speech. I associate it with a feeling I sometimes have when I am talking to a student—about his work, or his problems, or simply in an interview for admission to a course. I find myself trying to find out what makes him tick. You will know what I mean. I have my repertoire of questions, I collect my information, and I still feel that I haven't got down to anything that really matters to the student—anything that indicates the sort of person he is. So, in a more open-ended sort of talk I find myself looking deliberately for what it is that makes him tick. I believe *something* makes everybody tick and that the fine tuning device, if we could discover the secret of it, would have to do with *that something* among the individuals in a group.

All this is very vague and personal and low-level. But perhaps Carl Rogers could help to give the idea a little more shape. In his clinical work and in his writing about the applications of his ideas to education, Carl Rogers attaches considerable importance to what he calls an individual's "act of committal" and what the individual commits himself to is to "being himself."[10]

As English teachers, I think we can understand the notion of an *act of committal* because we have seen what may happen when a student chooses a book, reads it right through, and is "turned on" by it for the first time. Just one book, one event, but a key event in his life as a reader. But this other act, as Rogers sees it, is a more crucial one. Perhaps we have been too busily concerned with all the other things a student might be (a scholar, a good university entrant, a good citizen, or a tractable, cooperative member of the class) to notice whether he is able to be, above all, himself—and committed to it.

But, of course, a vast assumption underlies this whole idea—the assumption that, in our world history, civilisation where it has cropped up has been achieved because circumstances were favourable to man's achieving the best in himself. It has been achieved, in other words, because man is what he is and not in spite of that. The contrary assumption would be that civilisation has been achieved when some power greater than man, invoked by him, enabled him to overcome his nature and rise above himself.

You may well make that other assumption, and neither of us can offer proof. And if you do, you may think of the teacher as an ambassador of that superior power and at war with the nature of the students he teaches. The last thing he will want, in that case, is that they should be comitted to "being themselves."

I should apologize for bringing in such generalisations to explain why, in the end, I have to leave students to fashion their own futures. It goes back to the old question: "Am I my brother's keeper?" As I see it, "brother" and "keeper" are words from two different universes of discourse. Hence, in the long run, I can only hope so to arrange things that a student's curriculum—while he has been with me—makes sense to him afterwards, when he looks back on it.

But I ought to be able to find out, by some means, whether or not I am doing that.

References

1. George Kelly, "Humanistic Methodology in Psychological Research," in *Clinical Psychology and Personality*, ed. Brendan Maher, John Wiley & Sons, Inc., 1969, p. 135.
2. Ibid., pp. 135–6.
3. James Hoetker, "Limitations and Advantages of Behavioral Objectives in the Arts and Humanities," in *On Writing Behavioral Objectives for English*, ed. John Maxwell and Anthony Tovatt, National Council of Teachers of English, 1970, pp. 49–59.
4. George Kelly, "Behaviour Is an Experiment," in *Perspectives in Personal Construct Theory*, ed. D. Bannister, Academic Press, Inc., 1970, p. 260.
5. Quoted without source on the title page of Richard S. Peters et al., *Perspectives on Plowden*, Routledge and Kegan Paul Ltd., 1969.
6. Michael Polanyi, *Knowing and Being*, Routledge and Kegan Paul Ltd., 1969, p. 142.
7. Ibid., p. 146.

8. From the transcript of a lesson with a second year class at Sheredes School, Hoddesdon, Hertfordshire, England; by permission of Miss Elizabeth Cartland.

9. For "language in the role of spectator," see my article "Language and Experience," in *Explorations in Children's Writing*, ed. Eldonna L. Evertts, National Council of Teachers of English, 1970; for a fuller account, see Chapter 3 of my *Language and Learning*, Penguin Press, Ltd., 1970.

10. Carl R. Rogers, *On Becoming a Person*, Constable & Co. Ltd., 1967.

17

How We Got Here

I began my teaching career in a storm of controversy about the teaching of English grammar. It was not at that time a question of *whether* to teach it, but *how*. The mast my colours were nailed to was that of 'the reform of grammar reaching'. And certainly the enemy was a real one—the best-selling English textbooks were mines of unproductive busywork. No doubt my own zeal was sharpened by the fact that my department head when I began teaching presented me with a first-form syllabus that consisted of an unbroken chain of exercise numbers in Morgan's *Junior English Grammar*, with counterparts in other courses for other years. My role in the mystique was clearly that of acolyte, hers (the department head's) that of priest. Long after Mr. Morgan was dead, teachers used to write to him *via* his publishers asking him to settle a point of dispute that had arisen between colleagues. The schoolchild, I need not add, was cast in the role of *catechumenist*.

My first act of insurrection, then, was to write my own grammar book and go off, armed with it, to another job. *English on the Anvil* was published in 1934, and was an attempt to contribute to the work being done by Dr. Percy Gurrey, who had been my tutor during my professional training year at London Day Training College (now the University of London Institute of Education). Dr. Gurrey's influence on the teaching of English over the years I am considering has been enormous and invariably modest. If the study of grammar does not occupy today the place he saw for it in the English curriculum, it is in large part because other concerns he indicated to us have overtaken it.

English on the Anvil was available, to those who knew how to go about it, until a couple of years ago: as far as I was concerned, ship, mast and brave colours had sunk, almost without trace, long before that.

Published in *New Movements in the Study and Teaching of English*, Nicholas Bagnall (ed.), 1973. Reproduced by permission of Maurice Temple Smith, Ltd., London.

169

From a Grammar School English Syllabus, 1934.

A. English grammar is included in this syllabus as a means to an end. It is intended to lead to a skilful and effective use of the English language, spoken and written. Emphasis is therefore laid on the grammar of function and on exercises in the uses of the various parts of speech. . . .

B. . . . The aim therefore is to give the pupil as much liberty *as he can take:* to secure his co-operation and his interest; to develop in him as strong a self-discipline as possible; to encourage him to take as full responsibility for his own progress and his own future as he can.

Things had not vastly changed by the time we started the London Association for the Teaching of English in 1947, and we could always bet on the teaching of grammar as a topic to draw an audience of English teachers when all else failed. By then, however, it was as much a matter of whether to teach it as how. Professor Gurrey, the founding father of L.A.T.E., was one frequent contributor, and his friend and colleague, Professor Firth, was another—later to be joined by Dr. John Trim (before he left for Cambridge) and (as they successively arrived in London) Professors Randolph Quirk and Michael Halliday.

By 1955, when we had a day conference on the topic, we called it 'The Ancient and Wearisome Controversy on Grammar' and Mr. Hugh Sykes Davis opened the batting. But other issues had by then moved into the centre of focus.

*   *   *

Today, if I try (as I must) to make a map representing 'what goes on in English lessons', I need to begin by distinguishing sharply between *using* the mother tongue and *studying* it. And efforts, however strenuous and thought provoking, directed at coping with an utterance (whether to make one or respond to somebody else's) I should categorise as *use* and not *study*. Having made the distinction I should want to claim that the main stream of activity in English lessons will be using the mother tongue—using it to achieve some purpose on the part of the user.

In the second place, however, there must always be the possibility of moving out from an utterance into an *ad hoc* study of some feature or aspect of the utterance or its context. Such an *ad hoc* study might be grammatical, but it might likewise be phonological, lexical, semantic, rhetorical, stylistic, historical, psycholinguistic or sociolinguistic—and I must even so have left out several possibilities. I shall know when I move from use to study because, ignoring the purpose of the utterance I have in hand, I shall have some linguistic hypothesis in mind together with its exemplar from the utterance, and I shall be looking for parallel instances in other utterances: these 'observations' I shall then try to organise in such a way as to draw some inference. I believe such studies do deepen our understanding of language and may, as a kind of spin-off, improve our ability to use it. However, exactly in what circumstances it pays to make *explicit* what is known implicitly is a matter on which psychological evidence is scanty and inconclusive. Let me add that I value, both as worthwhile activities and for a possible spin-off, the kind of *ad hoc* studies that have been produced by Halliday's 'Linguistics and English Teaching Project' under the title *Language in Use.*[1]

Thirdly, there must always be the possibility of developing an *ad hoc* study into a systematic study in favourable circumstances. It seems to me that a systematic study of some aspect of language is an interesting and valuable undertaking providing the students are capable themselves of carrying out analyses of abstract data and provided they spend enough time on the study to reach the point where 'a system' begins to emerge. (So often in the past such courses have been all harrowing and no harvest.) I would regard such a study as what the Americans call 'an elective'—an alternative perhaps to economics in the Sixth form or biology in the fifth form: and while clearly it builds upon all that goes on in English lessons I do not see it as essentially or necessarily within the domain of subject English.

What is important is to recognize that a 'map' of English activities is of no value without an accompanying key representing priorities. There are teaching situations where, in my view, any *ad hoc* grammatical studies would be a form of Nero's fiddling. And we need above all to be clear about what we do when Rome is in flames.

*   *   *

Extract from lesson notes for a 'Matric' form at my teaching-practice school, 1929.

Aim. To get the class to appreciate the best qualities of Keats and Shelley's work, and to realise where those qualities lie in each case.

Presentation   Golden Treasury No 285, A Lament
Singing quality of Shelley's verse.
Let them read the poem silently first. Ask for the meaning of
'spontaneity'.
Why do you like it? Expresses a mood: How?
A lyric: *a snapshot* . . . . . . (etc. etc) . . .
  Blackboard:
  Shelley: Lyrical power   Keats: Descriptive power
            (Spontaneity)   (Word weaving)
            Snapshot `   Tapestry
            Men & world of   A dead world.
              today   Melancholy
            Belief in truth &   Belief in beauty
              knowledge

Application
Read as test St. 3 Ode to Autumn (G.T. 275)
Keats or Shelley? (Hands up).

It was in my first job, I remember, that I came to the solemn
conclusion that, if teaching were not demonstrably very inefficient
(less than 30% efficient it had been claimed), I would never dare to
face the responsibility of taking it up as a profession. And viewing the
statement in the terms in which I saw it then my self today would say
'amen'. But I see it differently now. I have shared in a movement
towards a conception of *learning* that gives quite a different meaning
to *teaching*—reduces it in fact to an ancillary of learning. And from this
perspective we can make our teaching as efficient as may be without
taking responsibility off the shoulders of the learner.

The counter-movement, however, is probably stronger and better
formulated today than it has ever been. Skinner's model of learning,
derived from experiments with animals but applied to human beings,
assigns to the teacher the full responsibility for deciding what is to be
learned and how. I am as likely to hear a writer of 'behavioural objectives' asking the student as to which responses to which stimuli are to
be reinforced as I am to hear Skinner asking a pigeon. I cannot accept
this emaciated view of the educational process; a view that marks
school learning off from all that goes on outside school—the pursuit of
curiosity, the random discovery, even the regime of asking and telling,
giving and taking, by which in daily life we profit from each other's
knowledge and wisdom. It is logical that Skinner should say, 'The
school of experience is no school at all, not because there is no learning
but because there is no teaching.'[2] It is surely nevertheless nonsense
to speak as though teaching could be thus disjoined from learning?

Psychologists, it seems to me, have usually tended to define learning too narrowly, to make it a special kind of human behaviour, tied to predetermined ends, associated with habit formation, and so on. I would prefer to recognize a learning aspect in a great variety of forms of human behaviour.

In fact, in recent years, another American psychologist, George Kelly, has elaborated a theory that does just that. His ideas are active in this country, though they have barely begun to make inroads where they are most needed—in psychology as a contribution to teacher education. George Kelly takes the scientist as his model for man, and sees learning in man as behaviour at its most typically human. Like the scientist, every man generates hypotheses from past experience, submits them to the test of actuality, and modifies his predictions in the light of what happens. All this is heady stuff as theoretical backing for what as teachers we have been learning from life; meanwhile, in practice, we need to model school learning upon the processes by which every helpless infant has become a more-or-less self-reliant individual before he reaches school at all.

One part of that transformation, of course, is of particular interest to us as English teachers. Moreover, it is on the grounds of this achievement—the way an infant learns to speak—that Noam Chomsky has launched the most formidable attack of all upon the Skinnerian model. Chomsky regards language as 'relatively stimulus-free behavior' and as such a mark of man's creativity. 'The child who learns a language,' he says, 'has in some sense constructed the grammar for himself on the basis of his observation of sentences and nonsentences.'[3] And John Lyons comments: 'Chomsky's criticisms of behaviourism are undoubtedly valid . . . There can be little doubt . . . that the behaviourist account of the acquisition of language, as formulated at present, fails to come to grips with, let alone, solve, the problem posed by what Chomsky calls "creativity".'[4]

The work of Chomsky and other linguists in recent years has certainly given strong support to a conviction on the part of English teachers that a child's own language is a precious means to his learning. To see how far this conviction has grown in the past forty years—despite Skinner and despite the opinions voiced in the Black Papers—one has only to compare, say the Plowden Report, with an official document issued in 1929, the year I began my teaching practice. Having recognized that 'Learning takes place through a continuous process of interaction between the learner and his environment' and that 'each new experience reorganises, however slightly, the structure of the mind and contributes to the child's world picture', the Plowden Report goes on to consider the role that talking plays in this interaction, and finds 'every justification for the conversation which is a characteristic feature of the contemporary primary school'.[5]

The 1929 document ('General Report on the Teaching of English in London Elementary Schools', published by H.M.S.O.) takes a very different view of language. It is based on the belief that 'the use of English . . . is a fine art, and must be taught as a fine art.' While the Report stresses the importance of developing in children 'the power to express themselves in speech and writing', the only assessment of work in spoken English carried out by the inspectors was in fact a test in 'recitation' and a test in reading aloud—from which we can draw few conclusions. It is in the comments on written work that the report really shows its hand. It makes a distinction here between 'the language of the home and the street' on the one hand, and 'the language the school is trying to secure' on the other: and it drives the point home by urging teachers to avoid setting young children subjects for writing which 'deliberately throw them into the atmosphere of their out of school life.' Instead, 'the child's exercises in writing English should be based upon what he reads and hears in school.'

From the report of Mr. John Trim's talk to LATE, 1953:

First, the dialect-speaking child should not be made to feel that his speech, which was to him after all an inherent part of his personality, is inherently bad, and that he consequently is inferior to someone else whose speech is not dialectal. . . . He should be taught, simply, that his kind of speech is that which Londoners use when talking ordinarily to each other. It is very good for this. We understand each other, and feel that we have something in common. . . .

Mr. Trim concluded by asking if this all seemed somewhat idealistic. It certainly made great demands on the teacher. It required of him knowledge, systematic knowledge about spoken English. . . . But by restricting the use of Standard Spoken English to those situations where it was required, it offered the possibility of avoiding inner and outer conflicts which must beset any child who undertook a fundamental revision of his speech in all aspects of life, cutting himself off from his past, and from his whole speech environment, the whole community in which he had had his being. In this way, by promoting bi-lingualism, (or multi-lingualism, since we had as many forms of speech as we had different personal relations) we made Standard Spoken English acceptable to a generation which was no longer afraid of being called working class.

The two policies represented by these documents are of course both alive in schools today. There are plenty of teachers whose energies are directed towards harnessing in the new situation the power of the language the children already possess—so legitimizing, confirming and extending learning processes already in existence. And there are plenty of other teachers who, as far as language is concerned, attempt something of a fresh start. A 'fresh start policy', though they do not realize it, will inevitably tend to cut off a child's principal means of entry into the new worlds that schools and teachers can offer.

*   *   *

There is one respect in which, from the thirties to the seventies, the whole perspective has changed. In the thirties, despite warning shots fired in 1926 by the Hadow Report—the grammar school was seen as a spearhead of social reform in education. It was the bright hope of the public sector, year by year eating away at the areas of privilege of the public schools, the private sector. It stood as it were alone in this democratic role, and all that seemed necessary was for more and more money to be devoted to providing such an education for children whose parents could not afford to pay for it. It was the 1944 Act that, in practice, crystallised out the 'dual system' (never more than nominally tripartite). The 1944 Act spelled out the planned provision at secondary level of a lower-grade education for lower-grade examinees.

> An LATE report reflects a view taken of literature and the VIth Form in 1952:
> The study of literature gives the moral training once given by the classics to all, but which now only a few continue into the Sixth Form. Literature helps to define right and wrong, and relates them to real life. It offers an experience of life and of human nature to the inexperienced; to the boys and girls we expect to be the future leaders, but whose sheltered studies at school and university seldom include those rough experiences they will not only meet, but be expected to control when they go out to work.

Even so, it was not till Floud and Halsey, Jackson and Marsden, and others in their wake, had demonstrated that the dual system, far from opening up new opportunities, was likely to have the effect of preserving the *status quo* in a (roughly) dual society, that the grammar school as democratic vision—if visions can do so—really turned sour.

> Another view of the Grammar School, twenty years earlier.
> From a Prize Day report, 1932:
> 'Take a little boy,' said Sir Percy Nunn, 'put him in a test-
> tube, pour in a little algebra, a little French, a little hand-
> work and so on, in the hope that the final product will be an
> educated man. It is a strange process, the chemistry of edu-
> cation, but it works.'

As in 1930 I looked for my first job in a state grammar school, so today I would look for it in a comprehensive school and for essentially the same reasons.

Reasons, too, no less fallible: something has certainly been achieved—the dual system has been recognized for what it is—but the problems indicated by Floud and Halsey, Jackson and Marsden, seem as far away as ever from solution. It is likely—as it has often been before—that English teachers will be the first to feel the increasing pressures, and the first who are constrained to look for alternative ap-proaches: and this by reason of the kind of preoccupations they share with the children they teach—their concern, among other things, with the quality and configuration of everyday experience.

The membership list for L.A.T.E. as it was first established looked, with a few exceptions, like a select gazetteer of London gram-mar schools. However, one of the first reports to be produced by a study group was on 'English in the Secondary Modern School', and by 1957 there was in existence a comprehensive school discussion group within L.A.T.E., holding regular meetings under the chairmanship of Guy Rogers, then headmaster of Walworth School. It represented a powerful extension of L.A.T.E.'s activities and brought into its mem-bership such people as John Dixon, whose book *Growth Through English*,[6] written some ten years later, must surely be the most widely influential book on the topic we are considering to be written within the period I have under review.

The story continues with the vastly enlarged opportunities that came with the formation of N.A.T.E., the National Association for the Teaching of English. As I remember it, it was a word dropped by Professor George Allen that sowed the first seed. An H.M.I. at the time, and chairman of the Secondary Schools Examinations Council's En-glish panel, George Allen took the opportunity of a panel meeting to remark that it was high time English teachers got together to form a national association: one panel member present was Denys Thompson—whose editorship of *The Use of English* dated back at least into the forties.

To tell the whole story, L.A.T.E. had several times been urged by groups of teachers in other parts of the country to set up a national association. Each time, after careful consideration, the committee had recommended that resources of time and energy were insufficient to allow us to take up the challenge. Each time they had, instead, encouraged the formation of a sister association and given what help they could to get it going. The first such group was the Forest A.T.E., formed in Essex in 1954; others followed in Fleet, (Lancashire) and Leicester, and finally in 1962, in Bristol.

At all events, Denys Thompson called together representatives of L.A.T.E. and the other A.T.E.'s, and of the 'Use of English Groups' that were by this time scattered about the country. They met, about twenty of them, on April 4th 1963, and as a result N.A.T.E. was born, with Professor Boris Ford as its first chairman.

Some of the most original and valuable work N.A.T.E. did in its early years concerned teaching in the primary school—the subject of its evidence to the Plowden Committee, and at the same time the object of a grant from the Calouste Gulbenkian Foundation, for the purposes of follow-up.[7] But my topic at the moment is the changing context of secondary school English—N.A.T.E. and the growth of comprehensive education.

That English panel meeting of the S.S.E.C. was one of the last to be held; it heralded, and not by coincidence, both the death of that body and the birth of the Certificate of Secondary Education, and N.A.T.E.'s early years were considerably taken up in the general hum of activity that brought teachers out of their classrooms and administrators out of their offices to get the C.S.E. Boards floated. N.A.T.E. made its voice effectively heard, publishing scrutinies both of the blue-prints and of the early achievements of the Boards, and turning some of its attention in a similar way to the G.C.E. machinery. No doubt it was the course of events that determined this focus upon examinations; yet, as we realised when we began to exchange ideas with English teachers in U.S.A., the role of public examinations in the secondary school system of this country is in subtle ways a key one.

Then came the Dartmouth Seminar, in the summer of 1966, and the transatlantic dialogue in our sphere began in earnest. Twenty representatives of English teaching in England were invited by NATE to meet a similar number of American representatives in New England and spend a strenuous month together. The whole affair was the brain-child of Dr. James Squire, then Executive Secretary of the National Council of Teachers of English. The Americans were our hosts, thanks to a grant from the Carnegie Foundation, and N.C.T.E. were joined in their sponsorship by the Modern Language Association of America. Frank Whitehead, NATE chairman, led the British contingent. The following year, largely as a result of the efforts of Merron

Chorny of Calgary (who had also attended the Dartmouth Seminar), a Canadian Council of Teachers of English was formed. Then in 1971 members of N.C.T.E., M.L.A., N.A.T.E. and C.C.T.E. met for a week's conference, 550 strong, at the University of York. Of the six 'commissions' planned for that conference, two were exclusively concerned with the secondary school and three more were concerned in part.

The transatlantic dialogue, highlighted by Dartmouth and York, has been an important source of new thinking about English teaching. We can look to America for the fruits of long experience of comprehensive education; from Britain we can contribute something of the dialectic of autonomous classrooms—disorganised often enough and sometimes ingenuous, but practical and comparatively free from dogma. Above all I think a ferment of ideas is likely to arise whenever diverse people experienced in widely different situations come together and discover common problems. (That is easy to say: but it takes genuine concern, commitment and sympathy to penetrate beyond alienating differences and find, from a common viewpoint, common problems.)

The dialogue at York, it appears to me, came to concentrate on two problems: that of 're-defining our subject *in the light of the needs of all children*'; and that of the relation between our conception of English teaching and the context—the educational system and beyond that the society—in which we tried to realise that conception.

Of the first it must be said that NATE had already amply demonstrated its commitment to the task. In 1968 it had organised, as a follow-up to Dartmouth, an Anglo-American Seminar on 'The Language of Failure': forty teachers, inspectors and administrators from both sides of the Atlantic spent twelve days at Walsall studying the relation between language and failure in school. Patrick Creber's recent book, *Lost for Words*,[8] is an important outcome of that seminar. The controversy now raging as to what is meant by 'language deficit' and 'cultural deficit' and what implications lie here for the re-definition, not of English alone but of the whole educational process— this is a far cry from the debate about grammar teaching:[9] the walls are down and we're facing some real weather—I hope.

The second problem from York is intimately related to the first and turns out no more comfortably. But I must make my own way towards it.

*   *   *

We have, I believe, made some real progress in recent years in this business of re-defining our subject. A kind of consensus is beginning to emerge and ideas and experience and research findings have seemed to fall in place behind it. It grows out of a concern for what language is and the many purposes for which we use it. Clearly we use it, in the first place, for all sorts of practical purposes: to inform or instruct or persuade people, and likewise to get information, to acquire knowledge or expertise, to consider the arguments and blandishments that others offer us. And these 'practical' purposes are not always so practical—they evolve into what we should probably call 'intellectual purposes': thus we may use language in an attempt to explain things to ourselves—to draw references, to construct theories, to speculate. The practical and the intellectual purposes share what I might call a common structure, a common mode of organisation. Psychologists, who have for generations been primarily interested in this kind of organisation, describe it as 'cognitive'. In using language in these ways, we take on responsibility for abiding by that organisation, obeying its rules. We take responsibility, for example, for the existence of the things we refer to in the real world, for the reasonableness of our generalisations, for the logic of our arguments.

But quite other rules seem to reflect quite a different kind of organisation when, let us say, we write (or read) poems, novels and plays. That these utterances are highly organised is something we feel certain about—in fact we might even feel that such writings primarily exist as an expression or experience *of order*. But it is a very difficult and perhaps impossible task—at present—to describe by what principle the order is achieved.[10] Perhaps the clearest thing about such writings is that they are *not* practical, they are not concerned to keep the world's affairs on the move. In fact they reflect above all our involvement in *what is not going on now*. For this reason we might say that when we use language in this way we are using it 'in the role of *spectator*'—and when we use it to keep the world's affairs moving, we use it in the role of *participant*.[11]

Then again we very frequently use language in ways where there seem to be very few rules applying of either kind, and where the 'organisation' seems loose or undemanding. When we chat with other people simply to enjoy their company, or to satisfy an interest in what they have been doing, or for the pleasure of recalling shared experiences, or to let off steam about things that have annoyed us or gloat over things that have pleased us—gossip or chat of this kind seems free to follow the personal whims and fancies of those taking part in it and to lay very few responsibilities upon them as speakers.

Such language has been called 'expressive'. To say that it is comparatively free of rules is to suggest that it is not very different from the kind of language we might use silently in speaking to ourselves. I would see it as a kind of 'matrix', a starting point from which the two other kinds develop. When the demands of a participant role—the need to get something done in the world—reach a certain point (and are met), I would call the resulting use of language *transactional;*

where the demands are of the other kind—those of spectator role—I would call the use that satisfies those demands *poetic*.[12] (As you might suppose, expressive language, loosely structured, is free to move at will from participant role to spectator or *vice versa:* it straddles, as it were, that dividing line.)

As English teachers we have more and more come to see our responsibilities as focussing upon the spectrum of language usage from the expressive to the poetic—language, in other words, in the role of spectator. Yes, we still recognize the difference between what Shakespeare wrote and what will come from the pen of a fourteen year old—in fact we are learning a little about the *nature* of those differences, the nature of the organisation that gives Shakespeare's writing so much power as *an experience of order*. Yet we value the ordering process the fourteen year old achieves in his writing as of the same *kind*. It follows that we see as essentially similar processes, directed towards a similar end, his response to Shakespeare's words and his shaping of his own experience in his own words. He can go further when he has Shakespeare at his elbow. Both his writing and his response are educationally important because they are assimilative processes—they reflect an individual's concern for the unity, coherence and order of his accumulated representation of the world he has lived in.

Of course this reflects a great deal that we have known for a long time about the importance of literature in a child's education. But it reflects it in a new way, relating it directly to the child's own use of language upon his own experience.

At this point we rub our eyes and realise that the other half of the spectrum of language uses—from expressive to transactional—is primarily the concern of those teachers and writing upon which the learning of their subjects relies. In fact, this conviction marked another milestone in the history of LATE. In a series of conferences and study-groups beginning in 1966 LATE worked up to a conference in 1968 on 'Language across the curriculum'. The ideas of Douglas Barnes, who had been looking at the language of teacher/pupil exchanges in the classroom, and of the Schools Council Writing Research Unit, were important contributions, but a principal outcome took a very practical form—an attempt to persuade school staffs to get together and thrash out 'a language policy' for work in their school throughout the curriculum. All this, and the thinking that led up to it, will be found set out in Harold Rosen's contribution to *Language, the Learner and the School*.[13]

In 1971 NATE devoted its annual conference to 'Language across the Curriculum'[14] and was able to secure the co-operation of teachers of other subjects and make valuable links with other subject associations. And the Schools Council Project, 'Writing across the Cur-

riculum, 11 to 13", set up that same year under Nancy Martin's direction, is actively exploring the implications of many of the ideas we
have touched on here—working with teachers in a variety of classroom
situations over a range of subjects and integrated programmes.[15]

Expressive speech, as we have seen, is the mode of language in
which we develop 'togetherness'—get to know people and enjoy the
company of those we know already. The expressive writing of personal
letters satisfies both writer and reader by using language *as though* in
each other's company, creating a virtual presence in absence. But expressive speech and writing embrace other purposes too: it is the form
of language in which we 'first-draft' our tentative or speculative ideas.
In other words, it is an essential mode for *learning*—for the tentative
exploration of new areas of knowledge. And it serves this purpose
precisely because it is free from constraints and uninhibiting. It be-
speaks a relationship of mutual trust between the parties, and it cannot
function adequately where that relationship does not exist. Thus, it is
not to be had simply on demand—any more than an angry call of
'Relax, will you!' can have the desired effect.

Of course, learning can take place wherever there is a motivated
learner and a teacher who knows. It has even been suggested that
conflict between the two may be helpful to the learning.[16] But all that
is no model for education in the broad sense. As school teachers we are
concerned with processes far more complex and more fundamental
than, for example, what passes between a learner-driver and his driv-
ing instructor. The achievement of a greater willingness to learn, the
achievement of a livelier curiosity—these are a part of the growth we
are trying to foster. Yet, as John Holt[17] and others have shown, what
comes through to the child is often the very reverse.

In general, teachers do not yet recognise the importance of language to the learning they are trying to secure, and this being so they
do not allow sufficient opportunities for the use of expressive speech
and writing. Central to the kind of understanding we need to promote
among all teachers will be the recognition that young children need to
use language almost wholly within the expressive band if they are to
build firm foundations; and that thereafter there should be a constant
returning to the expressive as exploratory stages on the way to a confident and efficient use of transactional language—the language of recording, reporting, arguing, theorising, speculating and any other
transaction required of scientists, geographers, historians and so on.
Then, having said that for all teachers, we need to add for the English
teacher that a similar relationship exists between the expressive and
poetic ends of that spectrum. The expressive is the natural medium for
talking or writing about our own experiences: its shaping, ordering
effect will be sharper as it moves towards and into the poetic; and the
expressive (both in spectator and participant roles) will be a principal

means by which students will enter into and interpret the stories, poems and plays that they read.

*   *   *

> From the recommendations made at the final plenary session of the York Conference in 1971:
> "We look for the opportunity to enquire further into such matters as the following:
>
> * the full implications of the non-authoritarian teacher role we are committed to, and how it relates to methods of control, school organisation and the form of the curriculum.
> * the re-defining of our subject in the light of the language needs of all children and their probable needs in a kind of society we cannot predict.

Clearly, what we have been looking at at some length is no more than the formulation from a limited linguistic point of view of a massive truth about the nature of the teaching/learning relationship. We have learnt from bitter experience that there is in the long run no means of enforcing learning. We have come to recognize that the most precious means to a child's progress in learning is his own acknowledged responsibility for it: and, complementary to that, that we have no diviner's powers or rights by which we could so predict the society he will live in that we dare take on that responsibility ourselves. We have come to accept that learning in school should be an extension and intensification of out-of-school learning, and that as a consequence we both seek to encourage students to learn from each other and recognise that we are constantly, as teachers, committed to reaping harvests we have not sown. And we know also that the kind of talk, writing and reading that best serves learning can flourish only in a situation of genuine trust.

(A massive 'truth', I have called it. Is it a truth? Is it a fallacy? What evidence am I offering? I can only, in the first place, state it as a growing conviction born of the experience of a growing number of teachers; and, in the second place, suggest that some of the evidence seems to support these ways of looking. Finally, I suppose, we have to live with a conception of our task that can satisfy us.)

What came forcibly home to us at York in 1971 was the fact that *teachers are where these things are to be learned:* where the experience of failure has often enough prepared the way for a revaluation, and the experience of individual successes—indeed experience in general in close contact with the learners—has suggested lines along which a revaluation must be made. Heads and administrators, however, have not that advantage. As a result, the system in which teachers' work grows less and less appropriate to what they are trying to do. It seemed clear to us at York that part of our efforts as associations must be directed towards influencing, not more teachers, but those who keep the educational system running.

Groups within the conference commissions were already concerned with such matters, but the conference's concern broke these bounds. As a result of action by individual members, the issue was raised for discussion in an open session, and following that a seventh un-planned commission was formed to devote itself wholly to the problem and its broader social implications. The work of 'Commission 7' goes on, and must do so. It may have a James Bondish ring to it, but there is nothing secret or sinister about it. It may run the danger of descending at times to pointless grumbling and destructive approaches. On the other hand, I know we have allies at all levels of the system: and we shall need them.

One thing is quite clear, there is no going back. The generation gap, teddy boys, the teenage cult, hippydom, the pill, the drug scene, the welfare state, student protest and student participation, earth-shrinking, electronic aids, and pigeons who play table-tennis—good and ill, they have all happened, or are happening. Get down to where it is all taking place and you will know that there is absolutely no future in trying to go back to the educational manners and methods that worked forty years ago.

References

1. *Language in Use*, by Peter Doughty, John Pearce and Geoffrey Thornton, Edward Arnold, 1971.
2. Quoted (without source) on the title-page of *Perspectives on Plowden* by R. Peters *et al.* Routledge and Kegan Paul, 1969.
3. Review of *Verbal Behaviour* (by B. F. Skinner) by Noam Chomsky, *Language*, Vol. 35, January–March, 1959. See page 57.
4. *Chomsky*, by John Lyons, Fontana Modern Masters Series, 1970, p. 85.
5. *Children and Their Primary Schools* (The Plowden Report). HMSO, 1967, pp. 521 and 535.
6. *Growth Through English*, by John Dixon, Oxford University Press, 1967, was a direct outcome of the Dartmouth Seminar I refer to later.

7. The publication produced by NATE as part of this follow-up was *Children Using Language,* edited by Anthony Jones and Jeremy Mulford, Oxford University Press, 1971.

8. *Lost for Words,* by J. W. P. Creber, Penguin Books, 1972.

9. See in this connection, *Language and Class* by Harold Rosen, Falling Wall Press, 1972.

10. Susanne Langer is concerned to explore this alternative form of organisation to the cognitive. See her *Philosophical Sketches,* Mentor Books, 1962, and *Mind: An Essay on Human Feeling,* Johns Hopkins Press, 1967.

11. For a fuller account see "The Role of the Onlooker" by D. W. Harding in *Scrutiny,* VI (3), 1937: and my *Language and Learning,* Penguin Books, 1972.

12. This description of language uses is drawn from the work of the Schools Council Writing Research Unit at the University of London Institute of Education, and I acknowledge my indebtedness to my colleagues in the unit, Miss Nancy Martin, Dr. Harold Rosen and Messrs. Tony Burgess, Dennis Griffiths, Alex McLeod, and Bernard Newsome.

13. *Language, the Learner and the School* by Douglas Barnes, James Britton and Harold Rosen. Penguin Books, Revised Edition, 1971. This also contains Douglas Barnes' contribution to the original.

14. For a full report see *English in Education,* Vol. 5 No. 2, 1971. Published for NATE by Oxford University Press.

15. Teachers are invited to write for further information to Writing Across the Curriculum Project, University of London Institute of Education, Malet Street, London WC1E 7HS.

16. See "Teaching" by Blanche Geer in *School and Society,* Open University Reader, Routledge and Kegan Paul, 1971.

17. *How Children Fail* by John Holt, Penguin Books, 1969.

18

Reflections on the Writing of the Bullock Report

The three years or so that separated the first meeting of the Bullock Committee from the publication of its Report in 1975 (*A Language for Life*, London, Her Majesty's Stationery Office) certainly provided me with a learning experience, perhaps a major one. Yet I do not relish the task of trying to say precisely what it is I learnt in that time.

I have, of course, a good deal of lumber: copies of papers produced by Committee members or presented to them; photostats of existing publications someone thought they ought to pay heed to; minutes of fifty-four meetings of the Committee and some twenty-five meetings of its sub-committees; successive drafts leading up to the final version of the Report; bundles of evidence submitted in writing, some of it brilliant, some fanatical, some blindingly obvious, and a lot of it modestly helpful to us at the time. I have called it lumber, but I preserve it with care since one day I may be able to turn the lumber into learning. Meanwhile, what do I know I have learnt?

I learnt, over many months, to question the possibility of affecting what goes on in schools through the particular means we were employing, that is, through the agency of a government-sponsored committee. It was at times exhilarating to find that ideas long nurtured in the various factions members belonged to had suddenly acquired the stamp of official approval, had been uttered, so to speak, in the establishment voice. But then followed a doubt as to whether the act of official formulation was in fact a further and enhancing stage in the long process of nurturing, or whether it might be a step in reverse. If nurturing an idea means getting more of the appropriate people to think about it for themselves, might its transmogrification into official dogma result in *less* of that thinking, more of a taking for granted? Ironically, one of the very ideas that gained this promotion into the establishment is itself a relevant principle to apply at this point: the

Foreword to *Teaching for Literacy: Reflections on the Bullock Report*, Frances Davis and Robert Parker (eds.), Ward Lock Educational, 1978. Reprinted by permission.

185

Report urges teachers to take more account of students' 'intentions' as a means of facilitating their learning. The context is that of learning to write:

> The solution lies in a recognition on the part of teachers that a writer's intention is prior to his need for techniques. The teacher who aims to extend the pupil's power as a writer must therefore work first upon his intentions, and *then* upon the techniques appropriate to them . . . Spontaneity then becomes capable of surviving the transition from artlessness to art; or in plainer terms, of supporting a writer in his search for new techniques appropriate to his novel intentions. (p. 104)

But if nurturing an idea about teaching and learning (such as that particular one) involves the generating of new insights and hence novel intentions on the part of teachers, is it not possible that an officially published brief injunction might appear to the teacher as no more than *other people's* intentions with respect to his behaviour?

I learnt to raise this question, but not to answer it. My doubts were not resolved when, after a brief round of debate in 'launching' the Bullock Report in this country, I went to Australia and attended a conference in which teachers and advisers and researchers were discussing the problems of 'language across the curriculum'. I discovered that a great deal of activity, of the 'nurturing' kind, was going on in many parts of the Australian Commonwealth, and I thought that maybe they were fortunate in *not* having an injunction laid at the door of every school to produce a 'language policy for the whole curriculum'. Such an injunction, at its most misunderstood, might result in no more than a concerted witch-hunt against bad spelling and punctuation!

Secondly, I have learnt something about the way people's theories relate to their practices. In a sense this is obvious and familiar enough, but confrontation regularly over a period with consistent differences between the way people behave and the way their theories (presumably) *explain* and *justify* that behaviour to themselves I did find illuminating. The matter is far more complex than the proverbial distinction between 'do as I say' and 'do as I do'. For example, someone who adheres to a conventional behaviourist theory of learning may consistently behave, as a learner and as a teacher—or, in the situation of a committee, in the strategies he uses to expound his own views and explore other people's—in ways that are far more adequately explained in terms of a humanistic, cognitive theory. Alternatively, someone who justifies the classroom practices in his school by appealing to humanistic psychology may seem consistently to employ techniques of reinforcement, positive and negative, in order to get the better of an argument. It follows that we cannot make a simple judgment upon the value of anyone's contribution to the educational enterprise; and that too ready recognition of educational 'factions' may obscure many of the subtleties of likeness and difference. (To accept 'neutrality' at this point as a way of solving the dilemma would be a gross misconstruction: rather we are forced back to reaffirm the importance for all practitioners of arriving at theories that will empower rather than frustrate their behaviour.) It is my overriding impression that teaching experience—the repeated intuitive response to teaching/learning confrontations—makes teachers much more alike in their behaviour than in the theories they rely on to explain and justify that behaviour. But the simple logic of behaviourist learning theory has an obvious appeal to administrators because it makes evaluating, accounting and planning seem much more feasible; and administrators, by persuading or overriding teachers, have frequently succeeded in having such theory applied in the classroom. Where this happens, 'intentions' (as we envisaged them above) have no place in the programme, and the gap thus created we feverishly try to fill under the label of 'motivation'. In my view, accountability should be truly seen as the teacher taking full responsibility for the behaviour of the daily confrontation; and only a learning theory that adequately explains both his successes and his failures in the confrontation can help him discharge that responsibility.

My experience on the Bullock Committee, then, serves to underline the importance to teachers of a rationale, a theory that is consistent with and supportive of their practices. It provides us with a running code of operational principles, a way of monitoring our own practice, a way of effectively influencing other people and defending our own position.

I learnt also a good deal about the nature of compromise and the ways in which it operates. The Chairman, Sir Alan Bullock (now Lord Bullock), repeatedly reminded members that they must resist the temptation to overstate their views for the sake of reducing the scope of wilful misrepresentation. It is a fair point: wilful misrepresentation is always possible and it is pointless to try to guard against it—and worse than pointless if in doing so we distort our views in stating them. And yet there is still a problem: a view that is innocently stated in good faith may be adequate communication to a reader who comes halfway to meet it, but if it is to challenge another reader to *change* his view, it will need to carry conviction by anticipating and countering his objections. Now it must surely be recognized that the language of establishment documents has been evolved, amongst other things, to give as little unnecessary offence as possible. This results very often in a general air of lack of conviction. In the case of the Bullock Report, I believe its establishment status, the size and diversity of views of the membership, the amount of data it was expected to handle, all militated against the production of a forthright and convincing document. Compare it, for example, with the Report of the Study Group on Linguistic Communication to the National Institute of Education (USA)[1]: in session at the same time as the Bullock Committee and working in the same field, ten members were able in less than two weeks to prepare a report that carries more conviction and more daring speculation than was possible in the full-scale British enquiry, with twenty members working for two years.

The compromise that creeps into the finally edited wording of a committee document is perhaps the most difficult kind to control. An individual writer's words will very often both make his statement and at the same time, by means which it may be difficult to identify, make clear the direction from which the statement is 'projected'. For the sake of stylistic uniformity, the corporate document must sacrifice these individual signposts and take on instead the tones of an echoing oracle, coming from everywhere. After making allowances for some inevitable toning down, however, it is disturbing to find that a member's original draft may undergo compromising amendment such as the following. In the chapter on writing, at a point where the relation between language study and performance in writing is being considered, the original draft ran:

> Explicit rules and facts about language (that is to say the outcomes of other people's studies) probably have direct practical value to the language user only insofar as they solve problems in the tasks he is engaged on, or insofar as he is able to reconstruct for himself the analysis that led to the rule. It is the neglect of these limiting conditions that has led to much profitless language work in schools.

But the version finally approved by the Committee has clearly lost *en route* something of its directed thrust:

> Explicit rules and facts about language, that is to say the outcomes of other people's studies, have direct practical value to a pupil when (a) they solve particular problems in the tasks he is engaged on, or (b) he is able to reconstruct for himself the analysis that led to the rule. (p. 162)

I believe the Bullock Committee was fortunate in that this kind of drafting drift into compromise was not a frequent occurrence, and I would add that these should be judged alongside a sense of amazement that with so vast an input to interpret and so diverse a company of interpreters the Report ever got written at all!

Where such changes did occur, however, they were symptomatic of a much more general and far-reaching impulse to compromise inherent in the whole situation. When Mrs. Margaret Thatcher, as Minister of Education, set up the Committee of Enquiry into Reading and the Use of English, she selected as members representatives of the principal factions, or schools of thought, in the field and chose a neutral chairman—someone not already credited with views on the controversial issues since his expertise lay in a different field. One must suppose that Mrs. Thatcher believed that what was important about the learning and teaching of the mother tongue lay at a deeper level, was more fundamental, than the issues over which people disagreed. In effect, she called together a disparate crew and told them she fervently hoped for a unanimous report. The Chairman, Sir Alan Bullock, seems to have shared this view, since from beginning to end he worked to have the Committee produce a report which all members would sign. He succeeded, though the substantial list of reservations itemised by one member after signing somewhat vitiates the success. In any case, its cost in time and effort was enormous: a majority view, as distinct from a unanimous one, would have been far easier to reach and would have constituted a document with more conviction. In other words, the situation created had the effect of ensuring that compromise was built into the production from the outset. I emerged from the experience more convinced than ever that the issues over which there are sharply conflicting views about English teaching are the fundamental, formative issues. Harold Rosen[2], in a published critique of the Report, makes the point very well. He writes:

> It is not difficult to detect behind the Report's fair and mostly dispassionate tones the fact that in matters of language and the teaching of English in particular the battle-lines have been drawn. However faint they may seem there is no doubt that the fiercest debates are between those who believe in carefully constructed linear programmes, buttressed by claims for sequence, system and structure, and those who believe that development in language can only be achieved by working in a much more flexible and open-ended way.

It was when the approved versions of the various chapters finally came together for the first time that I realized the full effect of the thousand and one particular compromises that had been made throughout the drafting. The picture that emerged seemed to me altogether too firmly drawn, as though the problems did not exist to which the Committee had no answer. The compromises, in other words, had been reductive in effect, an avoidance of many of the real complexities; what had been lost was precisely a sense of openness and flexibility. It was at this stage that I drafted my own reservations, which became, in the course of the ensuing argument, an appended 'Note of Extension' to the Report.

A few months after the Report was published, I retired and spent the next two years teaching mainly in Canada, with visits to the States and Australia. Back in England now, in 1977, I must say that the Bullock Report begins to look like a beacon that shines brighter and brighter as the skies around it darken. Amid all the talk of 'literacy' and 'evaluation', both very narrowly conceived, can it survive to keep before us a more enlightened view of language and learning? The darkening skies are certainly not a local phenomenon, but belong at least to the whole Western world: inflation brings anxiety, and anxiety will tend to reduce the number of factors we are prepared to take into account in making a judgment. In a time of shrinking perspectives, educational perspectives are particularly vulnerable if for no other reason than that schools constitute a large part of the national budget.

I do not believe that 'enlightened education' (meaning, in its true sense, 'progressive education') is part of any bandwagon, or fashion cycle, or pendulum swing; it is a slowly growing movement with philosophical roots way back in the past and pragmatic roots deep in the intuitive wisdom of the most successful teachers today. It has not been tried and found wanting: as the Bullock Committee Survey was able to indicate, it has as yet barely achieved a foothold in the schools of this country.[3] I doubt whether there was ever a time when it was more important, or more difficult, than it is today to keep these ideas alive. I hope the Bullock Report, despite all my earlier reservations, will finally prove its worth as an aid and support to those who are trying to do so.

References

1. G. A. Miller, ed., *Linguistic Communication: Perspectives for Research*, International Reading Association, 1974.
2. Harold Rosen, ed., *Language & Literacy in our Schools: Some Appraisals of the Bullock Report*, University of London Institute Studies in Education 1, 1975.
3. See Bullock, the tables on pp. 373 & 376 (where 'vertical grouping' may be taken as the formal indicator of a 'progressive school', whereas the data reported show little departure from traditional methods).

19

Language in the British
Primary School

Every thoughtful primary school teacher would agree, I believe, that it is a very difficult matter to assess the quality of learning that is going on in any classroom. But if it is difficult for the teacher, who is *there*, what of the parents and the public, who are not? No wonder they are so easily misled by the dogmatic pronouncements of the Black Paper campaigners. This may be one of the main reasons why popular opinion tends to fall in behind such views. Clearly, five minutes in a formal teaching situation is enough to demonstrate that useful information is being retailed: but to judge the quality of *learning* on this basis is like estimating the state of nurture of a nation by considering the size of its butter mountain or its reserves of dried milk. As every teacher knows, when you tell thirty children something, only some of them will have been told.

The 'British Primary School' has not lacked for enthusiastic supporters in many parts of the world. Long before the Plowden Report[1] came out this was true, but the 'image' and the Report have certainly sustained each other, and have made, I believe, an effective contribution to the work of innovators in other systems. Of course, when overseas visitors spend time themselves in our schools they often report that the 'image' and the reality fall far apart. It must be recalled that the survey of teaching procedures carried out for the Bullock Committee gave pretty convincing evidence that informal or 'progressive' methods had barely a foothold in our primary schools so far as language work was concerned. Yet the detractors continue to ignore this evidence. A recent *Times* reports publication of a document prepared by the Monday Club which reiterates the familiar charge: "Literacy and numeracy standards among 10-year-olds were a national disgrace, the paper says. It attributes the alleged decline in standards to too much 'progressive' teaching, and it calls for national standards to be set

Published in "Forum" 21 (2), Spring, 1979. First delivered at a conference on primary education organized by the educational journal, "Forum."

in both literacy and numeracy."[2] The focus of the reactionary attack is now on the primary school because the one view it shares with its protagonists is a belief that the most promising solution of our undoubted secondary school problem would be to get things right in the preceding stages.

The Bullock Report[3] has also been influential in other English-speaking countries, but it is, I believe, a less radical document than Plowden. The Bullock Committee was set up to represent all factions, yet both Mrs. Thatcher and the Chairman she appointed were eager to secure a unanimous report, presumably on the grounds that the issues that really matter lie at a more fundamental level than those that divide us. I don't think a reading of the Report bears out that view: what comes over, I believe, is a somewhat watered-down form of a 'progressive' view, with some important anomalies and ambiguities. In particular, I think it offers cold comfort to radical innovators who, in their classrooms, are beginning to devise solutions to the most difficult of the inner-city secondary-school problems.

The year the Report came out, 1975, was the year of my retirement and I spent most of the next two years teaching in Canada and Australia. I returned to what seemed, from the point of view of educational climate, a very different England. The 'Great Debate' was in full swing, launched by a speech from the Prime Minister which had a good deal to say about literacy but made no reference to the Bullock Committee's views on that topic. 'Literacy', in fact was one of the words on everybody's lips, and 'evaluation' was the other. I soon began to feel that the Bullock Report was a beacon that shone ever more brightly as the skies around it darkened. Not that 'literacy' and 'evaluation' as concerns are in themselves agents of darkness, but they require wise handling and are all too easily mishandled for ulterior purposes. A narrow focus on literacy may result in the rejection of the spoken uses of language from which literacy must grow; notions of evaluation become threatening when they see it, not as a way of generating information useful to the system, but as a means of enforcement, whether upon teachers or upon pupils. On both literacy and evaluation, the hidden protagonists are two sharply divided views of teaching and learning.

The Plowden Report was clear about the importance of talk as a means of learning. It placed a high value on "the direct impact of environment on the child and the child's individual response to it" (para. 544), recognised the unique role of language as an organiser of experience, and so found that there was "every justification for the conversation which is a characteristic feature of the contemporary primary school" (para. 535). The Bullock Report in its earlier chapters is equally forthright and pursues the ideas a little further: "(i) all genuine learning involves discovery, and it is as ridiculous to suppose that teaching begins and ends with instruction as it is to suppose that 'learning by discovery' means leaving children to their own resourses; (ii) language has a heuristic function; that is to say a child can learn by talking and writing as certainly as he can by listening and reading" (para. 4.10). To a teacher in the old tradition, as to the public, it is common knowledge that a child learns by listening to the teacher and reading the textbook, and there is no need to look any further. But this view is based on a misunderstanding of the processes involved: "Once it is understood that talking and writing are means to learning, those more obvious truths that we learn also from other people by listening and reading will take on a fuller meaning and fall into a proper perspective. Nothing has done more to confuse current educational debate than the simplistic notion that 'being told' is the polar opposite of 'finding out for oneself'. In order to accept what is offered when we are told something, we have to have somewhere to put it; and having somewhere to put it means that the framework of past knowledge and experience into which it must fit is adequate as a means of interpreting and apprehending it. Something approximating to 'finding out for ourselves' needs therefore to take place if we are to be successfully told. The development of this individual context for a new piece of information, the forging of the links that give it meaning, is a task that we customarily tackle by talking to other people". (4.9). Teaching by seminar, a strategy based on this principle of learning by talking, is sometimes ridiculed by its opponents as a "pooling of ignorances". But there is one sort of gain to be had from discussing a topic with those who share our ignorance, and our struggle to understand, and another complementary gain from discussing it with an expert, the teacher. Good teaching consists in relating these two processes in a productive manner. But this account of language in learning is incomplete until we have admitted also learning by reading, learning by listening to the teacher's monologue. Rightly phased, these can be crucial highlights: but that phasing implies that the reading and listening should be spaced out with intervals for the students' own talk, sometimes with the expert, sometimes with each other. Finally, learning by writing is most typically the 'harvesting' stage, when what has been talked about and thought about is worked on, solitarily, from the standpoint of the writer's own synthesis. A little hard evidence on the learning value of writing was shown in a report of an experiment by Howe[4]: half the students attending a lecture undertook to make notes, the other half not to; after a brief revision session, some little while later, at which the note-takers had their own notes and the others had the lecturer's notes, a series of recall tests demonstrated the superior recall of those who had undertaken the writing, that is, the note-taking.

The Black Paper retort to the paragraph I have quoted from the Bullock Report did not have to await the publication of the report; it was voiced by a Committee member in his 'Note of Dissent": "It is doubtful if children's talk in school does much to improve their knowledge, for free discussion as a learning process is notoriously unproductive. As for children learning by writing, this seems a very doubtful proposition. The writer can only write from his present knowledge and experience and in the case of children these are very limited" (p. 558). A similar view is put forward by Jeanette Williams (in the juggernaut she calls 'a critique' of our Writing Research), when she complains that encouraging a child to use expressive talk and writing is "in a sense imprisoning the child in a web of commonsense concepts"[5]. We must infer that behind the two opposing views of the nature of teaching and learning lie very different conceptions as to the nature of our knowledge of the world.

George Kelly[6] began one of his psychological papers: "This paper, throughout, deals with half-truths only. Nothing that it contains is, or is intended to be, wholly true. The theoretical statements propounded are no more than partially accurate constructions of events which, in turn, are no more than partially perceived". And he goes on to explain: "When a scientist propounds a theory he has two choices: he can claim that what he says has been dictated to him by the real nature of things, or he can take sole responsibility for what he says and claim only that he has offered one man's hopeful construction of the realities of nature." This agrees in substance with things said by Karl Popper, a philosopher whose conclusions in other respects have been very different from Kelly's. Popper[7] showed that scientific hypotheses cannot be established as true: they can be proved false, but unless and until that happens they "forever remain hypotheses or conjectures" For this part, he draws no hard and fast line between our commonsense and theoretical or scientific concepts: "I tried to show that our knowledge grows through trial and error-elimination, and that the main difference between its prescientific and its scientific growth is that on the scientific level we consciously search for errors: the conscious adoption of the critical method becomes the main instrument of growth" (p. 115). Such methods, he claims, are widely applicable beyond the bounds of science.

I believe a concern for the mastery of theoretical concepts begins with a respect for the commonsense concepts from which they must grow: that the mastery itself is a process of modifying commonsense concepts, and that mature thinking involves moving *back and forth* along a continuum from theoretical to commonsense, from abstract to concrete, from the fruits of analysis to the data of experience.

Here is a 9-year-old writing about his first 'scientific experiment' in school: "1. The *paper* crinkled up and then went smaller and black.

It was very brittle and thin at the end. It turned to ashes so if we breathed on it hard it flew all over the place. . . . 2. The *cotton cloth* burned and fringed at the same time. But the amazing thing was that the threads separated or in other words parted so that you could see through them like from the inside you can see through net curtains. 5. The *cotton yarn* at first looked like little worms crawling about and then the flame covered and smoothed it like a sheet covering your face."[8]

Learning to observe and record is an essential part of the learning process in science. It involves sorting the objective from the subjective aspects of the experience recorded and the rejection of the latter for the purpose of mustering and organising the former. But our everyday speech and expressive uses of writing demand no such separation; what happened and how what happened affected us, our feelings about the events, are intertwined in our experience and we normally expect our listeners or readers to be interested in both aspects. Expressive speech and writing naturally carries both: the very words that denote the events are likely also to carry something of our feelings about them (as when we say, "I hear Arsenal made mincemeat of Chelsea" rather than the announcer's "Arsenal 4, Chelsea Nil"). Thus scientific recording requires the use of informative writing, not expressive: but the move from one to the other on a child's part involves the difficult piece of learning I have been describing, and that must be given time. To allow expressive writing (like that of the nine-year-old above) in the early stages enables the teacher to monitor that learning in progress, and plots for the student its gradual achievement. It seems to me that attempts to hasten the process threaten to divorce the scientific facts to be handled from the experiences that give rise to them. It is all too likely then that rote learning from the textbook will replace the development of a true scientific understanding. What is true for science is true also for all environmental and historical studies. The philosopher Ernst Cassirer once said of learning in history: "If I put out the light of my own personal experience I cannot see and I cannot judge of the experience of others".[9]

Expressive speech and writing are forms of discourse which come naturally to us in situations of mutual trust, and as such they embody the teaching/learning relationship we try to establish with every child. Further, because there is trust there is also a willingness to take risks—and the exploration of new experiences, the acceptance of new information, the move to a new viewpoint, demand that a learner should take risks.[10] A campaign for literacy can all too easily be used as a weapon in the hands of those who oppose these educational processes because they do not understand them.

Among the things currently being said about evaluation is the statement that evaluation is an inseparable part of teaching. I want to

claim that while evaluation is part of a teacher's responsibility it
should be kept as distinct from teaching as possible, and we should
know when we are doing the one and when we are doing the other.
Clearly, we can take the argument no further until we have broken
down the term 'evaluation' and see the different things that it might
refer to.

Since education is a public expense, I believe it has to be ac-
countable to the public, and that there must therefore be some form of
national 'monitoring' to provide a comprehensible glimpse, as it were,
of what goes on in schools. The Bullock Report goes into some detail
as to how this might be done without interfering with the processes it
sets out to evaluate. The essential features are that it should assess
what teachers in fact try to teach (wherever this can be done), that
there should be no single test or 'instrument' which might have the
effect of distorting or restricting what they teach, and that no attempt
should be made to measure the whole performance (in a given subject)
of a particular pupil or a particular school. This form of national assessment is thus kept clear of other forms of evaluation and their purposes. From the evidence of the document "Language Performance"[11],
I am very happy with the plans devised by the Assessment of Performance Unit for carrying out this national evaluation of work in language.

Consider next the evaluation procedures required for the man-
agement of local resources—psychological services, additional teaching strength, specialist teachers, supplementary budgets and so on. I
think we need to keep a careful watch at this level: do the testing
procedures yield information which will be used to benefit
children?—both because it is the right information and because resources exist to respond to it. Evaluation of innovative
programmes—which might be within a school or Education Authority
or more widely—is yet another distinct purpose and one that need not
concern us here. Very little such work is done because very little is
known about how to do it. That brings us to the heart of the problem
for my purposes here—evaluation by the teacher.

Before tackling it, however, I want to suggest that in all these
other forms of evaluation there is a danger that the procedures will be
misused as instruments of enforcement upon teachers. This was nota-
bly the case with the behavioural objectives movement in North America. For many administrators the enforcement aspect was overt and
systematic: teachers were to formulate their objectives in accordance
with approved policies *in order to be held to them.* Similarly in this
country, Rhodes Boyson has expressed the view that H.M.I.s ought to
return to their one-time role and go round classrooms checking that the
teaching of the 3 R's is satisfactory—as a direct counter-measure, I

assume, to the spread of 'progressive' teaching methods. Claims of this sort at this time could, I believe, be multiplied. I think they are ill-based because enforcement by this means does not achieve what it sets out to do and because in the long run it lowers the quality of teaching. It is ineffective in the general sense that what happens in any classroom is the result of interacting teacher and pupil behaviours: the gap between any regulation, guideline or other sort of 'recipe' and the actual behaviour of the teacher is one that only the teacher can fill. At his most effective he fills that gap from *conviction*—indeed, so many second-by-second decisions contribute to it that anything more remote than inner conviction has little chance of being consistently applied. I would use this argument equally to oppose the notion of 'teacher-proof' project kits and enforcement by evaluative procedures. The long-term adverse effects are best described as the substitution of a 'regime of surveillance' for a 'regime of trust'. The productive value of a regime of trust between teacher and pupil can be matched by that expected from a relationship of trust between teachers and the public—and the intermediary agents, parents, principals and administration. Admittedly, it can be shown that not all teachers are trustworthy: but the loss we sustain when, in a more open regime, they are able to 'get away with things' is nothing, in my view, compared with the effects of loss of morale on the part of the average teacher and, more particularly, on the part of the best teachers in the system, when trust gives way to surveillance.

To deal briefly with evaluation in school, I think, as teachers, we have to accept responsibility for generating information about pupil performance which will be useful to parents, succeeding teachers, placement agencies, and, at a later stage, employers and admission agencies. If for the moment we can restrict the term evaluation (in school) to that process, I would stress that this evaluative function should be kept distinct from our teaching function. "Teacher didn't want to *read* my story, she only wanted to *mark* it!" was the comment of a six-year-old in an infant school, and it is the distinction he recognised that concerns me here. We are more than ever supported today in a belief that children demonstrate a mastery in achieving their own intentions that they do not show in working to somebody else's purposes. Linguists have discovered that a young child's mastery of syntactic structure cannot be truly assessed from their responses to presented test questions, but only by observing their spontaneous utterances[12]. With this support, primarily from cognitive psychologists, we have grown more expert in our attempts to tap children's own intentions in school, and at arousing new intentions in directions in which we foresee their developing needs and powers. Yet it is my contention that the 'evaluative frame of mind' that we have allowed to become a part of the teacher's stance—the readiness to 'mark' rather than 'read'—prevents us from reaping the full benefit of these attempts. Courtney Cazden comments on one aspect of this evaluative habit of mind: "But teachers, over the decades if not over the centuries, have somehow gotten into the habit of hearing with different ears once they go through the classroom doors. Language forms assume an opaque quality. We cannot hear through them; we hear only the errors to be corrected. One value of knowledge about language is not to make the language of our children more salient to our attention. Quite the opposite. That knowledge reassures, and it lets language forms recede into the transparency they deserve, enabling us to talk and listen in the classroom as outside, focussing full attention on the children's thoughts and feelings that those forms express."[13]

If we succeed in harnessing or arousing a child's intention—to write something, perhaps, or to read something—we shall release in him tacit powers favourable to his success, and it is in that process of satisfying his own intention that he will learn most effectively. But if we then 'evaluate' his performance—in my present sense of the word, that of giving a mark or grade or comment which will indicate a 'verdict' upon his performance—then we are in effect providing an alternative objective to his own satisfaction. In fact the evaluation becomes the real objective, his satisfaction no more than an ostensible one. The evaluating procedure, in fact, *drives a wedge between a child's intention and its satisfaction.* A typical intention for a piece of expressive writing on the part of a ten-year-old, for example, might be his wish to establish and maintain a relationship with the teacher who reads it: he will know whether his writing has succeeded by the way he feels about the growing relationship. The teacher's response will aim at maximising this aspect of the exchange as the best way of ensuring its learning value. In reading and responding appropriately he will have fulfilled his teaching function: for his evaluating function, he will, at the end of the term or the year, help the child select some of his writings (perhaps including this particular piece), and this work will be multiply marked (by the teacher and a colleague) to arrive at the informative evaluation of the child's progress which will go to parents, other teachers and so on. 'Responding appropriately' may, of course, include very helpful detailed 'feedback'—the comments of someone better able than the child to overcome the difficulties we meet in trying to say what we mean: but this, in my terms, is not 'evaluation' but 'guidance'—the heart of teaching.

That leaves one gap to be filled: since a teacher's intention is to teach, he must continually monitor his efforts in terms of the learning that goes on in those he teaches. This is indeed inseparable from teaching, but the information generated is for the teacher's guidance, is constantly sought, interpreted and applied, and may have no relevance to the child, his parents or any other agency.

I want in conclusion to remind readers that the 'enlightened' view of teaching and learning we profess is not an outmoded bandwagon, representative (as I have heard it said) of 'the dependent sixties'. It is, in fact, not a bandwagon at all, nor a pendulum swing. It is a steady, slow growing movement that has roots in philosophy back to Dewey and beyond; and is deep-rooted in the intuitions of the most successful teachers over a much longer period than that. It is under attack in many countries today as an effect, I believe, of the worldwide inflationary recession. I am not thinking primarily of budgets, a setback we can survive: I think the psychological effects of the recession are much more intractable. Psychologists have often enough pointed out that one of the first effects of anxiety in a person is a reduction in the number of factors he is prepared to take into account in arriving at a decision; and I believe the same can be seen at the level of whole societies. People today are asking difficult questions in all directions, but the educational system is particularly vulnerable. Typical of U.S.A., the question there has taken the form of 'How much for the dollar?'; but the formulation fits well enough what is going on elsewhere in the world. The narrowing of educational perspectives is variously reflected here in the views of the public, of parents, in the Black Papers, the administration at all levels, and in the views of many teachers themselves. However, I think we can already see signs of the worst being over: as recession itself recedes I believe perspectives will widen again. But meanwhile, in the difficult five years, say, that lie ahead, it seems to me more than ever important that the ideals that created the image of 'the British Primary School', and the practices that supported it, should be kept alive.

References

1. Central Advisory Committee for Education, *Children and Their Primary Schools* (Plowden Report), HMSO, 1967.
2. *The Times*, Educational Correspondent, 13th September 1978.
3. Department of Education and Science, *A Language for Life* (Bullock Report), HMSO, 1975.
4. M. J. A. Howe, "Taking Notes and Human Learning", *Bulletin* of the British Psychological Society, Vol. 28, April, 1975.
5. J. Williams, *Learning to Write or Writing to Learn?* N.F.E.R. Publishing Company, 1977, p. 47.
6. George A. Kelly, "Man's Construction of His Alternatives", 1958, reprinted in B. Maher, ed. *Clinical Psychology and Personality*, Wiley & Sons, 1969, p. 66.

7. Karl Popper, *Unended Quest,* Fontana, 1976, p. 79.
8. With grateful acknowledgements to Mrs. Heather Kay for permission to quote this extract.
9. Ernst Cassirer, *An Essay on Man,* Yale University Press, 1944, p. 187.
10. James Britton, Tony Burgess, Nancy Martin, Alex McLeod & Harold Rosen, *The Development of Writing Abilities, 11–18,* Macmillan, 1975, pp. 81–82.
11. Department of Education and Science, *Language Performance,* Assessment of Performance Unit, 1978.
12. D. I. Slobin and C. A. Welsh, "Elicited Imitation as a Research Tool in Developmental Psycholinguistics" in *Language Training in Early Childhood Education,* ed. C. S. Lavatelli, University of Illinois Press, 1971.
13. Courtney B. Cazden, "How Knowledge about Language Helps the Classroom Teacher—or Does It?" *Urban Review,* 1977, pp. 74–90.

20

English Teaching: Retrospect and Prospect

The James McAuley Memorial Lecture and Conference Opening Address [of the Third International Conference on the Teaching of English, Sydney, 1980].

My first contact with Professor James McAuley was in August 1971 when he traced me to the University of Connecticut and telephoned to invite me to the UNESCO Conference in Sydney in the summer of 1972. In April 1972 I was in New York for a meeting of the International Steering Committee (a post-Dartmouth committee representing USA, Canada and England) and from that meeting came a letter to Jim McAuley inviting AATE to be represented on that committee. Just a year later, the invitation having been accepted, Jim himself attended a meeting of the committee in London, and paid a visit to my home *en route*. There he met also Merron Chorny and John Dixon (both of them here today). It was a fascinating evening.

I remember him above all as poet and politician—and that's an interesting combination. He was, as you will know, a native of these parts and a graduate of this university. You may not know that his gifts as poet and politician made him notorious on one occasion, when with his fellow poet, Harold Stewart, he brought off a famous literary hoax: a modernist literary journal published the work of one "Ern Malley"—a random concoction drawn from diverse sources that included a scholarly American report on the drainage of mosquito breeding grounds. The motive—to protest the kind of verses being produced at that time in Britain by such writers as Dylan Thomas and Henry Treece.

Poet and politician. When James McAuley got on to politics he was liable, to quote a line of his own poetry, to "thrust his speech among them like a sword". On that evening in 1973 we had talked the politics of English teaching; but before the evening was over we per-

Published in *English in the Eighties*, papers given at the Third International Conference on the Teaching of English, Sydney, 1980. Edited by Robert D. Eagleson for the Australian Association for the Teaching of English, 1982. Reprinted by permission.

suaded him to round it off by reading some of his own poetry—and that is how I remember him best. It is appropriate, however, to remember that his political acumen lies behind the realisation today of a proposal he put before the International Steering Committee in 1973—that there should be, in 1979 or 1980—an international English conference in Australia.

I wonder what Jim McAuley would have said had he been standing here today, faced with this topic, "English Teaching: Retrospect and Prospect"? I certainly cannot speak for him. Nor shall I attempt a "state of the art" summative statement. The more I see of such oracular, even cabbalistic, statements—my own or other people's—the less am I tempted to embark on another one. I can offer you my retrospect, my perspective on the future and it will be no more than a personal statement—one man's hopeful construction of the realities of English teaching, as George Kelly would have put it.

I set up shop as an English teacher in a state secondary school fifty years ago next month. The year before I began, in 1929, there was published an official report on *The Teaching of English in the Elementary Schools of London*. A curious document. Among other recommendations it warned teachers to "draw a sharp distinction between the language of the home and the street and the language the school is trying to achieve". And it went so far as to suggest that teachers should not set children to talk or write about their homes or neighbourhoods, because that would be inviting them to use the wrong language. (Some of you have heard me refer to that before—how can I but repeat myself when I talk so much?)

There are plenty of teachers in our various countries who still operate "a fresh start policy" for language in their classrooms. But we have made some advances in fifty years: no official statement would dare to put forward so linguistically naive and ignorant a view today. Thirty years of intensive study of the way children acquire language in infancy—thirty years of watching and listening to children—have taught us a lesson we shall not forget.

"Watching and listening"—it is only in more recent years that we have begun to realise how language behaviour builds on earlier non-verbal behaviour: how cooperative routines set up between infant and adult, mostly in the form of play, increasingly generate *meaning* for the infant; and how early language comes in to highlight meanings already established in this way. Thereafter, language has a crucial role to play, enriching and extending cooperative behaviour, cumulatively reaping the harvest of earlier understandings, organising memory into narrative form, vastly increasing in scope and accessibility the body of expectations with which the child will meet every new event. Here is learning indeed, a model for all subsequent learning: using language to make sense of the world gives the child, Hey Presto!, a mastery of language. It is our task as teachers to build on that learning, to enrich and extend it, to harness it ever more closely to ever more complex modes of experience.

This challenge has never been greater than it is today in the multicultural classrooms we are facing. Wayne O'Neil, American linguist, broke into a learned discussion once to say:

> I think that any book that comes out of this conference ought to make it perfectly clear that all of what we talk about is for naught if in fact American education is going to proceed to be exactly what it has been, a way of drawing people away from their roots and cultures rather than a way of increasing their activity within those groups and cultures.[1]

I know no more promising way of increasing such activity within subcultural groups than by cherishing and nourishing the speech of the home and the neighbourhood and by helping it to find the kind of expression, in story, poem, play, which can communicate the spirit of the subculture to a multicultural audience. That nourishing means, of course, that we can no longer limit our concern for literature to a concern for any canon, be it classical or national. Standard English? Yes, that's on the agenda too, seen essentially as the written language in which information is stored and made available.

In the 'thirties we knew nothing about language learning in infancy. Such studies as there were were locked away in fat, unreadable psychology manuals. Clearly, our educational bosses were no wiser than we were, on the evidence of the 1929 report I have referred to. And that fixes my base-line.

The 'forties, among other events we have tended to forget, saw the teenage revolution. Young people gained, once and for all, a kind of independence (which, like the age of puberty, grows earlier every year). New attitudes to authority emerged: a teacher's authority could no longer be assumed but had to be earned, patiently and sometimes painfully. Martin Buber understood this very well: writing in 1947 he spoke of the period as "the time of the crumbling of bonds" and saw, in consequence, that the teacher could no longer represent "the ambassador of history to this intruder, the child", but "faces the child as individual to individual."[2]

If I have laboured this point, it is because it is so consistently forgotten by certain critics of enlightened educational policies today—including some of those who urge us "back to basics": nothing is more sadly futile than a belief that we can put the clock back.

The 'fifties I find difficult to recall in any clear focus. Perhaps that is because it was a decade of spadework; teachers in their classrooms patiently tackling the task of working out new methods of teaching and learning appropriate to the new relationships, the individual to individual stance of teacher to child. For the new relationships demanded a new conception of the learning process itself, a move from a unidirectional to an interactive view.

In England, I believe one important aspect of this movement was the increasing influence of primary school teachers on their secondary school colleagues. The secondary school subject specialist is more prone to seeing learning as a uni-directional process—something proceeding from teacher to pupil—than is the primary school teacher who must see himself as a facilitator of learning in all areas of the curriculum.

I do not imply that the problems of the secondary school can all be solved by applying the successful experience of primary school teachers—indeed some of the problems posed by attempting this rapprochement seem as far away from solution today as ever. But the recognition that learning is always an interactive process is a crucial first step: its implications—that talking and writing may be modes of learning, that a curriculum must be negotiable, that in-school and out-of-school learning should be inseparable parts of one pattern—the working out of these implications constitutes an area of active innovation in secondary schools today.

These were the ideas that blossomed in the 'sixties, a heady and dangerous decade. I see it as a "grand processional" from the Dartmouth Conference in America to the Bullock Report in England. It was heady to have ideas that had germinated in quiet processes and small circles suddenly come out into the open; and dangerous in the way that an institutionalised orthodoxy is always dangerous. The new orthodoxy was no exception: the grand processional swept into its wake many who were more in the swim than in the know, and they did much to supply ammunition to the critics, the nostalgic admirers of education in the "good old days". The term "child-centred education" came to be widely used, and it seems to me a highly ambiguous and even misleading term. Interactive learning (like the cooperative ploys of infant and adult) is a *joint* undertaking. Vygotsky[3], urging the social and cultural nature of learning, has put this very clearly, showing how operations and calculations originally carried out overtly in joint activity with an adult become internalised with the help of inner speech and so shape the child's consciousness. "Adult and child-centred" seems a more accurate description of the kind of education we have in mind, appropriate to an interactive view of learning, and highlighting the crucial role of language, in its many modes, as the principal instrument of interaction.

It is easy, I think, to characterise the 'seventies: it is the "age of anxiety". You remember that Auden wrote a "Baroque Eclogue" with

that title epitomising the years of the Second World War. But his definition of anxiety in that poem seems to me to fit exactly the mood of the
'seventies: "their vision shrinks as their dreams darken". A world recession creating basic uncertainty about the future—the darkening of
our dreams; and with that a shrinking of perspectives, a limiting of the
number of factors we are prepared to take account of in making a
judgment. In educational terms, this means a "back to basics" policy,
("rationalisation", as some administrators interpret the term) and, in
England, the anti-progressive views of the Black Papers.

By this view, my grand processional has been re-christened "the
decadent 'sixties". The movement, as I have suggested, draws ammunition from practices based on a laissez faire philosophy and other indi-
cations of the work of bandwagon progressives. I think there is an
urgent need for thorough study of the highly complex structure of the
open classroom, the highly complex demands of interactive learning
and negotiated curricula. And for that reason I welcome two recent
studies produced by your National Working Party on the role of language in learning, *Negotiating the Curriculum* and *Literacy Around
the Workbench*.

What we have learned must be preserved, even when it seems
like a soft sell in a hard market. We have learned that mastery of
language comes with its purposeful use and that attempts to teach the
bare skills by practice exercises is bound to fail. It is the user's own
intention that releases the powers of mastery: any practice will help
only in so far as it feeds directly into a mainstream of activity that is
purposeful.

Put at its broadest, we master language by using it to make the
most of our lives. Within the school context, this suggests three major
intentions or purposes for language to fulfil. *First*, that of establishing
and maintaining relationships. If learning is an interactive process, we
can't teach people we don't know, so the building of a personal relationship comes logically first.

Here are some extracts from a journal written by a nine-year-old
in an elementary school in Toronto where I spent some weeks two
years ago. The school is in an area largely occupied by Chinese and
Greek families and the writer, Linda, is a Chinese Canadian. The
words in italics are her teacher's responses:

Friday, Jan 18th, 1978. After my rough copy of my project I am
going to rerange my project around. I am going to put growing up
first page, What monkeys do to eat in second page. Why do monkeys make faces page three. *Sounds interesting!*

Jan. 25. It was interesting. Did you think it was very interesting or interesting or just a little interesting? Mrs. E., I'm sorry

your husband wouldn't let you have another dog but anyways someone already took the dog . . . How's Malcolm? I hope he isn't sick or anything. *Malcolm is fine, thank you—he cries when I leave in the morning and gets very excited when I come home!*

. . .

Feb. 14. The last time I wrote I told you that I was school sick and you asked me why. Well now I will tell you why because I like to learn, I also like you, I like to do work and when I was away I miss the class. Today I am glad to be here because I wouldn't want to miss the Valentine party. Mrs. E., can you give me a few suggests for the party. *(1) a sharp knife to cut apples, (2) serviettes, (3) little bags to take goodies home in.*

Feb. 20. Mrs. E., thank you very much for the suggests for the Valentine party. I'm sorry you were away. What did you come up with? *I was very sick!* When you were away the class had other teachers. The first teacher's name was Mrs. G., and the second teacher's name was Mr. M. They were both nice teachers. You know sometimes I wish you were my mother. *Lots of the time I wish I had a little girl like you!*

Feb. 21. It's too bad I'm Chinese because if I was English you could adopt me. . . .

March 29. It's my birthday today! Ouch! I hate getting my patty-whacks. Mrs. E., can you tell the people who are going to give me my patty-whacks to do it lightly. I have a tender ass. Just a joke, but please tell them. *O.K.*

The children in that class enjoyed writing their journals because they clearly fulfilled a purpose—that of making them feel happy about their teacher and about the way she felt about them. ("Yes, we kind of *communicate*", Linda told me.)

The *second* purpose to be achieved through using language is that of *learning* in its accepted sense. Teachers of all subjects are discovering the value of expressive talk and writing as a means of coming to understand, of making your own the material of the curriculum. I shall call that Learning I and see it as part of the process of organising the objective aspects of experience. That leaves the *third* purpose of using language or what I call Learning II—often not recognised as learning at all. This is the process of organising the subjective aspects of experience; of using talk and writing and reading to explore and shape our inner lives. It covers the stories and poems—fictional and autobiographical—that children write, as well as the stories and other forms of literature that they read, and a great deal of valuable talk. It is by such means that an individual preserves his picture of the world as a world worth living in.

We are already looking at the future—retrospect has become prospect by a silent change of gear. The nature of this gathering tonight, the nature of the programmes for this conference, suggests that we may well be unanimous in resisting the retrenchment, the shrunken perspectives of the "age of anxiety". But I think we have also another problem on our hands, and a more troublesome one: the threat of a polarisation in our views as to the nature of our subject, English. Let me go back to the last International Conference in this series, at York University in 1971. I think there emerged from that conference a kind of synthesis, a way of bridging the traditional gap in English teaching between a concern for language and a concern for literature. This is how a US participant wrote about it:

> I have been looking for an over-riding structural principle for my English program. At the York Conference I was exposed to the British concept of "language" and the work being done to use growth and communication models and language theories to understand and organise the sequence and type of language experiences students have. It will now be possible for me to create beneficial and appropriate language environments and situations for my students, recognising that the previously fragmented aspects of the English program are related by their common denominator—language.

A threat to that emerging synthesis was foreseen by Garth Boomer in 1973:

> If the old controversies were predicated on content versus experience and grammar versus growth, there are now indications that the 'seventies will generate polemics on the place and value of literature, and, on a wider scale, the position of English itself as a separate subject on the curriculum. It will be a pity if, as a blacklash at the 'sixties, the old dichotomy between language and literature is re-established. What seems to be required is a re-valuation of the relationship between language and literature and society, along with a thorough analysis of our teaching of English literature in the universities.[4]

One approach to a synthesis is based on the distinction between using language in the role of participant and in the role of spectator. It is a notion that has been much discussed and much misunderstood. It originated as an attempt to see the relationship between the language of literature and non-literary uses of language. Or, to put it another way, are there uses of language which could be seen as brother, sister or second cousin to the mode of language usage we call "literature"?

As participants in the world's affairs we use language to get things done—to buy or sell, to inform or seek information, to persuade or instruct. But much of our daily talk does not seem *useful* in this way, does not seem concerned to get anything done. For example, when we go home in the evening, we chat or gossip about the day's events. The events we talk about are over, so we cannot be participating in them. Rather, we are reviewing, rehearsing, reconstructing, contemplating past events—and it is an obvious metaphor to say that we have taken up the role of "spectator" of those events. But we don't chat about all that has happened—we select from the day's events and that selection implies an evaluation, a highlighting of what is important or interesting or worth talking about.

The way we recount these events is even more strongly evaluative: if we feel sorry for ourselves we tell the story in such a way as to evoke sympathy on the part of our listener; if we have had a red-letter day, we try to get our listener to share our exhilaration. D. W. Harding has suggested that there is a deep-seated motive for this kind of talk: that in offering an evaluation of events we are in fact seeking the approval, or the modification, of *the way we evaluate.* Putting that more broadly, we are trying out our value systems in order to have them sanctioned by other people—not of course by anybody and everybody, but by our intimates, since close associations are built upon shared values. The "deep-seated motive" is what Harding calls "a basic social satisfaction" in knowing that we are not alone in feeling the way we do about the world.[5]

When we participate in events, we have to evaluate in order to know how to act, but in this case, because we are concerned "to get something done", we shall evaluate under the constraints of self-interest. As spectators we are free from those constraints and evaluate more deeply, more openly. To put it briefly, as participants we *apply* our value systems, as spectators we are concerned to *generate* values and *refine* our value systems.

When we chat about things that have happened to us, we are in the role of spectator; but so also is our listener. That is to say, we may be onlookers on other people's experiences. By the same token, we are in the role of spectator when we contemplate the imagined experiences recounted in fiction (or contemplate possible or impossible future events in our day-dreaming). The language of literature has, then, a second cousin in the language we use in chatting about events, real or imagined.

All this is, I think, consistent with George Kelly's "theory of personal constructs". Kelly[6] who takes the scientist as his model for man, sees human behaviour as essentially experimental. We draw from past experience to form hypotheses about any present encounter, test out those hypotheses and reform then in the light of what actually happens. But I think there are two aspects to our personal construct systems. There is a knowledge aspect—an organisation of the inferences from experience as to what the world is like. (If our experimental behaviour has been to treat a plate-glass door as though it were an open access, we need to amend our knowledge of what the world is like.) And there is a value aspect—an organisation of how much and in what ways we *care* (in D. H. Lawrence's words, "the way our sympathies flow and recoil").

From the knowledge aspect, we need a rational, logical, consistent set of constructs, not one riddled with incompatibilities. But it is the value aspect that makes us the sort of people we are, and our need to *be one person* is at least as pressing as the need for a consistent world representation. Empirical, scientific, philosophical modes of enquiry help us to extend and refine the knowledge aspects of our system: the value aspect requires another mode of enquiry, one that in its perfected form we call "art".

Gossip, chatting about events, reflects a concern for the value aspect, the ways in which we care. The more that gossip moves towards the forms of art, of literature, the more effectively shall we work upon that aspect. What a work of art gives us, whether as reader or writer, is *an experience of order.*

That introduces the second distinction I need in order to characterise a work of literature. First, it is, in the terms I have been describing, a piece of spectator role discourse; but, secondly, it has achieved artistic *form*, that particular and little understood mode of organisation that is common to all the arts—a unity and inner coherence of all the forms, perceptible or conceivable, that the medium offers. Gossip and the child's unshaped narrative, autobiographical or fictional, is art-like but not art. To take an extreme example, here is a piece of writing by an eleven-year-old Melbourne boy, asked by his teacher to write a story:

> Teacher wouldn't know if you broke your arm. They just pile the work up. It gets harder every day. Third term is the most boringest time I know of. The days are long and boring.
> This story is my life more than a story.
> Cause I didn't know what to write.

You could hardly have a more un-shaped narrative, yet it is a human voice, a human cry, an evaluation!

When we read and respond to a work of literature, we are, again, working on the unity and coherence of our value systems, our feelings about the world, but we are doing so in double harness with the artist. To look at it this way is to see literature in a social context, to recognise the role of the artist as the apex of a pyramid, to recognise the importance of a readership that gives currency to the values arrived at by the most sensitive members of a society.

Speculatively, and perhaps in digression, I want to add one point. In the very process of perceiving the world, we give and find shape, pattern, order. In our talk and writing—the way we tell the stories of our lives—we give and find further shape. *"Give"* and *"find"*. Yes, there is shape, pattern, order in the world irrespective of our human perceiving and interpreting. Recall the shape of a front of fern, the "record", as Susanne Langer has said, of the slow movement of its growth. At the biological level, man shares that order; but in his behaviour, in the narrative of his actions, when we compare it with pattens of instinctual behaviour in the lesser creatures, we find randomness and even chaos rather than order. Mankind has achieved freedom in the way he acts, and that is the price.

If Susanne Langer[7] is right, a primary principle of all the arts is that they embody, in their build-up and resolution of tensions, the rhythm of every living act—a pattern characteristic of every living organism. This introduces what seems to me a fascinating speculation: we shape our lives into a kind of narrative in order more fully to possess our experiences; the shape we give in the art narrative is an attempt to recapture, or at least to approximate to, a natural order, an order found in living creatures, but something that in our actual daily lives we have lost.

Is there in all this the basis for a synthesis, a way of unifying our conception of subject English? A way of relating the learning that goes on in English lessons with the learning appropriate to the whole curriculum? (The one thing we must not do in the 'eighties is to go back to attempts to define subject English in isolation from the rest of a student's learning experiences, out of context in the curriculum as a whole. Such failure on the part of subject specialists to consider the whole curriculum has, it seems to me, left a gap that vacuous, doctrinaire theories have been only too apt to fill.)

Garth Boomer, looking at the Australian scene, foresaw a threat to the synthesis. Certainly that threat—a language/literature polarisation—is strongly in evidence in England. Our attempt to place literature in a context, to explore its relationship with other uses of language, is rejected because it is interpreted as taking literature down from its pedestal, or removing the railings that protect the sacred from the profane. Thus, Frank Whitehead commenting on the spectator/participant distinction writes:

> What then can have been the motive for Britton to wrench so cavalierly from their context these two terms to form the cornerstone of his over-ambitious theorising? I suggest that the attraction was the opportunity to postulate a continuity between

"gossip" and "literature" in a way which tacitly exalts the significance in human life of the former and at the same time subtly
denigrates the distinctive characteristics of the latter.[8]

The cause is taken up, though in a much more reasonable tone, in
the recent publication by David Allen, *English Teaching Since 1965:
How Much Growth?*[9] Allen perceives and regrets the tendency to
polarise, or so I interpret it. Nevertheless, he echoes Whitehead in
criticising my position as showing no concern for values. My retort
here, particularly to Whitehead, is that he appears slow to recognise
any concern for values that does not arise in the context of a work of
literature. And I suspect that Allen both wishes for a synthesis and on
the other hand assigns so unique a place to literature that he finds it
difficult to admit any other element alongside it. While off his guard (I
suggest) he writes:

> It would require a very strong appreciation of literature's own
> demands to resist the temptation to merge literature into a gen-
> eral "unity", whether that dictated by the needs of a particular
> pupil or the organisation of the English curriculum into themes of
> general importance.

Does he see "merging literature into a general unity" as something to
be aimed at, or "a temptation to be resisted"?

The synthesis he finally suggests is what, after Whitehead, he
calls "art-speech", and that, as he describes it, covers the reading of
literature, work in drama, and the students' own speech and writing of
an art-like nature.

It is a central point in what I have said over the years that as far as
using language is concerned, the focus in English lessons should be on
language in the spectator role—and that would account for most of
what goes on. It is not, however, the whole of the synthesis. Spelling
that out in skeleton form:

1. Wherever *study* of language is appropriate, fostering an understanding of how it works (across all its uses), that is a part of the
   work in English lessons.
2. Wherever intensive practice of some language technique will
   feed directly into a mainstream of purposive activity (in any part
   of the curriculum), that—at least until the millenium arrives of an
   effective, universally adopted, language across the curriculum
   policy—is the responsibility of the English teacher.
3. As far as language *use* is concerned—speaking, listening, writing,
   reading—the principal area of operations in English lessons is in
   the Expressive to Poetic spectrum, that is, language in the role of
   spectator.

Since this last seems to me precisely the synthesis covered by "art-speech" as David Allen describes it, it seems unfair that he should, *en route* to this conclusion, regard me as a malign influence. "Britton's achievement," he writes, "has been great; but at very great cost." (p. 67)

The threat of polarisation is certainly real—a move to set up a literature-based concept of English over and against what I have been calling the synthesis. I call this a threat because I believe that, *in practice,* such a concept tends to move towards an exclusive kind of specialism. I shall always remember L. C. Knights telling a group of teachers how he introduces students to his English Honours courses in literature. "You have to remember," he tells them, "that we are not specialists: we are simply people who have more time and better opportunities to go into what belongs to everybody." Though the proponents may not want it that way, in effect, I think it happens. I shall raise my objection in words that George Kelly once used:

> Some of my literary colleagues leave me with the impression that "the nature of man" puts more out of my reach than within my grasp. I expect better of them. This is crucial. . . . Humanity needs to be implemented, not merely characterised and eulogized.[10]

Art Vickers[11], truck driver turned teacher, taught for a while in a community school in Calgary. He ran writing classes for high-school dropouts and others with similarly limited objectives. His method was to begin every session with a ten minute free writing period, and the expressive nature of his responses to that writing usually succeeded in releasing the block set up by previous failure. In what follows he introduces the work of one of his students, Jean, aged twenty-six, separated from her husband, bringing up her child. Her ambition was to enter training as a registered nurse:

> Jean had a lot of trouble freeing herself from the habit of writing and re-writing her work in the ten minute writing period. Consequently, her work was never done. Finally, after I had spent an unsatisfactory three weeks in trying to draw her out nicely, I simply wrote on her work, 'Okay, so now you can go back to writing your own thoughts in your own words.' The very next day I received the following work:
>
> "He's rather an insignificant looking little bear. His once fluffy two-toned brown fur has been almost completely worn off by five years of cuddling and abuse. He's been sewn innumerable times with a variety of different colours of thread, to save his foam stuffing from falling out. His two little green glass eyes are on the verge of being replaced by two plastic shirt buttons. He goes by

the name of Thomas, a label given as soon as his young companion could speak. He cannot be replaced, for the older and more ragged he becomes, Thomas becomes that much more important to the child whom he has helped for some years to get through a long and lonely night." (Sept. 22, 1975)

On December 1st, Jean wrote this:

"This is for my son

"I know there are times that I've let you down, and in more ways than one. Times when I should have been with you when you were with a baby-sitter because I was out on a date. The men that have not only been a hurtful part of my life, but yours too. The things you miss out on because you don't have a full-time father, like hockey and Saturday afternoon baseball games. Being a single parent is not easy for me nor is it easy for you being the child of a single parent. Sometimes when I yell at you or punish you for trivial things it's because I'm in a bad mood or I had a bad day, or I was out too late the night before or I just wish I had someone to share you with. You know that I love you more than anyone or anything, but unfortunately sometimes that isn't enough or at least I don't feel like it is. Maybe someday when you've children of your own you'll realise that my shortcomings are only those of a person trying as hard as possible to make a good life for another person. To share the good times and help you through the bad, to help you understand right from wrong isn't always a simple task. I guess what I'm trying to say is bear with me through the hard times and all the mistakes I'll make with you and my own life too because I love you and although it may not seem like it to you I am doing my very best for both of us."

We cannot call that writing "literature"; it is art-like but not art. But I believe you will feel with me that a concern for values is reflected, that both in the teaching and in the student's writing "humanity is being implemented".

So, as we resist the polarisation, we must work on the synthesis, correct it, extend it—and for a start we might work on the misunderstandings that have arisen from misinterpretation of it. It is, finally, in the classrooms that the problems will be resolved and the synthesis achieved, and subject English will emerge to be described.

I once heard a Canadian Dean of Education lecture for an hour on "change in the elementary school"; he argued that the elementary school was so conservative an institution that change was impossible. Within his own terms, he proved his point, because he was thinking of change from outside, change from the top. But he would have found a very different picture had he looked at change from within, change by contagion from teacher to teacher.

If this were not an assembly but a more convivial occasion, I should ask you now, with "English in the 'Eighties" in mind, to raise your glasses and drink a toast to the *decade of the teacher*. As we have developed our view of learning as interactive, and that of the curriculum as negotiable; as we have recognised the dramatic effect of intentions upon performance, by teachers as well as by students; as it has become clear that teaching consists of moment-by-moment interactive behaviour, behaviour that can only spring from inner conviction—I think we are, perhaps for the first time, ready to admit that what the teacher can't do in the classroom can't be achieved by any other means. Not the "grand processional" then, not the "age of anxiety", but the "age of the classroom teacher".

No, I do not mean that nobody else matters, nobody else can help. I think there are great opportunities for people like me—in professional development, initial and in-service training, whatever you call it—provided we see that interactive learning applies to teachers as well as to those they teach; provided we see our role as helping them to theorise from their own experience, and build their own rationale and their own body of convictions. For it is when they are actively theorising from their own experience that they can, selectively, take and use other people's experiences and other people's theories.

I see a vital role for administrators, once it is realised that they are teacher supporters rather than building superintendents or systems analysts—and teacher support means helping teachers to learn as well as helping them to teach.

Walking down Euston Road ten days ago, I was thinking about this occasion and wondering whether "the age of the classroom teacher" was altogether too optimistic an idea to be realistic. Then I saw, outside Friends' House (the Quaker Headquarters), a poster which seemed to me as I read it to be putting my thoughts into words. It contained a quotation from Rufus Jones, an American Quaker in the early years of this century: "I pin my hopes to quiet processes and small circles in which vital and transforming events take place."

Moving into the 'eighties, into rough waters with plenty of problems educational, social and political, I am not pessimistic. I pin my hopes to quiet processes and small circles in which I believe I shall see, if I'm still alive at the end, vital and transforming events taking place.

References

1. J. F. Kavanagh and I. G. Mattingly, *Language by Ear and by Eye*, M. I. T. Press, 1972, p. 156.

2. Martin Buber, *Between Man and Man*, Routledge and Kegan Paul, 1947, pp. 93–94.
3. L. S. Vygotsky, *Mind in Society*, Harvard University Press, 1978.
4. Nicholas Bagnall, *New Movements in the Study and Teaching of English*, Temple Smith, 1973, p. 75.
5. James Britton, 'What's the Use? A Schematic Account of Language Functions', *Educational Review*, 23 (3), 1971, pp. 205–219. D. W. Harding, 'The Role of the Onlooker', *Scrutiny*, 6 (3), 1937, pp. 247–258.
6. George A. Kelly, *A Theory of Personality*, Norton, 1963.
7. Susanne K. Langer, *Mind: An Essay on Human Feeling*, Johns Hopkins, 1967, Chap. 7.
8. Frank Whitehead, 'What's the Use Indeed?' *Use of English*, 29 (2), Spring, 1978, p. 17.
9. Heinemann Educational, 1980.
10. George A. Kelly, 'Humanistic Methodology in Psychological Research' in B. Mahler, ed. *Clinical Psychology and Personality*, John Wiley, 1969, p. 135.
11. Art Vickers, *Language in the Center*, No. 10 in *Language in the Classroom: A Series*, Department of Curriculum and Instruction, University of Calgary, 1977.

A Selected Bibliography of Other Britton Publications

1934 English on the Anvil: A Language and Composition Course for Secondary Schools. London, Foyles Educational; Eighth printing, London, John Murray, 1952.

1950 "The Meaning and Marking of Imaginative Composition," *The New Era*, 31(7), pp 137–143.

1951 "Books about Shakespeare," *The Use of English*, 2(4), pp 190–197.

1954 "Evidence of Improvement in Poetic Judgment," *The British Journal of Psychology*, 45(3), pp 196–208.

1957 (Editor) *The Oxford Books of Verse for Juniors*, Books 1 to 4, Oxford, The Oxford University Press.
"The Teaching of Grammar," *Education*, 6(3), Wellington, the New Zealand Department of Education, pp 49–53.

1960 "Growing Up in Writing," in Boris Ford (Ed.), *Young Writers, Young Readers*, London, Hutchinson, pp 53–73.

1963 "Literature," in James Britton (Ed.), *The Arts and Current Trends in Education*, London, Evans Brothers, pp 34–61.
"Experimental Marking of English Compositions written by 15-year-olds," *Educational Review*, 16(1), pp 17–23.

1964 (Editor) *The Oxford Books of Stories for Juniors*, Books 1 to 3 and Teachers' Books, Oxford, Oxford University Press.
"The Aims of Teaching English in the Senior School," "The Language of the Imagination," and "Poetry in the Junior School," in F. R. Copeland (Ed.), *English Teaching in South Africa*, Grahamstown, Grahamstown Publications, pp 24–40, 152–169 & 228–247.

1966 (With N. C. Martin & H. Rosen), *Multiple Marking of English Compositions*, London, Schools Council Examinations Bulletin 12, H.M.S.O. "The Language of Poetry," *The English Teacher*, 6(1) Alberta Teachers Association, pp 6–14.

1968 "Odysseus and Commuters: A Note on Myth," *Didaskalos*, 2(3), pp 106–113.
(With Bernard Newsome), "What Is Learnt in English Lessons?" *Journal of Curriculum Studies*, 1(1), pp 68–78.

1969 "Talking to Learn," in *Language, the Learner and the School*, Harmondsworth, Penguin Education, pp 81–115.

1970 Language and Learning, London, Allen Lane, The Penguin Press; Pelican Edition, 1972.
"The Student's Writing," in Eldonna Everetts (Ed.), *Explorations in Children's Writing*, Urbana, N.C.T.E., pp 21–74.
"Their Language and our Teaching," *English in Education* 4(2), pp 5–13.

1971 "What's the Use? A Schematic Account of Language Functions," *Educational Review*, 23(3), pp 205–219. (Reprinted in Barrie Wade (Ed) *Language Perspectives*, London, Heinemann, 1982, pp 110–124.)

1972 "The York International Conference, 1971," *English in Education* 6(1), pp 2–6.

1973 "What Does the School Do with Language?" and "The Present State of Theory and Knowledge Relating to English Teaching," in *The Teaching of English*, Canberra, The Australian Government Publishing Service, pp 4–20.

1974 "English in the Curriculum," in *The Space Between: English and Foreign Languages at School*, London, Centre for Information on Language Teaching and Research, pp 25–45.
"What Is English?" *Trends in Education*, 36, London, Department of Education and Science, pp 24–28.

1975 (Editor and co-author with Tony Burgess, Nancy Martin, Alec McLeod & Harold Rosen), *The Development of Writing Abilities, 11–18*, London, Macmillan Education for the Schools Council, and (1977) Urbana, N.C.T.E.
"Teaching Writing" in Alan Davies (Ed.), *Problems of Language and Learning*, London, Heinemann Educational for the Social Science Research Council, pp 113–128.

1976 "Language Out of School," *English in Australia*, 35, pp 2–15.

1977 "Language and the Nature of Learning: An Individual Perspective," in James R. Squire (Ed), *The Teaching of English:* 76th Yearbook of the National Association for Studies in Education, Part 1, Chicago, University of Chicago Press, pp 1–38.

1978 "The Composing Process and the Functions of Writing," in C. Cooper & L. Odell (Eds.), *Research on Composing*, Urbana, N.C.T.E., pp 13–22.
"I'm Listening," *Journal of the Canadian Association for Young Children*, 4(1), pp 33–36.

1979 "Learning to Use Language in Two Modes," in Nancy Smith & Margery Franklin (Eds.), *Symbolic Functioning in Childhood*, Hillsdale, N.J., Lawrence Erlbaum Associates, pp 185–196.

"No, No, Jeanette! A reply to Jeanette Williams' Critique of the Schools Council Writing Research Project," *Language for Learning*, 1(1), pp 23–41.

1981 "Language and Learning Across the Curriculum," *fforum*, 2(2), University of Michigan, pp 55–6 & 93–4.

In the press

"Writing and the Story World," in Gordon Wells & Barry Kroll (Eds.) *Explorations of Children's Writing Development*, Chichester, John Wiley & Sons.

"Reading and Writing Poetry," in Rosalind Arnold (Ed), *Timely Voices*, Oxford University Press, Australia.